The Rise of Populism in Western Europe

Timo Lochocki

# The Rise of Populism in Western Europe

A Media Analysis on Failed Political Messaging

 Springer

Timo Lochocki
The German Marshall Fund of the United States
Berlin, Germany

ISBN 978-3-319-62854-7      ISBN 978-3-319-62855-4    (eBook)
DOI 10.1007/978-3-319-62855-4

Library of Congress Control Number: 2017946175

Printed on acid-free paper

This Springer imprint is published by Springer Nature
The registered company is Springer International Publishing AG
The registered company address is: Gewerbestrasse 11, 6330 Cham, Switzerland

# Testimonials

Timo Lochocki's book is fascinating because it is ambitiously comparative. *The Rise of Populism in Western Europe* systematically shows that the fortunes of populist parties depend, at least in part, on the positions adopted by their more mainstream competitors. With new media data, he can specify the mechanisms and sequences in more detail than ever before. Eventually, this allows him to stress convincingly that the radical right's electoral success isn't necessarily inevitable.

Tim Bale
Professor of Politics, Queen Mary University of London, UK

*The Rise of Populist Parties in Western Europe* really advances our understanding on populist radical right parties. Timo Lochocki can refute economic explanations for the rise of nationalist parties like the Front National (FN) or the Alternative for Germany (AfD). Instead, he argues that a "crisis of conservatism" created the perfect context for their advances. This book will provide both less and more informed scholars and practitioners with an excellent insight into populist radical right politics in Western Europe.

Cas Mudde
Associate Professor, University of Georgia, GA, USA

Conventional wisdom and mistaken assumptions taint the debate about the rise and persistence of populist parties across Europe. Timo Lochocki's book takes on plenty of these misperceptions with high-quality comparative research. As he manages to present his findings in very accessible language, *The Rise of Populist Parties in Western Europe* is a must-read for anybody who is following the debate about where Europe is today and where it might be tomorrow.

Matthew Goodwin
Professor, University of Kent, UK

# Foreword

The shocking outcomes of the British EU referendum and the US presidential elections have made "the rise of populism" the dominant story of 2016. If one is to believe the international media, politics in Western democracies are now a struggle of life and death between an embattled status quo and an emboldened populism. All the European elections of 2017 have been framed this way, despite fundamental differences in the electoral contests and the strength of the populist challengers. So, while the frame holds some truth for the second round of the French presidential elections, between centrist Emmanuel Macron and populist radical rightist Marine Le Pen, it falls flat in the German elections, which are a classic contest between center-right and center-left with only a marginal role for the internally divided, populist Alternative for Germany (AfD).

A casual reader of international media could also be forgiven for thinking that populism is a recent phenomenon. US media seem to suggest that everything started with the rise of Donald Trump, referring to the different European populist radical right parties as [insert name of specific country] Trumpism, as if Europe didn't have a populist radical right tradition that predates the election of Trump by several decades. Similarly, many media exaggerate the novelty and success of Marine Le Pen by describing her predecessor as leader of the Front National (FN), her father Jean-Marie, as some sort of "marginal" extremist.

The reality is that the so-called third wave of right-wing extremism has been in motion since the 1980s and parties like the FN were far from marginal before today—under Jean-Marie Le Pen the party regularly won more than 10% of the national vote and even made it to the run-off of the presidential elections in 2002. The Austrian Freedom Party (FPÖ) gained a shocking 27% in the 1999 parliamentary elections, entering the Austrian coalition government as a junior partner the next year. In fact, the "rise of the radical right," as it was called then, has been a major topic of political and public debate since the late 1980s.

Not surprising, then, that the study of the populist radical right in Europe is far from new either. In fact, in the last three decades, populist radical right parties have been studied more than all other party families combined, despite being much less successful than Christian Democratic or Social Democratic parties. Not a month goes by without a new book or journal article on the topic. Much of the work has become repetitive, focusing on the same few cross-national and cross-temporal datasets to figure out "who votes for the populist radical right?"

And while "economic anxiety" versus "cultural backlash" is still playing out in the media, academic research has long settled this question (spoiler alert: it is mainly cultural backlash) and has concluded that these demand-side explanations only provide partial answers to the question. To advance our understanding, supply-side factors have to be taken into account. What do populist radical right parties *offer* voters and how does this relate to what other political parties present? This is where Timo Lochocki's highly original book comes in.

*The Rise of Populist Parties in Western Europe* focuses exclusively on the supply side of both populist radical right and centrist politics. It does so in an original way, by arguing that the populist radical right's "political messaging" on identity issues such as the European Union and immigration is the key to its success (and failure). When populist radical right parties put forward a so-called winning formula that is "for the nation, against the elite," they increase their chances of electoral success.

However, the supply of other political parties, particularly of the center-right, plays a role as well. Where most authors consider the crisis of social democratic parties as crucial to the rise of populist radical right parties, Lochocki argues that it is instead a "crisis of conservatism" that creates the perfect context for the rise of the populist radical right. This resembles Piero Ignazi's seminal "silent counter-revolution" argument, made 25 years ago, which contended that the rise of neo-conservatism in the 1980s created a breeding ground for the "extreme right" parties of the 1990s.

In short, Timo Lochocki has written a highly accessible and original book, which should provide both less and more informed scholars and practitioners with an excellent insight into populist radical right politics in Western Europe. While it won't be the last word said on the subject, this book advances our understanding of an excessively studied topic, a rare feat these days.

Athens, GA                                                            Cas Mudde
29 April 2017

# Preface

How the world has changed since I started working on this book in 2010. Seven years ago, Germany and Sweden seemed to react calmly to external challenges such as immigration and the European Union. In contrast, France and Norway were home to highly polarized debates about their national identity. These differences intrigued me during my stays in these places. I do not know what came first, my personal astonishment when I listened to friends from these countries or my academic curiosity about these empirically palpable differences.

Why was the Sweden of 2010 home to such a significant share of migrants relative to its population but deprived of a polarizing debate on the matter? Why was the debate on immigration in the Netherlands so aggressive? Why was Germany embracing the EU, but a large part of Great Britain rejecting it?

None of the explanations I encountered convinced me. Each theory seemed to work for one country only, due to the difference between each country's historical trajectories, crucial political figures, degrees of racism or nationalism, and economic crises.

Having spent years studying social and psychological processes I was strongly inclined to assume that human behavior to a large extent follows comparable mechanisms. "To understand is to perceive patterns," Isaiah Berlin wrote. But nobody could offer a pattern that could account for the differences I was so flabbergasted by.

I hypothesized an extremely complex interplay of factors behind these differing phenomena. To better understand why some countries react with far more hostility to external challenges (such as immigration or EU matters) than others, I wanted to reveal the factors that explain how societies negotiate belonging and national identity in the twenty-first century. Thus, my PhD thesis was originally aimed at establishing a new theory of social change.

However, I quickly realized that the best proxy for measuring polarizing and aggressive debates over national identity was the strength of a country's populist radical right party. This is how I turned to comparative party politics and, ultimately, how my book came to focus on variation in the electoral advances of populist radical right parties in Western Europe.

In the first months of my PhD, this constituted a setback, because I had spent little time focusing on this topic during my previous studies. Eventually, however, incorporating a wider set of literature allowed me to see a broader picture. At the end of the writing process, I saw that I could not have understood the rise and fall of populist radical right parties as thoroughly without a background in Social Psychology and Social Theory.

In 2017, I am tempted to smirk when I remember these considerations, because since finishing my PhD in 2014 and starting work as an expert on European party politics, I am never asked about Robert Gould or Anthony Giddens any more... Instead, nearly all questions concern the AfD, Geert Wilders, Marine Le Pen, and their peers.

But not only has my work changed over the last years but also the world. When I started working on this book in 2010, very few populist radical right parties made the headlines. What a different world we are living in now!

After various Eurozone and refugee crises, Brexit, Donald Trump's victory in the USA, the rise of the Alternative for Germany (AfD), and Marine Le Pen's Front National making it to the second round of the French Presidential Election in 2017, the world now seems to be driven by populist movements. None of this could have been foreseen in 2010.

Nonetheless, the patterns and mechanisms visible over the last 30 years are indeed still the driving factors behind the rise and fall of populist parties today. Studying the rise and fall of the German Republikaner around 1990 or the political earthquake Pim Fortuyn triggered in 2002 in the Netherlands helps a great deal in understanding Brexit or Donald Trump. The empirics in this book will prove that Isaiah Berlin was indeed right: social behavior—whether debating national belonging or voting for a far right party—is rooted in patterns.

These patterns needed to be altered slightly at times to adapt to changing political circumstances but nonetheless remained largely unchanged at their core: the rise and fall of populist radical parties follow measurable and comparable patterns across Western European countries.

However, what astonishes me as much as these patterns are two different phenomena. Firstly, that comparative party politics has meanwhile established a pretty clear consensus on this subject, while the public is still relatively unaware of it. As I will show throughout the book, the rise and fall of populist radical right parties have very little to do with economics or historical particularities, yet countless commentaries insinuate exactly that. To me, this explains a large part of their rise. The outspokenness of many "experts" seems to be indirectly correlated with the degree of their knowledge on the subject. How should our political elites react to such a phenomena successfully if a large share of public commentaries on the subject are largely misleading?

Secondly, this seems to hint just how far the Social Sciences in Western democracies have drifted apart from the issues with which these societies are actually concerned. Research in Political Science and Sociology discusses many topics that have very little relevance in the daily life of citizens, and the researchers in the field who deal with hands-on topics (e.g., party politics, though there are of course many more) struggle to devote enough time to communicate their knowledge to a broader audience.

In this sense, the rise of populist radical right parties might be a sign not only of political elites growing apart from their voters but also of researchers having lost contact with the "real world" and being deprived of time to communicate with the people they research. In this vein, I hope that this book is a small contribution offering academically grounded knowledge on an important topic to a broader audience.

The book relies on my PhD thesis completed in 2014 but extends and updates the text based on the historical events of recent years. The theoretical and empirical chapters have been shortened, and the case studies and practical implications at the end have been extended to make the book accessible beyond academic audiences. I am sure that in this undertaking I have disappointed both sides: academics will complain about the lack of detail, while informed citizens may struggle to cope with some of the remaining complexities. I hereby apologize to both in advance.

While my apologies go to researchers and readers alike, I owe the greatest gratitude to my academic mentors. My two senior advisors Prof. Dr. Klaus Eder from Humboldt University Berlin and Prof. Dr. Bernhard Wessels from the Berlin Social Science Center always supported me and guided me through very, very treacherous waters at times. Not only their expertise but also and especially their wisdom guided this young researcher. Their calmness, constant encouragement, and especially their empathy are the foundations of this book.

Additionally, this book could have never been written without Prof. Dr. Elisabeth Ivarsflaten from the University of Bergen and Prof. Dr. Claudius Wagemann from Goethe University Frankfurt (and, previously, the European University Institute in Florence). Their insights on methodical and party political questions has been a major asset. I owe the greatest thanks to both of them for their never-ending patience, knowledge, and constant support.

After handing in my PhD in 2014, I began working at the German Marshall Fund of the United States (GMF). This professional environment enabled me to continue my work on European party politics and to spread the news on what was happening in contemporary liberal democracies. For this chance, I am indebted to my former superior, Dr. Daniela Schwarzer, and even more to my colleague and very dear friend Astrid Ziebarth.

To list all the friends whose help and support was essential to maintaining my sanity while first writing a PhD and then working at a think tank while the entire world was turning upside down would not be possible. I dedicate this book to all of you. Thanks for everything.

Paris, France                                                                                      Timo Lochocki
4 May 2017

# Contents

# Abbreviations

| | |
|---|---|
| AfD | Alternative für Deutschland |
| Brexit | The United Kingdom's prospective withdrawal from the EU |
| B90/Die Grünen | Bündnis 90/Die Grünen |
| C | Centerpartiet |
| CDA | Christen-Democratisch Appèl |
| CDU | Christlich Demokratische Union Deutschlands |
| CMP | Comparative Manifestos Project |
| Corr | Correlation |
| CSU | Christlich-Soziale Union |
| D66 | Democraten 66 |
| EFSF | European Financial Stability Facility |
| ESM | European Stability Mechanism |
| FAZ | Frankfurter Allgemeine Zeitung |
| FDP | Freie Demokratische Partei |
| FP | Folkpartiet liberalerna |
| FN | Front National |
| GER | Germany |
| KD | Kristdemokraterna |
| LPF | Lijst Pim Fortuyn |
| M | Moderata samlingspartiet |
| MP | Miljöpartiet de Gröna |
| NL | Netherlands |
| NPD | Nationaldemokratische Partei Deutschlands |
| NyD | Ny Demokrati |
| OECD | Organisation for Economic Co-Operation and Development |
| PDS/Die Linke | Linkspartei |
| PRRP | Populist Radical Right Party |
| PvdA | Partij van de Arbeid |
| PVV | Partij voor de Vrijheid |
| REP | Die Republikaner |
| SAP | Sveriges socialdemokratiska arbetareparti |

| | |
|---|---|
| SD | Sverigedemokraterna |
| SE | Sweden |
| Sig | Significance |
| SPD | Sozialdemokratische Partei Deutschlands |
| UKIP | United Kingdom Independence Party |
| V | Vänsterpartiet |
| VVD | Volkspartij voor Vrijheid en Democratie |
| QCA | Qualitative Comparative Analysis |

# Chapter 1
# Introduction: How the Failed Political Messaging of Moderate Political Actors Strengthens Populist Radical Right Parties

Western European populist radical right parties (PRRP) such as the French Front National (FN) or the United Kingdom Independence Party (UKIP) are perhaps the most influential political forces of the last decade. UKIP played a major role in the United Kingdom leaving the European Union ("Brexit"); the FN has not only reached the second round in the French presidential elections in 2017, threatening Europe with a similar exit from the EU ("Frexit"), but was also the model for Steve Bannon's campaigning that underpinned Donald Trump's election as US president.

As is common with social phenomena, the more a phenomenon grows in importance, the more 'experts' come to the fore offering explanations for what is happening. In recent years, international newspapers have been full of 'explanations' for the rise of populist right-wing parties in Europe. Most of them have been highly subjective and hardly taken into consideration the academic knowledge on the subject. Two 'explanations' have become especially widespread; firstly, the infamous 'historical argument': Country A is especially prone to populism because of historic event B (and conversely, country C is immune to populism due to historical lessons learned from D); secondly, the rise of nationalist parties is a result of the economic crises that have shaken Europe since 2008. Both 'arguments' are fundamentally wrong. Populist radical right parties have attracted substantial vote shares in nearly every European country, with very different historical trajectories; so history can hardly explain what is happening. These nationalist parties have attracted the most votes in the richer northern European countries, where voters are hardly moved by economics; and they have hardly made any ground in southern Europe or Ireland, which were heavily hit by the EU's austerity politics. It is not the economy, stupid! This has led some commentators to resort to underlining how complex and multifaceted the rise of PRRPs is as a phenomenon. While this is true, their rise is neither unexplainable, nor unavoidable. Instead, the electoral ups and downs of nationalist parties in Western Europe follow measurable, comparable and thus generalizable patterns.

Research in comparative party politics scrutinizing the reasons for the rise and fall of nationalist parties has made remarkable advances in recent years. The key

© Springer International Publishing AG 2018
T. Lochocki, *The Rise of Populism in Western Europe*,
DOI 10.1007/978-3-319-62855-4_1

explanation for why voters opt for populist radical right parties seems to be found in the so-called 'supply-side' of political competition. The programmatic offer of established, moderate parties is key. However, comparative research has struggled to explain how exactly the offers of established parties affect the advances of PRRPs. For instance, some studies have suggested that when conservatives 'move to the right', the PRRPs benefit, because their agenda is legitimized. However, others claim the opposite is true, because voters then have a conservative alternative to the populists. The prime reason why comparative research got stuck here lies with the lack of a precise measurement of *how* the agenda of established parties affects the voter and *why* moderate parties alter their political messaging. This book addresses these issues and explains the political mechanisms that stand behind the rise and fall of populist radical right parties in Western Europe.

This study relies on a unique research design that ensures high validity (properly measuring party-voter linkages), high reliability (the findings are independent of the author's political opinion) and high generalizability (the mechanisms revealed hold for all Western European countries). It works with a most-similar case design and data on political messaging based on nearly 10,000 political claims obtained from reports in national newspapers of record. The data mirrors salience and party positioning with identity politics in the three countries embracing comparable scope conditions for populist radical right parties but variation with their electoral advances: the Netherlands, Sweden and (West) Germany. A triangulation based on deterministic (QCA) and probabilistic logic (correlational models) supports a two-level theory, explaining the factors defining varying party rationales that either lead to advances or losses for populist radical right parties.

These nationalist parties present themselves as sole defenders of the national identity. They accuse the established parties of selling out the nation's cultural core to migrants and the European Union. Their winning formula reads 'For the Nation, Against the Elite'. Fitting the hypothesis of stable demand, this study finds that the necessary conditions for the ups and downs of populist radical right parties lie within the political messaging of established parties. Even in times of social media and 'fake news' the electoral fortunes of populist radical right parties primarily depend on how moderate parties frame issues of national identity—embodied by immigration and EU topics.

Bourgeois parties politicize identity politics when they want to mobilize conservative voters. When identity politics are salient, the bourgeois party must stick with its conservative messages to prevent the electoral gains of the far right. This is facilitated substantially by social democrats accommodating the conservative standpoints of the bourgeois party, resulting in a conservative compromise in political messaging. Whether the center-left opposes or appeases the conservatives' messages depends on what voters think about the economy. If the electorate is largely freed of economic concerns, the center-left is likely to oppose the demands of the conservatives. If the social democrats are then polling well ahead of the center-right for longer, the bourgeois party drops their conservative messages trying to attract voters of the center-left. Then the bourgeois party can be accused of

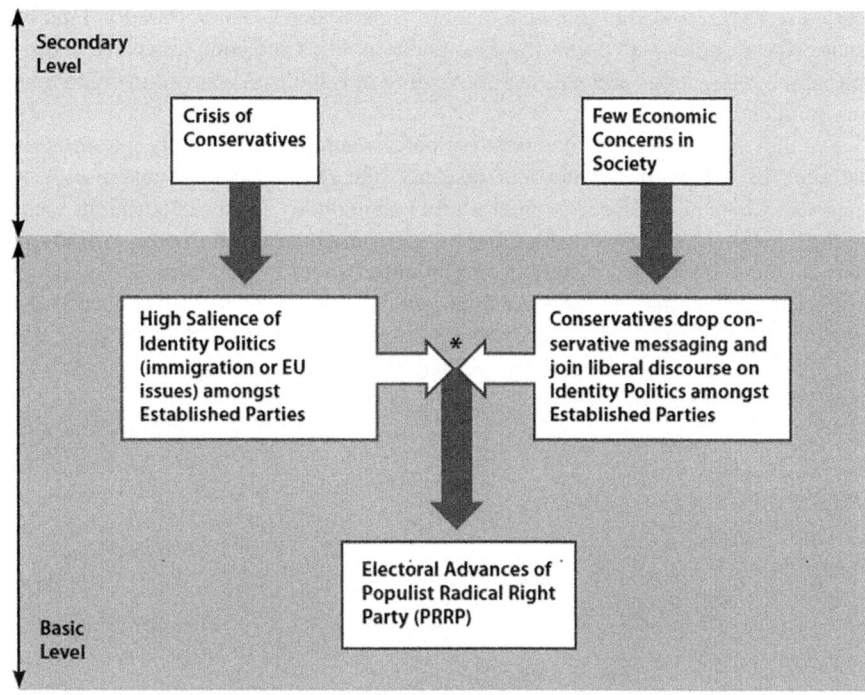

necessary cause        conjunction of        *  logical AND
                       necessary causes

**Fig. 1.1** A two-level theory of populist radical right parties in Western Europe—high extension, low intension

overpromising and under-delivering; of selling out the national identity. Then populist radical right parties rise in the polls (Fig. 1.1).

This book traces the steps from reviewing the state of the literature to the eventual political consequences of its findings. The second chapter shows the importance of explaining variation in electoral advances of populist radical right parties and outlines the research questions in detail. The state of research is summarized in Chap. 3. In contrast to other studies in comparative politics, the literature review also puts a heavy emphasis on studies in social conflict. Ultimately, these studies are key in the operationalization of the research design, which is dealt with in Chap. 4. Chapter 5 reviews the findings of the statistical analyses and offers the two-level theory explaining variation in the electoral advances of populist radical right parties in Western Europe. Chapters 6–8 present detailed case studies of the Netherlands, Sweden and (West) Germany. Chapter 9 proves the generalizability of the findings across Western Europe in explaining the electoral advances of the Alternative for

Germany (AfD) and the United Kingdom Independence Party (UKIP). Finally, Chap. 10 concludes with a new theory on party politics and emphasizes the pivotal role of the interactions and political messaging of established parties in contemporary politics.

Scholars and students of comparative politics might be especially interested in the state of the public debate and research, the research design and the QCA analyses (Chaps. 2–5). Readers interested in one country in particular might focus on the case studies (Chaps. 6–8). Observers of contemporary European politics, in Germany and the United Kingdom in particular, should read Chap. 9. Campaign strategists and journalists short on time could focus on the introduction and the concluding Chap. 10. Both summarize the political mechanisms leading to the rise and fall of populist radical right parties that can be summarized with the headline: 'It's political messaging, stupid!'

# Chapter 2
# The Riddle: Why Are Some Populist Radical Right Parties More Successful than Others?

## 2.1 The Curious Rise of a New Star in Western Politics

The election of Donald Trump in the USA and the departure of the United Kingdom from the European Union ('Brexit') showcase the power of populist radical right parties (PRRP). Donald Trump reaped the rewards of the decade-long campaigning of the right-wing extremist Tea Party (Dionne 2016), while the United Kingdom Independence Party (UKIP) was the strongest proponent of the UK leaving the EU (Lochocki 2015b). The impact of PRRPs across democratic politics in continental Western Europe has also been substantial. In Austria, Denmark, France, the Netherlands, Norway, Sweden and Switzerland, PRRPs have reshaped a once bipolar party structure into a tripolar system. PRRP parties poll on equal footing with conservatives and social democrats. In contrast, up to summer of 2017 they have remained relatively weak in Belgium, Germany, Greece, Ireland, Portugal and Spain (Table 2.1).

The differences in electoral advances are remarkable. When Europeans are asked for their sympathy towards the agenda of PRRP parties, 10–25% of voters have expressed consistent support for their program, regardless of time and country (Giugni and Koopmans 2007; Van der Brug and Fennema 2007; Fieschi et al. 2012). This has led one of the most well-read scholars of populism, Cas Mudde, to state: 'Widespread demand is a given, rather than the main puzzle, in contemporary western democracies. Provocatively stated, the real research question should be: why have so few [populist radical right] parties been successful given the generally fertile breeding ground?' (Mudde 2010, 1179).

Given that the demand for PRRPs' agendas remains stable, but their advances vary substantially, what seems to vary instead is voters' demand for a new political player. It appears that in some countries, at certain times, this demand for a new political player remains significantly lower due to the sufficient programmatic supply of established political parties (Rydgren 2007). Accordingly, the variation in the electoral advances of PRRPs could be accounted for by understanding when

T. Lochocki, *The Rise of Populism in Western Europe*,
DOI 10.1007/978-3-319-62855-4_2

**Table 2.1** Electoral fortunes of PRRPs in Western Europe

| Country | PRRP crossing electoral threshold | Votes last federal election, in % (year) | Polls in February 2017 |
|---|---|---|---|
| Austria | Freiheitliche Partei Österreich (since 1986) | 20.5 (2013) | 30–34 |
| | Bündnis Zukunft Österreich (since 2005) | 3.5 (2013) | Less than 3 |
| Belgium | Vlaams Blok (since 2004) | 3.7 (2015) | 8–12 |
| Denmark | Danske Folkeparti (since 1998) | 21.1 (2011) | 14–18 |
| Germany | Alternative für Deutschland (since 2012) | 4.7 (2013) | 8–12 |
| Greece | Anexartitoi Ellines (since 2012) | 3.7 (2015) | 2–4 |
| England | UK Independence Party | 12.7 (2015) | 10–14 |
| Finland | Perussuomalaiset (since 2007) | 17.7 (2015) | 7–11 |
| France[a] | Front National (since 1986) | 17.9 (2012) | 24–28 |
| Ireland | – | – | – |
| Italy | Lega Nord (since 1992) | 4.0 (2013) | 11–15 |
| Luxembourg | Alternativ Demokratesch Reformpartei (since 1989) | 6.6 (2013) | 3–7 |
| Netherlands | Partij voor de Vrijheid (since 2006) | 10.1 (2012) | 17–21 |
| Norway | Fremskrittspartiet (since 1981) | 16.3 (2013) | 11–15 |
| Portugal | Partido Popular (since 1974) | 7.8 (2015) | 4–8 |
| Spain | – | – | – |
| Sweden | Sverigedemokraterna (since 2006) | 12.9 (2014) | 17–27 |
| Switzerland | Schweizerische Volkspartei (since 1986) | 29.4 (2015) | 26–30 |

[a]Numbers based on first round of French presidential election

and why voters' stable demand for their program is insufficiently catered to by established political parties. The guiding research question of this book thus reads: *When—and why—does an electoral niche open for a populist radical right party?*

## 2.2   Defining Populist Radical Right Parties

But what program are European PRRPs allegedly catering to so compellingly? According to studies scrutinizing the motivation of their voters (Arzheimer 2009b), as much as the campaigns of successful PRRPs (Ivarsflaten 2008), the key factor behind their electoral advances is their firmly conservative position in matters affecting the national identity—the political debates about identity politics or, as others say, cultural matters—in particular, their fierce rejection of any form of multiculturalism. Simon Bornschier summarizes the core of their program vividly:

First, [...PRRPs] challenge the societal changes brought about by the libertarian left, and question the legitimacy of political decisions that enact universalistic values. Second, and more importantly, the populist right has promoted new issues and developed new discourses, for example concerning immigration. This does not involve ethnic racism, but rather what Betz (2004) and Betz and Johnson (2004) have called 'differentialist nativism' or 'cultural differentialism', which represents a counter-vision to multicultural models of society (Bornschier 2010, 5).

This very elaboration is crucial to understanding what distinguishes PRRPs from right-wing extremist parties (e.g. the National Democratic Party, NPD, in Germany). Right-wing extremist parties are anti-democratic movements, running on a platform of ethnic, blood and soil racism (e.g. only people with national ancestors can be 'real Frenchmen'). In contrast, PRRPs are anti-elite parties that campaign on a very strict definition of national interest and national belonging, cumulated in a very narrow understanding of national culture. However, this very definition might apply to people without parents and grandparents born in the respective country, too, for example if they strictly assimilate into a defined set of alleged national values, customs and traditions. The society PRRPs envision is therefore best defined as 'Illiberal Democracy'.

Scholars have put forward various definitions to capture this party family. They are referred to as 'radical' (Minkenberg 2001; Norris 2005), 'extreme' (Bale 2003; Eatwell 2003), 'nationalist' (Ellinas 2010) or 'anti-immigration' (Spanje 2010). These definitions are all valid in their own way. However, the crucial points of the PRRPs' program are their populist rhetoric (evoking emotions, blaming the 'elite' and using aggravating wording), and their radical exclusionism based on cultural markers of distinction through democratic decision-making, as captured by the term 'illiberal democracy'. In the light of these considerations, this book will refer to the party group under scrutiny as *populist radical right parties*, PRRPs (Mudde 2016).

In trying to compare this party family to other political actors, it is helpful to rely on the model of the two-dimensional space (as used for instance by Kriesi et al. 2008). The political space is divided in a socio-economic axis of conflict (with the opposing poles left and right defining redistribution and no redistribution by the welfare state) and a cultural axis of conflict, where identity politics play out (with a liberal and a conservative pole, defining multiculturalism and international cooperation on the one side and nationalist policies on the other). Most PRRPs do not have a very thought-through economic program; neither do they receive many votes for their economic platform—their appeal almost entirely rests on their cultural agenda (Arzheimer 2009b; Ivarsflaten 2008). Given that this agenda remains in the democratic spectrum, it is helpful to define the position of PRRPs as closest to the conservative/traditional-communitarian pole on the cultural axis of political competition (where identity politics are discussed) within the democratic spectrum. It is important to note that established moderate parties—especially center-right parties—at times embrace the same position (Fig. 2.1). The prime goal of populist radical right parties thus seems to be the establishment of an Illiberal Democracy.

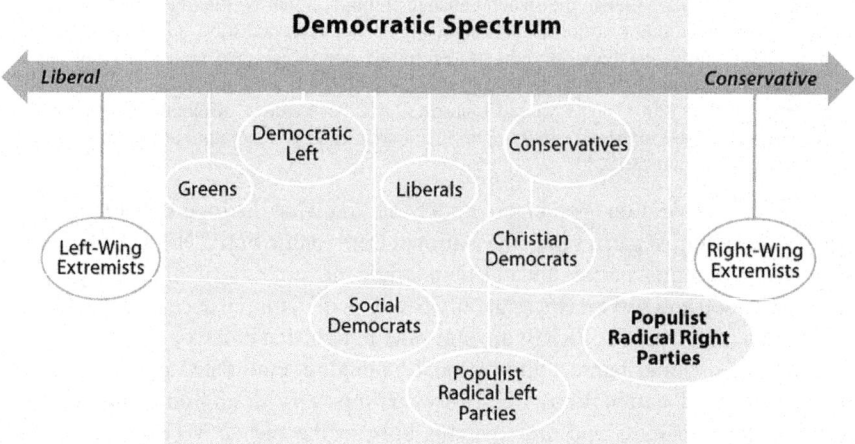

**Fig. 2.1** The position of European parties on the cultural axis, mainly consisting of issues of immigration and European integration

## 2.3   The Winning Formula: For the Nation, Against the Elite

Various scholars have understood PRRPs as institutionalized counter-movements to the salient multicultural discourses that have informed various European societies over the last 30 years (Kriesi et al. 2008; Bornschier 2010). These liberal discourses diverged from an exclusion mechanism based on ethnic premises that defined modern nation states (Wimmer 2000). The post-Cold War, post-modern Europe was supposed to be based on a 'civic turn' (Mouritsen 2008), outlining forms of belonging beyond markers of ethnic distinction. A post-national age, deconstructing former national boundaries, should have been based on liberal policies of integration and immigration and international cooperation across national borders, reified by the European Union (Inglehart and Welzel 2005; Joppke 2007; Howard 2009). The high tide of these debates can be located in the mid-1990s, leading to Nathan Glazer's famous statement that 'we are all multiculturalists now!' (Glazer 1997). Since then, a 're-nationalization' has been witnessed in almost all Western democracies, on the discursive as much as the legal level. Post-modern and post-national ideas have shifted the emphasis from ethnic to civic means of integration 'culture' (whatever that is in the respective author's opinion), continuing to crystallize as the pivotal marker of distinction in contemporary discourses on the integration of migrants and in delineation towards other states (Brubaker 2001).

Immigration and integration play a key role in this respect. Firstly, the migrant and asylum seeker function as clearly visible symbols of an otherwise difficult to grasp social change. Secondly, the role of the state can be defined comparatively clearly in regard to immigration and integration: it is the state's primary task to control who or what enters, what happens within its realm and to define what and who may stay and go. Debates on immigration and integration thus offer the perfect symbolic interaction where voters can easily cast an opinion on whether they appreciate how the state organs deal with social change or not (Bornschier 2011). This link explains why PRRPs' programs merge very conservative positions with anti-elite sentiments: PRRPs understand the national culture as being under siege due to social changes linked to immigration and European integration and blame the established moderate parties—who hold control over the state's organs—as harbingers of these very changes. The national elite has not halted these changes; even worse—in the eyes of the populists—they have perpetuated the social changes with liberal migration policies or pro-European stances. This connection explains the two parts of the PRRPs' winning formula: *for the nation, against the elite.*

Populist radical right parties thus portray the external challenge (usually the migrant, at times the EU or international trade) as a primary threat to the national culture, which the national elites did nothing to stop; on the contrary, they even perpetuated the threat: UKIP portrayed the EU as endangering the prime symbol of British post-war identity—the NHS (National Health Service)—and thus blamed the established parties for ransacking British culture (Ford and Goodwin 2014). Especially in its early years, the Alternative for Germany (AfD) accused the governing parties of bailing out Greece using German taxpayers' money. The narrative that Greeks are lazy and untrustworthy was perpetuated, while it was reiterated that Germans had to undergo massive social cuts in the 1990s to enable their economic recovery in the 2000s. The story in conservative camps was that supporting Greek laissez-faire economics was an attack on core German narratives: industriousness and tough economic reforms. In turn, the AfD accused established German parties—who reluctantly backed the financial aid—as selling out the cultural core of the German nation, instead of defending it (Lochocki 2015a). Ultimately, debates about national culture are about national identity politics.

## 2.4  Why Bother?

After the election of Donald Trump and Brexit, the impact of PRRPs seems beyond question. However, although in the US and the UK populists won a majority of the Electoral College and the popular vote respectively, PRRPs can have a substantial influence in democracies without reaching 50% of the votes, and also without participating in national governments.

While we lack concrete studies on the topic, the electoral advances of PRRPs seem especially harmful for social democratic parties in proportional representation systems. This is for two reasons: firstly, because roughly half of PRRP sympathizers previously opted for a social democratic party (Ivarsflaten 2005); and secondly, because strategic options for center-right parties increase substantially after the entrenchment of a PRRP. The dominant center-right party (usually conservatives or Christian democrats) gains another coalition partner, and/or are able to center their focus on the political competition with the social democrats around the political center, while conservative voters opt for the possible coalition partner on the far right (Bale et al. 2010). It comes as no surprise that the massive problems of social democracy in northern Europe correspond strikingly with the substantial increase of vote shares for PRRPs. In turn, the countries in which center-left governments are still arithmetically feasible have weak PRRPs: e.g. Germany, Portugal and Spain.

PRRP's winning formula *'for the nation, against the elite'* breeds the assumption that leaders in democratic institutions are not trustworthy. The infamous 'protest vote' is meant to cast one's general dissatisfaction with the general state of affairs. If this sentiment is filtered into the system on a daily basis under the auspices of an entrenched PRRP, it undermines democratic trust per se. It comes as no surprise that Russian intelligence is considering PRRPs as a perfect tool to destabilize Western democracies (Wesslau 2016). Migrants and asylum seekers are defined as prime symbols of undesired social change brought about by allegedly unresponsive elites. Consequently, PRRPs also present the solution: a very conservative immigration and integration policy calling for very limited inflows of migrants and the assimilation of those already living in the country. PRRPs thus do not reject immigration per se, but call for very low numbers and reject multiculturalism. While most European societies are already home to millions of migrants, and even more citizens with migration backgrounds, this rejection of multiculturalism can trigger a culture war: a conflict between citizens supporting multiculturalism and international cooperation and those calling for assimilation and national solutions (Bornschier 2010). The rise of PRRPs thus perpetuates two societal grievances: the cleavage between elites and the electorate and the cleavage between liberal and conservative citizens. The growing influence of PRRPs thus leads to growing polarization, social fragmentation and hampers the smooth functioning of representative democracies.

PRRPs do not alter immigration policies in government, but rather in pushing mainstream parties to the right. As illustrated in citizenship studies, the presence of a successfully entrenched populist radical right party basically forestalls a liberalization of citizenship legislation (Howard 2006, 2010). But PRRPs do not only hamper liberalization, they also spark a conservative turn in immigration policies as they can set the national agenda (Minkenberg 2001) and influence various actors at the level of parties, policies and polities (Mudde 2013). PRRPs thus push mainstream parties to the right on the—for PRRPs—crucial issues of immigration and integration policies (Akkerman 2015; Carvalho 2014). Similar to the constant decrease of trust towards democratic institutions due to the interventions of PRRPs, the national debate is substantially influenced by the far right's permanent calls for very conservative immigration policies. In this climate, it is very difficult to formulate an alternative vision of a multicultural vivre ensemble. As Yilmaz Ferruh writes, the growing salience of immigration topics and the scapegoating of migrants for undesired social challenges

> is the result of the far-right's intervention in discourse through sustained crises and moral panics around Muslim immigrants and their 'cultural practices.' Their political parties have succeeded in making immigration, culture and religion central issues for all mainstream parties, including those on the left side of the traditional political spectrum. [...] Whatever the differences between political platforms, the basic antagonism produces its own culturally defined social divisions, making it impossible to articulate alternative visions under given conditions (Yilmaz 2012, 337/8).

How populist forces affect other policy areas, e.g. foreign policies, has not been examined with any clear-cut research findings as yet (Balfour et al. 2016), but the Brexit and the polarization across the EU lets us assume that the rise of populist forces benefits a revival of nationalist foreign policies.

The impact of growing PRRPs in the democracies of Western Europe can be illustrated by three processes. Their rise benefits the center-right of the political spectrum; witnessed by the weakness of social democracy in nearly all states in northern Europe. PRRPs' constant infusion of anti-elite sentiments and calls for very conservative policies in identity politics widens the gap between the electorate and the elites and between liberal and conservative citizens. Finally, the conservative turn in migration policies as much as the scapegoating of migrants and the EU due to the far right's rhetoric forges a climate in which migrants and international cooperation appear on the losing side. The rise of PRRPs seems to push Western democracies towards center-right governments, perpetuates a revival of conservative identity politics and propels a polarization of the respective societies along cultural cleavages.

## 2.5   Why Are Populists Not Winning Everywhere?

If the PRRPs' prime selling points are constantly supported by up to 25% of the European electorate (Compare Sect. 2.1), the question indeed reads: why have *so few* parties made it big? Why did the Front National (FN) manage to become a major player in France in the 1990s, while it took the Sweden Democrats (SD) 20 years longer? And why are there no PRRPs in Spain and Ireland, but rather successful ones in neighboring Italy and the UK? And if the Germans have hardly changed their opinion on the EU and migration over the last 20 years, why has it taken up to 2013 for the AfD to be able to harvest this stable demand?

Understanding this conundrum has brought a 'minor industry' (Arzheimer 2009a, 259) to the fore. However, as will be shown in detail, a substantial answer to what political mechanisms really enable and block the rise of PRRPs is still lacking. Various studies stress the importance of discussions of cultural topics for PRRPs' rise. The *form* of this very debate seems pivotal. Quantitative studies argue that a debate with high salience over identity politics, as immigration, must show a void on the conservative position so a PRRP can seize its electoral niche (Arzheimer 2009a, b; Ivarsflaten 2005; Giugni and Koopmans 2007; Kitschelt 1995; Rydgren 2007; Van der Brug and Spanje 2009). Qualitative studies offer further insights, arguing that there must not only be an opening in the conservative position, but a conservative position must be offered by an established political actor in the first place and then dropped over the course of the salient debate before a PRRP can mobilize on that position (Ellinas 2010; Muis 2012). Moderate parties must have first legitimized topics and positions via which PRRPs mobilize; these established parties must then have switched position over the course of the salient debate, in turn opening the political space for the PRRP.

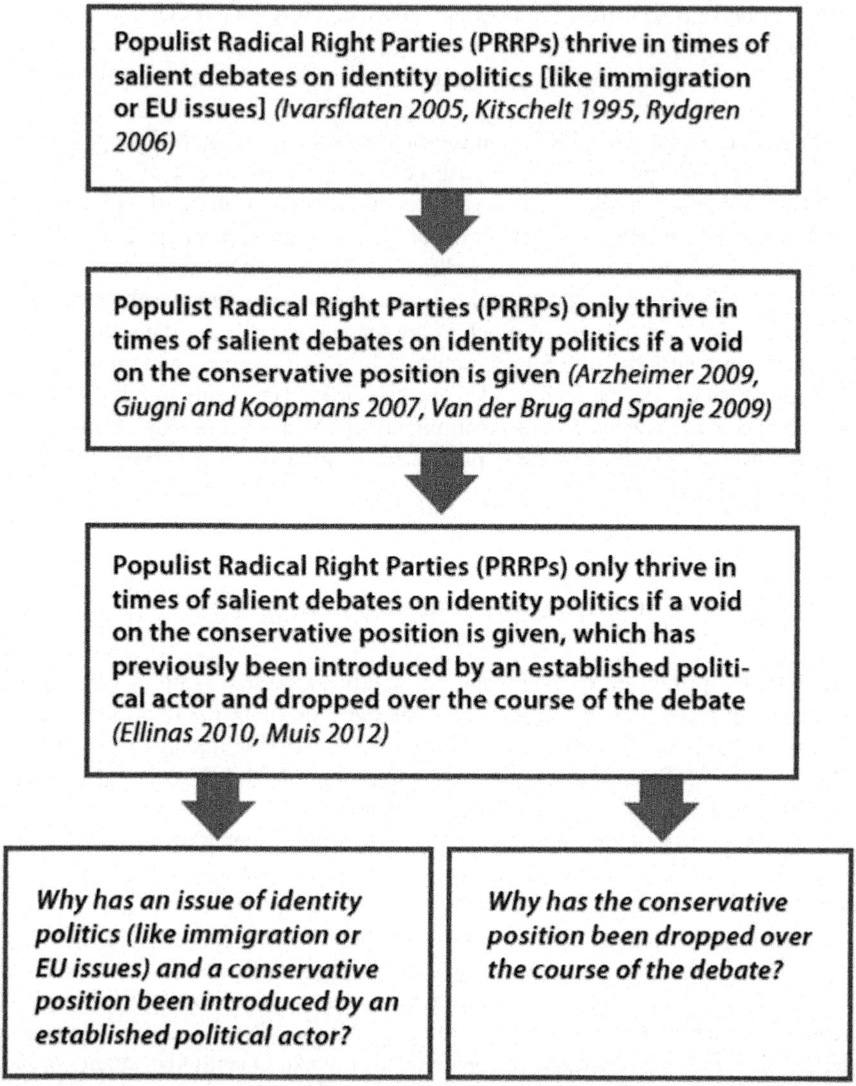

Populist Radical Right Parties (PRRPs) thrive in times of salient debates on identity politics [like immigration or EU issues] *(Ivarsflaten 2005, Kitschelt 1995, Rydgren 2006)*

Populist Radical Right Parties (PRRPs) only thrive in times of salient debates on identity politics if a void on the conservative position is given *(Arzheimer 2009, Giugni and Koopmans 2007, Van der Brug and Spanje 2009)*

Populist Radical Right Parties (PRRPs) only thrive in times of salient debates on identity politics if a void on the conservative position is given, which has previously been introduced by an established political actor and dropped over the course of the debate *(Ellinas 2010, Muis 2012)*

*Why has an issue of identity politics (like immigration or EU issues) and a conservative position been introduced by an established political actor?*

*Why has the conservative position been dropped over the course of the debate?*

**Fig. 2.2** Explanations for the rise of PRRPs in Western Europe and derived research questions

The research puzzle thus reads: how do you account for the striking difference between the stable and substantial demand for strictly conservative positions in identity politics, covering areas such as immigration, of up to 25% of the European electorate, on the one hand; and on the other, established parties' varying rationales for (1) increasing the salience of identity politics and (2) opening the electoral niche for PRRPs in dropping their conservative messages over the course of the debates (Fig. 2.2)?

## 2.6   Methodological Challenges: The Call for Comparative Case Studies

The challenge in answering these questions lies with *methodological* complexities. Given that PRRPs present themselves as alleged protectors of a distinct national identity, an analysis of their electoral fortunes requires country studies (Wimmer 2002). These alone, however, are not well suited to decipher generalizable political mechanisms (King et al. 1994). On the other hand, studies trying to elucidate variation of that party family with larger samples lack data sources that reliably and validly mirror party interactions (Helbling and Tresch 2011). This explains why Cas Mudde calls for moving away from the 'comfort zone of detached quantitative electoral studies of the same problematic data sources (e.g. Eurobarometer, World Value Survey) and descriptive historical studies of the same parties (e.g. British National Party, Front National)' (Mudde 2016, 10).

Proposing a solution, Charles Tilly offers a way to largely avoid both shortcomings. He emphasizes that the 'analysis of social and institutional change should be 'concrete'—referring to concrete units of analysis—and 'historical'—limiting their scope to an era bound to clearly defined processes' (Tilly 1984, 14). He argues for comparisons among large numbers of cases, if detailed information about each case is given, in calling 'for comparisons of various large entities, with one prime caveat: familiarity with cases needs to remain being given' (Tilly 1984, 77). Tilly is advocating for a medium-sized sample and mid-range theories in *comparative case studies*. This should ensure a substantial potential to generalize the findings, and also a rather high degree of validity and reliability, in turn, ameliorating the challenges of relying on either single case or large n-studies (Table 2.2). This study will adhere to these elaborations and work with comparative case studies.

**Table 2.2**   Challenges in the study of variation in the electoral advances of PRRPs

|  | Qualitative, single case studies | Quantitative, large-N studies | Comparative case studies |
|---|---|---|---|
| Advantage | Higher degree of validity | Higher degree of reliability and generalizability | Relatively high degree of reliability, validity and generalizability |
| Disadvantage | Lower degree of generalizability and reliability | Lower degree of validity | |

# References

Akkerman T (2015) Immigration policy and electoral competition in Western Europe: a fine-grained analysis of party positions over two decades. Party Polit 21(1):54–67

Arzheimer K (2009a) Contextual factors and the extreme right vote in Western Europe. Am J Polit Sci 53(2):259–275

Arzheimer K (2009b) Protest, neo-liberalism or anti-immigrant sentiment: what motivates the voters of the extreme right in Western Europe? Zeitschrift für Vergleichende Politikwissenschaft/Comp Gov Polit 2:173–197

Bale T (2003) Cinderella and her ugly sisters: the mainstream and extreme right in Europe's bipolarising party systems. West Eur Polit 26(3):67–90

Bale T et al (2010) If you can't beat them, join them? Explaining social democratic responses to the challenge from the populist radical right in Western Europe. Polit Stud 58:410–426

Balfour R et al (2016) Europe's troublemakers. The populist challenge to foreign policy. European Policy Centre (EPC). Available at: http://www.epc.eu/documents/uploads/pub_6377_europe_s_troublemakers.pdf. Last accessed 7 May 2017

Bornschier S (2010) The new cultural divide and the two-dimensional political space in Western Europe. West Eur Polit 33(3):419–444

Bornschier S (2011) Why a right-wing populist party emerged in France but not in Germany: cleavages and actors in the formation of a newcultural divide. Eur Polit Sci Rev. Available on CJO 2011. doi:10.1017/S1755773911000117

Brubaker R (2001) The return of assimilation? Changing perspectives on immigration and its sequels in France, Germany, and the United States. Ethn Racial Stud 24(4):531–548

Carvalho J (2014) Impact of extreme right parties on immigration policy: comparing Britain, France and Italy. Routledge, London

Dionne EJ (2016) Why the right went wrong. Simon & Schuster Paperbacks, New York

Eatwell R (2003) Theorising the rise of the European extreme right: towards a three-dimensional model. In: Merkl PH, Weinberg L (eds) Right-wing extremism in the twenty-first century. Frank Cass, London

Ellinas A (2010) The media and the far right in Western Europe: playing the nationalist card. University Press, Cambridge

Fieschi C et al (2012) Recapturing the reluctant radical: how to win back Europe's populist vote. Counterpoint

Ford R, Goodwin M (2014) Revolt on the right: explaining support for the radical right in Britain. Routledge, London

Giugni M, Koopmans R (2007) What causes people to vote for a radical right party? A rejoinder to van der Brug and Fennema. Int J Public Opin Res 19(4):488–491

Glazer N (1997) We are all multiculturalists now. Harvard University Press, Harvard

Helbling M, Tresch A (2011) Measuring party positions and issue salience from media coverage: discussing and cross-validating new indicators. Elect Stud 30:174–183

Howard MM (2006) Comparative citizenship: an agenda for cross-national research. Perspect Polit 4(3):443–454

Howard MM (2009) The politics of citizenship in Europe. Cambridge University Press, Cambridge

Howard MM (2010) The impact of the far right on citizenship policy in Europe: explaining continuity and change. J Ethn Migr Stud 36(5):735–751

Inglehart R, Welzel C (2005) Modernization, cultural change and democracy: the human development sequence. Cambridge University Press, Cambridge

Ivarsflaten E (2005) The vulnerable populist right parties: no economic realignment fuelling their electoral success. Eur J Polit Res 44:465–492

Ivarsflaten E (2008) What unites right-wing populists in Western Europe? Re-examining grievance mobilization models in seven successful cases. Comp Polit Stud 41:3–23

Joppke C (2007) Beyond national models: civic integration policies for immigrants in Western Europe. West Eur Polit 30(1):1–22

King G et al (1994) Designing social inquiry: scientific inference in qualitative research. Oxford University Press, Oxford

Kitschelt H (1995) The radical right in Western Europe: a comparative analysis. Michigan University Press, Ann Arbor

Kriesi H et al (2008) West European politics in the age of globalization. Cambridge University Press, Cambridge

Lochocki T (2015a) Countering right-wing populism. The AfD and the strategic dilemma for Germany's moderate parties. GMF Policy Brief 1/2015. Available at: http://www.gmfus.org/publications/countering-right-wing-populism. Last accessed 7 May 2017

Lochocki T (2015b) How the United Kingdom independence party's one seat has the power to change British and European politics. GMF Policy Brief 2/2015. Available at: http://www.gmfus.org/publications/how-UKIPs-one-seat-has-power. Last accessed 7 May 2017

Minkenberg M (2001) The radical right in public office: agenda-setting and policy effects. West Eur Polit 24(4):1–21

Mouritsen P (2008) Political responses to cultural conflict: reflections on the ambiguities of the civic turn. In: Mouritsen P (ed) Constituting communities: political solutions to cultural conflict. Palgrave Macmillan, London, pp 1–30

Mudde C (2010) The populist radical right: a pathological normalcy. West Eur Polit 33 (6):1167–1186

Mudde C (2013) The 2012 Stein Rokkan lecture. Three decades of populist radical right parties in Western Europe: so what? Eur J Polit Res:1–12

Mudde C (2016) The study of populist radical right parties: towards a fourth wave. C-Rex Working Paper Series 1/2016. Available at: https://www.sv.uio.no/c-rex/english/publications/c-rex-working-paper-series/Cas%20Mudde:%20The%20Study%20of%20Populist%20Radical%20Right%20Parties.pdf. Last accessed 7 May 2017

Muis J (2012) Pim Fortuyn: the evolution of a media phenomenon. Ridderkerk

Norris P (2005) Radical right: voters and parties in the electoral market. Cambridge University Press, New York

Rydgren J (2007) The sociology of the radical right. Ann Rev Sociol 33:241–262

Tilly C (1984) Big structures, large processes, huge comparisons. Sage Foundation, New York

Van der Brug W, Fennema M (2007) What causes people to vote for a radical-right party? A review of recent work. J Public Opin Res 19(4):474–487

Van Der Brug W, van Spanje J (2009) Immigration, Europe and the 'new' cultural dimension. Eur J Polit Res 48:309–334

van Spanje J (2010) Contagious parties: anti-immigration parties and their impact on other parties' immigration stances in contemporary Western Europe. Party Polit 16(5):563–586

Wesslau F (2016) Putin's friends in Europe. European Council on Foreign Relations Commentary, Oct 19. Available at: http://www.ecfr.eu/article/commentary_putins_friends_in_europe7153. Last accessed 7 May 2017

Wimmer A (2000) Racism in nationalised states: a framework for comparative research. In: Verkuyten M, Ter Wal J (eds) Comparative perspectives on racism. Ashgate, Aldershot, pp 41–72

Wimmer A (2002) Nationalist exclusion and ethnic conflict: shadows of modernity. Cambridge University Press, Cambridge

Yilmaz F (2012) Right-wing hegemony and immigration: how the populist far-right achieved hegemony through the immigration debate in Europe. Curr Sociol 60:368–382

# Chapter 3
# State of Research: Linking Social Theory with Comparative Politics

## 3.1 From Social Theory to Party Politics

Populist radical right parties thrive if they can present themselves as sole defenders of the nation. Then their winning formula 'for the nation, against the elite' is attractive to voters. However, before PRRPs can rely on this agenda, a conflict about the national identity has to erupt in the first place. Why and how identity conflicts unfold is a paramount issue in the social sciences (e.g. in Social Theory or Social Psychology). These studies will be reviewed before turning to the literature on PRRPs with comparative party politics. The most important outcome of this review lies in understanding the importance of perceptions; of perceived social structures and perceived discourses on identity in understanding far right parties. Any 'objective' data—be it unemployment figures, immigration statistics or assumed common historical interpretations—are thus of limited help in explaining the rise and fall of PRRPs. These perceptions must be included in understanding the varying conduct of established political parties, which is key in understanding PRRPs' electoral advances. These elaborations lead to fine-grain analysis and the formulation of a hypothesis to answer the major research question.

## 3.2 Theories of Social Conflict: Structures and Discourses Matter

Social conflict as organizing principle in modern societies has been theorized on various noteworthy levels. The godfather of the discipline is without a doubt Georg Simmel; the work of Lewis Coser set the tone in post-war social theory; the most recent overarching theoretical pieces stem from Robert Gould and Zygmunt Bauman.

© Springer International Publishing AG 2018
T. Lochocki, *The Rise of Populism in Western Europe*,
DOI 10.1007/978-3-319-62855-4_3

Georg Simmel understands social conflict as based in the organizing principles of the respective society. He argues that the more similar the competitors within the social structure are, the lower the levels of tolerance will be. The reason lies in the actors' *perception* of each other: two similar actors become involved in a conflict 'because there is only little that is different between them; hence even the slightest antagonism has a relative significance quite other than that between strangers, who count with all kinds of mutual differences to begin with' (Simmel 1955, 44). That means that conflict is all the more pronounced the closer the *felt proximity* between two actors. How the conflict between these two actors plays is then dependent on *subjective evaluation* of their own position vis a vis the other: 'Where it is a matter of attaining, we shall here speak of envy; where of keeping, of jealousy. The jealous person has a 'rightful claim' to the possession, whereas the envious person has no 'legitimacy of any claim'' (Simmel 1955, 50). He emphasizes that the case of jealousy hardens the social conflict: the feeling of envy focuses on the possession itself, while the feeling of jealousy is concerned with the possessor; the problem shifts from the good to its keeper (Simmel 1955, 51). A person feels jealous (thus focusing on the keeper, not the good) if he thinks his claim and legal right is hurt (Simmel 1955, 53). In consequence, social conflict turns aggressive if an actor—who feels entitled—feels stripped of access to valuable resources by another actor whose legal right or claim for a scarce good can be disputed as the social order stands in question. The key variables in explaining social conflict are thus the *perceived* organizational principles of a society and what has been *defined* as legitimate behavior within its realm.

Similarly to Georg Simmel, Lewis Coser argues that social conflict only occurs if the organizing principles of a society are questioned. He claims that groups that can avoid conflicts over core values tend to be the most stable. Groups that are not making strong claims on people's identity and not establishing rigid criteria for membership are more likely to function smoothly (Coser 1956, 87–110). If these criteria become too rigid, meaning too narrowly defined, they must necessarily divide the group. A divided group will eventually develop different interests within a shared realm. This eventually leads to one group being defined as disloyal towards once commonly shared goals; then the conflict breaks out into the open (Coser 1956, 128–137). Eventually, these intra-group conflicts perpetuate themselves as the conflict becomes a means to identify with either group: 'Conflict acts as a stimulus for establishing new rules, norms, and institutions, thus serving as an agent of socialization for both contending parties' (Coser 1956, 128). In essence, Coser argues that the construction of conflicting group identity defines their interest within the social structure they share and vice versa.

Taking a related stance, Robert Gould emphasizes that social conflicts are rooted in competitions about rank that turn hostile if using aggressive means forms of communication. Similarly to Simmel and Coser, he also underscores that a stable social order reduces the likelihood of conflict; only a disruption of the social order and its hierarchies can spark a social conflict (Gould 2003, 60 and 163/4). To what extent such a conflict then turns aggressive to the largest extent depends on the tone of the debate. It is not so much the origin of the conflict, defining its outcome, but to what extent the conflict is turned into a heated debate (Gould 2003, 136/7). Echoing Simmel and Coser, Gould thus emphasizes that the origin of a conflict lies with changes in the social structure, but that its outcome is defined by the departing *communication*.

Zygmunt Bauman understands the prime contemporary social conflict over immigration as rooted in people's craving for a kind of certainty the modern nation state can no longer deliver. In an attempt to cover up this incapacity, the modern nation state scapegoats and persecutes immigrants to create the illusion of power. To the state, the prime source of political power lies in the capacity to reduce subjectively-felt uncertainty and to organize social cohesion (Bauman 1987). If state institutions lose this power, the state would have cause to fear the rise of competing forces, which would then strip the state of its power. As globalization rendered the former power projections of nation states obsolete (Bauman 2000), the nation state needs to cover up its loss of power in forging a stable and secure environment for its citizens: 'The influx of foreign elements into the nation, particularly when made easy by the 'open arms' hospitable attitude of the host nation, casts doubt on the 'naturalness' of national membership and thus saps the very foundation of national unity and solidarity [...] [I]n the process foreigners are constructed as threat to order and security' (Bauman and May 2001, 143/4). The prime drivers of debates over immigration are thus *felt* endangering changes in the social cohesion due to globalization that the nation state cannot tackle. In turn, the state tries to *camouflage* its institutions' inability to manage contemporary diversity and to shape society's outlook by *scapegoating* migrants.

In all theories social conflict is conceived as symbolizing an increase in perceived complexity (Bauman) and/or a recalibration of felt social stratification (Simmel, Coser and Gould). How societies deal with these challenges is dependent on two factors (comp. Table 3.1): (1) the perceived organizing principles, the felt social structure of the host societies; and (2), the discursive processes framing the

**Table 3.1**  Theories of social conflict in comparison

| Scholar of social conflict | Reason for social conflict | Reaction of receiving society | Explanatory concepts | |
|---|---|---|---|---|
| | | | Social structure | Discursive processes |
| Georg Simmel | Challenging the 'legitimate order' | Striving to sustain the 'legitimate order' | Definition of 'legitimate order' | Organization or redefinition of 'legitimate order' |
| Lewis Coser and Robert Gould | Stimulates group conflict over rank | Recalibration of social stratification | Defines level of group solidarity | Form of communication explains degree of conflict |
| Zygmunt Bauman | Increasing complexity | Postmodern state institutions scapegoating migrants for an increase in complexity | Limits of diversity in post-modern societies have been reached | Migrants as alleged symbols of hyper-complexity |

identity of the society (referred to as 'discourse over complexity' by Bauman and 'struggles over loyalty and social order' by Simmel, Coser and Gould). How societies react to social conflict—(here: whether they turn to a populist radical right party or not) seems to depend on the perceived social structure and how the national debate on increased diversity unfolds.


## 3.3    Comparative Social Sciences: It's Not About Facts but Debates

The studies of social conflict recommend focusing on the perceived organizational principles in which the conflict occurs—the economic, institutional and discursive arrangements. These scope conditions are centered on the contemporary nation state. Studies analyzing changes in nation-states' social structure thus offer insights into how these conflicts play out in more detail.

In this vein, various studies have investigated to what extent the size of the immigrant group in each country has an impact on the response of the host society. Curiously, neither the actual size (Schlueter and Scheepers 2010) of the immigrant group, nor its perceived size (Hjerm 2007) can explain the varying responses of a host society. For an overview of this debate, see Pettigrew and colleagues: an effect is visible only in some countries, but not in general (Pettigrew et al. 2010). Country particularities seem especially important here because the national perception of immigration varies substantially (Herda 2010). If the size of immigrant groups cannot account for variation in the reactions of the host society, maybe the degree of economic competition can? Yet neither the actual nor the perceived degree of economic competition explains societies' varying responses here either. Again, an effect is visible in some countries, but not in others—and different institutions and discourses mediate the effects to a substantial degree (Coenders and Scheepers 2008).

A key concept used in explaining social cohesion in European societies is the level of social capital and social trust. Therefore, a wide array of studies scrutinize the effect of social capital and social trust on responses to social changes; again, an overview of the debate offers no general pattern as to whether an increasing diversity decreases social capital or not (Hooghe et al. 2009). Even more interesting, whether a high degree of social capital and social trust increases or decreases hostile reactions towards social change seems to depend largely on context, and on context-particularities—be it forms of domestic stratification, dominant discourses or state identity (Blad and Couton 2009).

Because levels of social capital and social trust tend to correlate with welfare state types, the question arises to what extent welfare state regimes have a say in societies' responses to social change. Esping-Andersen defined three welfare state regimes: the liberal, the conservative and the social-democratic/Nordic type (Esping-Andersen 1990). Based on these regime distinctions, previous studies describe a link between regimes of immigration and welfare. Studies focusing on the Nordic type claim that universal distribution increases hostility towards migrants because immigrants are conceived of as a clearly defined economic threat, while this is the case to a far lesser extent in the less generous liberal and conservative welfare regimes (Amna et al. 2000). Despite these tendencies, a general causal relation between welfare state regimes, patterns of redistribution and responses to social change does not exist (Finseraas 2007). Country particularities seem to be decisive here (Bloemraad and Kesler 2009); in particular, forms of the construction of solidarity (Keating 2009) and state institutions (Lecours and Béland 2005) are noted as intermediating factors.

Studies scrutinizing the link between social capital, social trust and welfare regimes and societies' responses to social change point out that the *form* of competition over scarce resources indeed accounts for varying reactions to an increase of diversity. However, these processes cannot be generalized, but are dependent on institutional and discursive particularities—the form salient national debates over social change take amongst key national opinion makers. In turn, accounting for variation in the electoral advances of PRRPs seems to depend on how salient national debates on social change are framed dependent on perceived socio-economic parameters.

## 3.4  How Societies Negotiate Belonging: Context and Perceptions Are Key

Societies' responses to social change seem to be based on their perceived social structure and debates over their identity. These, in turn, determine the framing of the issue in salient debates. This begs the question: how do groups negotiate belonging in the twenty-first century?

How an individual perceives a possible out-group depends largely on his standing in the alleged in-group (Schiefer et al. 2010). The individual's will to culturally adjust to a new group surrounding seems to be negatively correlated with the appreciation of his or her status in his or her own group. Simply put: the more you appreciate your status in your own group, the lower your incentives to adapt to another group's stratifications of status (Terry et al. 2006). The more cohesive the group structure, the more inter-group bias can be witnessed (Peterson 2009). Conversely, the more diverse the group's structure, the more tolerant the group towards out-groups, and, accordingly, the more tolerant of general diversity are the group's members; however, extremely diverse groups react rather negatively to the influence of out-groups (Bodenhausen 2010). The strategies and emotions that characterize in-group interactions thus heavily influence inter-group contact. 'These considerations point to the importance of considering subjective or perceived diversity as a causal variable having its own importance—perhaps having more immediate causal significance in shaping group dynamics and performance outcomes than 'objective' diversity; however that is defined' (Bodenhausen 2010, 9).

How this *perceived diversity* is negotiated depends on highly complex outcomes of regular interactions (Bratt 2005). However, a durability of difference remains in place even when 'deep-level similarities' are revealed: certain distinction markers, once placed, appear to be resistant to other influences and trump similarities in other daily interactions (Philipps et al. 2006). These phenomena might be termed as 'essentializing the others' (Chirot and McCauley 2006, 81–87). In spite of these claims, communication studies reconfirm the assumption that permanent inter-group communication enhances mutual understanding (Nagda and Zuniga 2003). However, this conclusion is limited to realms of communication that are 'neutral' (Guinote and Fiske 2003). Once the influences of out-/in-group settings are miti-gated, 'ingroup favoritism [...] does not imply 'outgroup hostility' but rather a cultural group selection in terms of 'differential cooperativeness" (Koopmans and Rebers 2009, 208). Individual-individual contacts between members of in- and out-groups always lead to a higher degree of cooperation than when a member of one group is confronted by the other group in its entirety, and this goes for both sides (McGlynn et al. 2009). Therefore, the perceptions groups have of each other depend on the context of the interaction between the groups.

The context is least favorable to reach an agreement between groups if one group ascribes unjust or threatening behavior to the out-group; for instance, in perceptions of violations of the 'reciprocity principle.' If you think a group is of help, you or your group will be in debt to this group. If you think someone caused you or your group harm, this behavior is not tolerated without retaliation (Cialdini 2001). In contrast, an individual's perception of threat leads to a stronger association between the individual and his/her proclaimed group. This, in turn, leads to greater polari-zation between the in-group and the out-group in times of uncertainty (Sherman et al. 2009). Conversely, the higher the affiliation of the individual with his/her in-group, the higher the perceived threat by the out-group (Cameron et al. 2005). This is explained by the fact that those who identify strongly with the group are most concerned with sustaining the identity and the structure of the group; they are averse to changes in its self-perception and structure (Chirot and McCauley 2006, 62). The most favorable in-group attitudes stem from individuals most frequently exposed to the potential out-group, while at the same time perceiving the contact with the out-group as 'typical' (Liebkind et al. 2004).

Accordingly, in-groups are expected to define and sanction alleged out-groups if they are considered a threat to the in-group. As the perception of harm/good is based on cultural and institutional settings, it can be argued that 'legitimized' behavior is rewarded, while behavior deviant from the allegedly legitimate order is punished. The perceived contexts in which the conflict occurs and the extent to which intra-group difference is considered a threat for one group's core organiza-tional principle defines the outcome of the conflict to the largest extent.

A strong counter-reaction to social change, reified by the electoral advances of PRRPs, thus depends on the extent to which the national debate leaves the impres-sion that the change is a threat to a core appreciated and perceived organizational principle of the receiving state.

## 3.5   Relational Approaches: The Migrant as the Perfect Threat

Social change is rejected if perceived as running counter to core organizational principles of the nation. This begs the question: how is this organizational principle defined and when is it conceived as being under siege?

The organizational principles of a group can be summarized as the crucial difference between groups. This mode of organization is the group's core from which the interaction within the group as much as its structure departs. Consequently, this difference defines the boundary between groups. Boundaries of the nation states of the nineteenth and twentieth centuries have been subject to seminal scholarship (Anderson 1991; Gellner 1994; Brubaker 1996). Scholars have also thoroughly examined to what extent modern nation states deal with immigrants based on these distinct historical trajectories (Reitz 2004; Joppke 2005, 2008; Wimmer 2002, 2006, 2008). However, contemporary Western states adhere to a post-modern logic of exclusion and inclusion. The important symbolic boundaries in contemporary democracies are not found in ethnic forms of belonging but in a context-dependent 'national culture' (Giesen 2007, 173). This 'national culture' is (re-)constructed continuously and explains the increase of struggles over symbolic boundaries to a hitherto unprecedented extent (Eder 2008). These deconstructions led to conservative Europeans feeling an increasing 'craving for roots and undisputed anchors of certainties' (Giesen 2007, 173) and alleged symbols of security and nostalgia (Fieschi et al. 2012, 9–13). And here the migration issue fits perfectly, as migrants and asylum seekers can be perfectly utilized to construct a boundary *against*.

Simon Bornschier's summary of this mechanism is worth quoting at length (italics mine):

> This opposition is, at heart, a conflict over the role of community. [...] Philosophical currents of the European New Right have borrowed from communitarian conceptions of community and justice in their propagation of the concept of 'cultural differentialism,' claiming not the superiority of any nationality or race, but instead stressing the right of peoples to preserve their distinctive traditions. [...] *Immigration is directly linked to this conception since the inflow of people from other cultural backgrounds endangers the cultural homogeneity* that thinkers of the New Right, as well as exponents of right-wing populist parties deem necessary to preserve (Bornschier 2010, 422/3).

In understanding PRRPs as a 'backlash against diversity' (Grillo 2007) stemming from a liberal and multicultural conception of community in the public discourse, their rejection of multiculturalism thus appears as the perfect symbol, the exclusionary boundary, the sound narrative to portray themselves as safeguarding societies' symbolic boundaries. A take on Ireland illustrates the point vividly: 'The object of the discourse might well be the redefinition of the nation, that is, what happens after immigration, yet it is being conducted through the language of immigration' (Garner 2007, 128). It has been barely possible to reinforce nations' boundaries in recent decades, because the diminishing possibility of rallying against neighboring states in post-war Europe came along with a lack of 'others' an identity could be formed against. Immigration offers the perfect narrative to define community—by pointing to those who do not belong to it.

Turning to the literature on comparative politics, the crucial role of the immigration issue is further supported. Before new parties are capable of entrenching themselves in the political spectrum, they are—nolens volens—dependent on the conduct of established parties. The issues the new party focuses on need to be politicized and then—in the eyes of the voters—dropped by established parties in a way that leaves voters' demands unsatisfied (Bale 2008; Ellinas 2010). The issues via which new contenders want to gain votes thus need to first be 'legitimized' by established parties. This mechanism is nicely shown in a case study on Pim Fortuyn's rise in the Netherlands in 2002: it was, similarly, established politicians' airing of anti-multiculturalism statements that fueled his electoral success. In this context, Pim Fortuyn's claims were justified and he was conceived as a 'regular,' 'legitimate' politician (Muis 2012).

Still, one might ask, why should immigration and especially anti-multiculturalism be the major issue for PRRPs? In general, these parties mobilize around three issues: strict welfare policies, anti-elite protest and extremely conservative migration policies (Ivarsflaten 2008; Arzheimer 2009b). Elisabeth Ivarsflaten found that PRRPs mobilizing on migration topics are far more successful (Ivarsflaten 2008). Descriptive large-N studies further show a high salience of immigration-related issues between established political parties *before* the electoral breakthroughs of PRRPs all over Europe (Alonso and Claro da Fonseca 2011). In turn, a heated debate on migration issues between *established moderate* parties seems to precede electoral advances of populist radical right parties. Scrutinizing the motivation of voters turning to PRRPs mirrors these findings: they are hardly mobilized by anti-elite sentiments or welfare state policies, but by PRRPs' stances on immigration (Arzheimer 2009b). A widely read study published by the Bertelsmann Foundation arrived at the same finding: supporters of PRRPs are primarily mobilized by fears over immigration (De Vries and Hoffmann 2016).

Historically speaking, nationalist parties have campaigned on militaristic expansion against their neighbors. However, after the Second World War, the 'lessons learned' (for the Allied occupational forces and during the Cold War) prevented this history repeating. Instead, disputes over national identity focused on the *domestic* realm. Famous examples include the rise of the separatist parties Vlaams Blok in Belgium and the Lega Nord in Italy around 1990. The transformation of the Austrian Freiheitliche Partei Österreich in the late 1980s can also be explained by taking into consideration debates about Austrian guilt and responsibility during the Second World War that heated up in the 1980s (Ellinas 2010). Although not directed against another state, but against the impact of the European Union, the transformed liberal-agrarian parties in Switzerland and Finland relied on nationalism during the rise of Schweizerische Volkspartei in the late 1980s and Perussuomalaiset (True Finns) in recent years (Fieschi et al. 2012). Thus, before the EU turned into a salient political issue in recent years, national identity—the core program of PRRPs—was hardly threatened by an 'external intruder'. National identity as such has never been put to test by another state. In this zeitgeist an *inclusive* national identity could hardly be forged. If everything is deconstructed that once gave it meaning (e.g. religion, conflicts between nation states, the fight between capitalism and communism, traditional gender roles), what can the roots of national belonging be? This explains why the PRRPs's core program rests on nativism (Mudde 2010, 2013), specifically ethno-nationalism (Rydgren 2004a, b, 2007). Migrants and immigration thus serve as perfect symbols PRRPs 'need' in order to mobilize for their nostalgic 'counterrevolution' against multicultural societies (Eatwell 2000, 2003). Migrants are easily constructed as the weakest link in an identity construction because they lack strong agency and can easily be scapegoated (Mouritsen 2008, 4/5). How symbolic boundaries are drawn against migrants depends on the national context (Lamont and Molnar 2002), but they cluster around society-wide similarities (Bail 2008). National elites have strong incentives to redefine these boundaries. They are enticed 'to distinguish, both in the political arena and in their private lives, between ethnic 'us' and 'them,' rather than between men and women, rich or poor, carpenters and college professors, and the like' (Wimmer 2008, 1007).

Rallying against multiculturalism, and campaigning on very conservative policies of migration and integration, is the raison d'etre of populist radical right parties. This campaign topic can be introduced and then withdrawn by established actors, it mobilizes conservative voters and serves as perfect narrative to call for an exclusive national identity many European voters crave for. Rallying against multiculturalism allegedly brought about by the national elites lies at the core of the nostalgic counterrevolutions of PRRPs. Voters of these parties hope to replace the 'borderlessness' and hypercomplexity of contemporary societies with clear-cut cultural markers of distinctions to find calm and clarity in strict national borders. They blame the established elites for not having reinforced these exclusionary markers in the first place, and instead of protecting their voters, exposing them to all this uncertainty. This is why PRRPs shout out loud: 'For the nation, against the elite!' (see Sect. 2.3).

Therefore, the extent to which the perceived organizational principle of a nation state is conceived as threatened by immigrants largely depends on how national elites frame the nation's symbolic boundaries in delineation towards migrants.

## 3.6   The Analytical Moment: What Entices Established Political Parties?

Who are the national elites in the leading positions of public opinion-making? One might consider various public figures (such as actors, anchor(wo)men or artists), the media as mediator (as gatekeeper of the public realm of communication) and political parties as key actors in the political process. The lion's share of concerned studies point to the pivotal role of one actor: established political parties (Rydgren 2004a, b, 2007; Helbling et al. 2010; Helbling 2012).

While one might accept that political parties are the prime opinion-makers in comparison to other public figures (actors, etc.), one might doubt whether the prime transmitter in the public realm—the media—does not also have a pivotal say in this respect. Maybe it is not politicians who shape the discursive realm, as reported by the media, but the media which controls it, in shaping the interval in which politicians must operate. A classic chicken and egg problem. One media study argues that the salience of immigration topics in national media benefitted the breakthrough of PRRPs in the Netherlands. In this case, the media set the agenda, not established politicians (Boomgarden and Vliegenhart 2007). Curiously, in duplicating the study with the same data, Dutch scholars found that the causal relation was interpreted in the wrong direction: media attributed a high salience to

---

**Populist Radical Right Parties (PRRPs) thrive in times of salient debates on identity politics [like immigration or EU issues]** *(Ivarsflaten 2005, Kitschelt 1995, Rydgren 2006)*

**Populist Radical Right Parties (PRRPs) only thrive in times of salient debates on identity politics if a void on the conservative position is given** *(Arzheimer 2009, Giugni and Koopmans 2007, Van der Brug and Spanje 2009)*

**Populist Radical Right Parties (PRRPs) only thrive in times of salient debates on identity politics if a void on the conservative position is given, which has previously been introduced by an established political actor and dropped over the course of the debate** *(Ellinas 2010, Muis 2012)*

*Why has an issue of identity politics (like immigration or EU issues) and a conservative position been introduced by an established political actor?*

*Why has the conservative position been dropped over the course of the debate?*

**Fig. 3.1** Explanations for the rise of populist radical right parties and derived research questions

the immigration issue only after established parties had already done so (Pauwels 2010). Public figures or the media are therefore unlikely to be capable of increasing the salience of immigration issues alone; the necessary attention comes from political actors: 'Political actors may not be able to inhibit structural conflicts from manifesting themselves politically. How they manifest themselves, however, is largely the result of politics. Thus, mainstream party behavior impinges on how polarizing these conflicts become' (Bornschier 2012, 142).

The discursive processes among established political actors are referred to as the shape of the 'political-opportunity-structure' (Kitschelt 1986) or the 'discursive-opportunity-structure' (Koopmans 1996). How the shape of these debates might lead to or prevent the rise of a PRRP support various hypotheses: Jens Rydgren and Elisabeth Ivarsflaten argue that the salience of economic topics, in combination with a strong polarization of the major political players over economic questions, prevents the advances of PRRPs (Ivarsflaten 2005; Rydgren 2007). This stands in line with Herbert Kitschelt's claim, arguing that PRRPs can only thrive if cultural topics become more salient than economic questions (Kitschelt 1995, 275).

Briefly repeating the elaborations that led to the formulation of the research questions, the issues seems not only whether or not immigration-related topics are discussed among established political actors; instead, the form of the debate is essential to determining whether or not it benefits a non-established political actor—a PRRP. Quantitative studies argue that there must be an absence of conservative voices in the debate over immigration in order for a PRRP to seize its electoral niche (Arzheimer 2009a; Giugni and Koopmans 2007; Van der Brug and Spanje 2009). Qualitative studies argue there must not only be an absence of conservative voices; a conservative position must also have been offered by an established political actor in the first place, then dropped over the course of the debate, so a PRRP can mobilize on that position (Ellinas 2010; Muis 2012) (see Fig. 3.1).

## 3.7  Conclusion: The Understudied Link Between Discourse and Structure

Comparative politics cannot yet give a convincing answer for how and why these changes take place. Cas Mudde has made the case that how political issues are framed by established parties is dependent on events, but first and foremost on how political elites want to utilize the issue for political gain (Mudde 2007, 299/300). Issue *salience* seems indeed highly context-dependent (Green-Pedersen 2012). One must therefore look at the cases in detail to understand variation in the salience of immigration-related topics in the party discourse. After the topic is salient, the party *position* is crucial. Parties' position changes seem rooted in the 'desire to be in office and the competition among parties' (Schumacher et al. 2013, 475). This rather tautological account cannot explain changes with party positions over time or across countries. Aren't all parties in all democracies keen on gaining access to office and maximizing their votes at all times? The 'causes of the causes' (Goertz and Mahoney 2006, 241) cannot be assessed.

And here the merits of the extensive literature review come into play: in revisiting the concepts outlined by various strains of the social sciences, it seems the more emphasis is placed on the debates amongst opinion leaders, the more structural circumstances are downplayed. However, these debates play out in a perceived organizational framework, which in turn must define the strategic incentives of political parties. The debate on national identity politics—like immigration—seems key to explaining the rise and fall of populist radical right parties; however, the timing and the form of this debate seems to depend on the perceived social structures the crucial political actors operate in.

This connection is the theoretical foundation of the research design (Fig. 3.2) and the understudied link between 'objective' and perceived structure and discourse (Fig. 3.3).

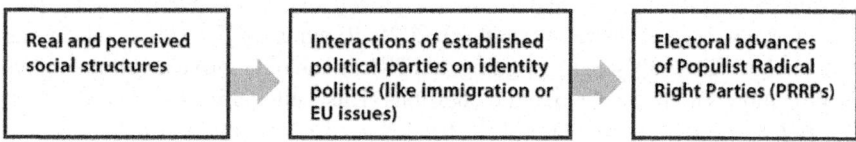

**Fig. 3.2** Theoretical foundation of research design

| LEVEL OF ANALYSIS | THEORETICAL INSIGHTS | PIVOTAL CONCEPTS | |
|---|---|---|---|
| **MACRO** | Social Conflict | Discourse | Structure |
| | | *On what?* | |
| | Comparative Social Sciences | Perception of competition over scarce national resources | |
| | | *How?* | |
| | Studies on Group Conflict | Perceived boundary conflicts | |
| | | *By Whom?* | |
| | Boundary Studies | Pivotal actors defining the symbolic boundary (national identity) | |
| | | *Why?* | |
| **MICRO** | Party Politics | Varying interests of established parties with political messaging on identity politics (like immigration or EU issues) | Varying patterns of 'objective' and perceived social structure |

**Fig. 3.3** The understudied link between discourse and structure in party politics

# References

Alonso S, Claro da Fonseca S (2011) Immigration, left and right. Party Polit:1–20
Amna E et al (2000) Volunteerism and culture in the Nordic welfare states: three essays on volunteerism and voluntary organizations. Sköndalsinstitutets Arbetsrapportserie Nr 9. Ersta Sköndal Högskola, Stockholm
Anderson B (1991) Imagined communities. Verso, Oxford
Arzheimer K (2009a) Contextual factors and the extreme right vote in Western Europe. Am J Polit Sci 53(2):259–275
Arzheimer K (2009b) Protest, neo-liberalism or anti-immigrant sentiment: what motivates the voters of the extreme right in Western Europe? Zeitschrift für Vergleichende Politikwissenschaft/Comp Gov Polit 2:173–197
Bail C (2008) The configuration of symbolic boundaries against immigrants in Europe. Am Sociol Rev 73(1):37–59
Bale T (2008) Politics matters: a conclusion. J Eur Public Policy 15(3):453–464
Bauman Z (1987) Legislators and interpreters. Polity Press, Cambridge
Bauman Z (2000) Liquid modernity. Polity Press, Cambridge
Bauman Z, May T (2001) Thinking sociologically. Blackwell, Oxford
Blad C, Couton P (2009) The rise of an intercultural nation: immigration, diversity and nationhood in Quebec. J Ethn Migr Stud 35(4):645–667
Bloemraad I, Kesler C (2009) Does immigration erode social capital? The conditional effects of immigration-generated diversity on trust, membership, and participation across 19 countries, 1981–2000
Bodenhausen GV (2010) Diversity in the person, diversity in the group: challenges of identity complexity for social perception and social interaction. Eur J Soc Psychol 40:1–16
Boomgarden HG, Vliegenhart R (2007) Explaining the rise of anti-immigrant parties: the role of news media content. Elect Stud 26(2):404–417
Bornschier S (2010) The new cultural divide and the two-dimensional political space in Western Europe. West Eur Polit 33(3):419–444
Bornschier S (2012) Why a right-wing populist party emerged in France but not in Germany: cleavages and actors in the formation of a new cultural divide. Eur Polit Sci Rev 4(1):121–145
Bratt C (2005) The structure of attitudes toward non-western immigrant groups: second order factor analysis of attitudes among Norwegian adolescents. Group Process Intergroup Relat 8 (4):447–469
Brubaker R (1996) Nationalism reframed: nationhood and the national question in the New Europe. Cambridge University Press, London
Cameron JE et al (2005) Perceptions of self and group in the context of a threatened national identity: a field study. Group Process Intergroup Relat 8(1):73–88
Chirot D, McCauley C (2006) Why not kill them all? The logic and prevention of mass political murder. Princeton, Princeton University Press
Cialdini R (2001) Influence: science and practice. Allyn and Bacon, Boston
Coenders M, Scheepers P (2008) Changes in resistance to the social integration of foreigners in Germany 1980–2000: individual and contextual determinants. J Ethn Migr Stud 34(1):1–26
Coser L (1956) The functions of social conflict. Free Press, New York
De Vries C, Hoffmann I (2016) Fear not values. Public opinion and the populist vote in Europe. Eupinions 2016/3. Bertelsmann Foundation. Available at: https://www.bertelsmann-stiftung.de/en/publications/publication/did/fear-not-values/. Last accessed 7 May 2017
Eatwell R (2000) The rebirth of the 'extreme right' in Western Europe. Parliam Aff 53(July 2000):407–425
Eatwell R (2003) Theorizing the rise of the European extreme right: towards a three-dimensional model. In: Merkl PH, Weinberg L (eds) Right-Wing extremism in the twenty-first century. Frank Cass, London

Eder K (2008) Symbolic power and cultural differences: a power model of political solutions to cultural differences. In: Mouritsen P, Jörgensen KE (eds) Constituting communities: political solutions to cultural conflict. Palgrave Macmillan, London, pp 31–52

Ellinas A (2010) The media and the far right in Western Europe: playing the nationalist card. University Press, Cambridge

Esping-Andersen G (1990) The three worlds of welfare capitalism. Princeton University Press, Princeton

Fieschi C et al (2012) Recapturing the reluctant radical: How to win back Europe's populist vote. Counterpoint

Finseraas H (2007) Immigration and preference for redistribution: an empirical analysis of European survey data. Annual Meeting of the Midwest Political Science Association 2007. Chicago

Garner S (2007) Ireland and immigration: explaining the absence of the far right. Patterns Prejudice 41(2):109–130

Gellner E (1994) Nations and nationalism. Cornell University Press, Ithaca

Giesen B (2007) Entgrenzung und Beschleunigung—Einige Bemerkungen über die kulturelle Vielfalt der Moderne. In: Bonacker T, Reckwitz A (eds) Kulturen der Moderne. Soziologische Perspektiven der Moderne. Campus Verlag, Frankfurt, pp 173–182

Giugni M, Koopmans R (2007) What causes people to vote for a radical right party? A rejoinder to Van der Brug and Fennema. Int J Public Opin Res 19(4):488–491

Goertz G, Mahoney J (2006) Social science concepts. A user's guide. Princeton University Press, Princeton

Gould R (2003) Collision of wills: how ambiguity about social rank breeds conflict. University of Chicago Press, Chicago

Green-Pedersen C (2012) A giant fast asleep? Party incentives and the politicisation of European integration. Polit Stud 60:115–130

Grillo R (2007) An excess of alterity? Debating difference in a multicultural society. Ethn Racial Stud 30(6):979–998

Guinote A, Fiske ST (2003) Being in the outgroup territory increases stereotypic perceptions of outgroups: situational sources of category activation. Group Process Intergroup Relat 6 (4):323–331

Helbling M (2012) Public debates, integration models and transnationalism in Western Europe. J Immigrants Refug Stud 10(3):241–259

Helbling M et al (2010) How political parties frame European integration. Eur J Polit Res 49:496–521

Herda D (2010) How many immigrants? Foreign-born population innumeracy in Europe. Public Opin Q 74(3):1–22

Hjerm M (2007) Do numbers really count? Group threat theory revisited. J Ethn Migr Stud 33 (8):1253–1275

Hooghe M et al (2009) Ethnic diversity and generalized trust in Europe: a cross-national multilevel study. Comp Polit Stud 42:198–223

Ivarsflaten E (2005) The vulnerable populist right parties: no economic realignment fuelling their electoral success. Eur J Polit Res 44:465–492

Ivarsflaten E (2008) What unites right-wing populists in Western Europe? Re-examining grievance mobilization models in seven successful cases. Comp Polit Stud 41:3–23

Joppke C (2005) Selecting by origin: ethnic migration in the liberal state. Harvard University Press, Harvard

Joppke C (2008) Immigration and the identity of citizenship: the paradox of universalism. Citizenship Stud 12(6):533–546

Keating M (2009) Social citizenship, solidarity and welfare in regionalized and plurinational states. Citizenship Stud 13(5):501–513

Kitschelt H (1986) Political opportunity structures and political protest: anti-nuclear movements in four democracies. Br J Polit Sci 16:57–85

Kitschelt H (1995) The radical right in Western Europe: a comparative analysis. Michigan University Press, Ann Arbor

Koopmans R (1996) Explaining the rise of racist and extreme right violence in Western Europe: grievances or opportunities? Eur J Polit Res 30:185–216

Koopmans R, Rebers S (2009) Collective action in culturally similar and dissimilar groups: an experiment on parochialism, conditional cooperation, and their linkages. Evol Hum Behav 30:201–211

Lamont M, Molnar V (2002) The study of boundaries in the social sciences. Ann Rev Sociol 28:167–195

Lecours A, Béland D (2005) The politics of territorial solidarity: nationalism and social policy reform in Canada, the United Kingdom. Comp Pol Stud 38:676–703

Liebkind K et al (2004) Group size, group status and dimensions of contact as predictors of intergroup attitudes. Group Process Intergroup Relat 7(2):145–159

McGlynn RP et al (2009) Individual-group discontinuity in group-individual interactions: does size matter? Group Process Intergroup Relat 12(1):129–143

Mouritsen P (2008) Political responses to cultural conflict: reflections on the ambiguities of the civic turn. In: Mouritsen P (ed) Constituting communities: political solutions to cultural conflict. Palgrave Macmillan, London, pp 1–30

Mudde C (2007) Populist radical right parties in Europe. Cambridge University Press, Cambridge

Mudde C (2010) The populist radical right: a pathological normalcy. West Eur Polit 33 (6):1167–1186

Mudde C (2013) The 2012 Stein Rokkan lecture. Three decades of populist radical right parties in Western Europe: so what? Eur J Polit Res:1–12

Muis J (2012) Pim Fortuyn: the evolution of a media phenomenon. Ridderkerk

Nagda B, Zuniga X (2003) Fostering meaningful racial engagement through intergroup dialogues. Group Process Intergroup Relat 6(1):111–128

Pauwels T (2010) Reassessing conceptionalization, data and causality: a critique of Boomgardens and Vliegenhart's study on the relationship between media and the rise of anti-immigrant parties. Elect Stud 29:269–275

Peterson B (2009) Hot conflict and everyday banality: enemy images, scapegoats and stereotypes. Soc Int Dev 52(4):460–465

Pettigrew TF et al (2010) Population ratios and prejudice: modelling both contact and threat effects. J Ethn Migr Stud 36(4):635–650

Philipps KW et al (2006) Surface-level diversity and decision-making in groups: when does deep-level similarity help? Group Process Intergroup Relat 9(4):467–482

Reitz J (2004) Canada: immigration and nation-building in the transititon to a knowledge economy. In: Cornelius W, Tsuda T, Martin P, Hollifield J (eds) Controlling immigration: a global perspective. Stanford University Press, Stanford

Rydgren J (2004a) Explaining the emergence of radical right-wing populist parties: the case of Denmark. West Eur Polit 27(3):474–502

Rydgren J (2004b) The logic of xenophobia. Ration Soc 16(2):123–148

Rydgren J (2007) The sociology of the radical right. Ann Rev Sociol 33:241–262

Schiefer D et al (2010) Cultural values and outgroup negativity: a cross-cultural analysis of early and late adolescents. Eur J Soc Psychol 40:635–651

Schlueter E, Scheepers P (2010) The relationship between outgroup size and anti-outgroup attitudes: a theoretical synthesis and empirical test of group-threat- and intergroup contact theory. Soc Sci Res 39(2):285–295

Schumacher G, De Vries C, Vis B (2013) Why do parties change position? Party organization and environmental incentives. J Polit 75(2):464–477

Sherman DK et al (2009) Perceived polarization: reconciling ingroup and intergroup perceptions under uncertainty. Group Proces Intergroup Relat 12(1):95–109

Simmel G (1955) Conflict and the web of group affiliations. The Free Press, New York

Terry DJ et al (2006) Predictors of cultural adjustment: intergroup status relations and boundary permeability. Group Process Intergroup Relat 9(2):249–264

Van der Brug W, van Spanje J (2009) Immigration, Europe and the 'new' cultural dimension. Eur J Polit Res 48:309–334

Wimmer A (2002) Nationalist exclusion and ethnic conflict. Shadows of modernity. Cambridge University Press, Cambridge

Wimmer A (2006) Ethnic exclusion in nationalizing states. The Sage handbook of nations and nationalism. Sage, London

Wimmer A (2008) The making and unmaking of ethnic boundaries: a multilevel process theory. Am J Sociol 113(4):970–1022

# Chapter 4
# Research Design: Ensuring High Validity and High Reliability Under the Auspices of Comparative Case Studies

## 4.1 Operationalizing the Hypothesis: Lessons from Charles Tilly

One variable seems especially crucial in explaining the varying advances of populist radical right parties: the immigration debate between established moderate parties. How this debates unfolds, in turn, seems dependent on how established parties perceive the social structures around them (Fig. 4.1). Established political actors observe two social structures: the society at large (1) and the party political competition (2). The key independent variable, 'debate about immigration', is a social construct, almost entirely dependent on how established parties frame immigration. Similarly, the 'objective' social structures hardly inform the decisions of established political actors; rather how the social structures are perceived. Consequently, the variables capturing various aspects of the social structures need to be operationalized insofar as they capture what people *think* about them, not how they 'really are'.

The guiding research hypothesis stands in line with Charles Tilly's seminal works on political competition and research logic. In his view the understanding of the evolution of political structures calls for understanding the *interactions* of established political actors (Tilly 1984, 30 and 143). In order to assess these interactions reliably, the selection of interactions is pivotal.

He argues that the 'analyses of social and institutional change should be 'concrete'—referring to concrete units of analysis—and 'historical'—limiting their scope to an era bound to clearly defined processes' (Tilly 1984, 30). This guidance means focusing on interactions in comparable scope conditions, refraining for example from comparing party political developments in Weimar Germany with those in the Federal Republic of Germany in the twenty-first century; here, the institutional scope conditions have changed too substantially (e.g. the international context and the German constitution). He calls for comparing as many cases as possible, *if* all the necessary detailed information about each

© Springer International Publishing AG 2018
T. Lochocki, *The Rise of Populism in Western Europe*,
DOI 10.1007/978-3-319-62855-4_4

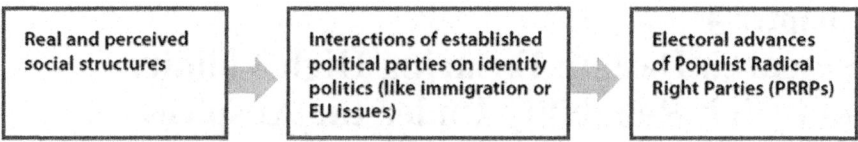

**Fig. 4.1** Theoretical foundations of the research design

**Table 4.1** Challenges in the study of variation in the electoral advances of PRRPs

|  | Qualitative, single case studies | Quantitative, large-N studies | Comparative case studies |
|---|---|---|---|
| Advantage | Higher degree of validity | Higher degree of reliability and generalizability | Relatively high degree of reliability, validity and generalizability |
| Disadvantage | Lower degree of generalizability and reliability | Lower degree of validity | |

case under scrutiny is available. He therefore aims 'for comparisons of various large entities, with one prime caveat: familiarity with cases needs to remain being given' (Tilly 1984, 77).

These two remarks come back the methodological challenges in the study of PRRPs. On the one hand there are many studies that rely on quantitative, statistical data. This is problematic because we cannot access the key nuances in between cases that cannot be accounted for by large-n studies; secondly, it might well happen that the data cannot measure what is the main interest—a classic issue of validity. On the other hand, fine-grained qualitative studies focus on one country or one party. But one can hardly determine whether a different scholar would reach the same conclusions because such data is especially prone to subjective interpretation; secondly, it is difficult to deduct from one particular case to another because what is found might only apply to very narrow scope conditions (Mudde 2016, 11). In essence, the study of PRRPs suffers from the known trade-offs of empirical social sciences: large-N studies struggle with the validity of their findings, but score high on reliability and generalization; in turn, single case studies suffer from low reliability and substantive problems with generalization, but offer high validity (Table 4.1).

In order to ameliorate these trade-offs, Charles Tilly calls for detailed *comparative case studies*. If the cases are selected properly, the findings ensure a high potential for generalization; if data collection is as detailed as necessary, the validity of the findings is high; finally, if the data withstands reliability tests, it is also reliable (Table 4.1). Consequently, this study will rely on comparative case studies in order to elucidate the varying electoral advances of populist radical right parties.

## 4.2 Case Selection: Sharpening the Scope

In order to decipher the reasons for varying party conduct and how this presumably corresponds with electoral variation amongst PRRPs, the question of which party interactions should be scrutinized arises. This study relies on a *most-similar system design* as proposed by Adam Przeworski and Henry Teune, grounded in the belief that cases 'as similar as possible with respect to as many features as possible constitute the optimal samples for comparative inquiry' (Przeworski and Teune 1970, 32). In order to select countries (where the party interactions take place) based on this rationale, rules of inclusion and exclusion of cases as proposed by Gary Goertz prove useful: the rule of inclusion calls for the relevance of cases if the value of at least one independent variable is positively related to the outcome of interest; the rule of exclusion defines cases as irrelevant if the value of any eliminatory independent variable predicts the nonoccurrence of the outcome of interest. This rule takes precedence over the rule of inclusion (Goertz and Mahoney 2006, 187/8). Therefore, the excluding criteria must be defined first and might as it decide the case selection alone.

The first excluding criteria are the omission of democracies stemming from the transformed countries of Central and Eastern Europe. The party-evolutions of these young democracies follow very different paths from those in Western Europe, especially concerning populism in general, whether on the left or the right side of the political spectrum (Di Tella 1997). This study will therefore focus on Western European countries.

The second excluding criterion rules out countries that have been home to an established PRRP since the 1980s. What sounds at first like a tautology merely adheres to the fact that—as elaborated in the earlier chapters—immigration-related issues have functioned as a prime narrative of the cultural conflict in modern democracies since the 1980s. Therefore, the advances of PRRPs before the 1980s were most likely dependent on cultural issues other than immigration-related topics; respectively, after a party has been part of the political spectrum for decades, other factors might influence their electoral advances (Bornschier 2010). Countries already exposed to successful PRRPs in the mid-1980s will consequently exhibit different patterns of party interaction on immigration-related matters because—as elaborated in previous chapters—the electoral entrenchment of a PRRP is a game-changer. This study will therefore focus on Western European countries that were not home to an entrenched PRRP at the end of the 1980s.

The third excluding criterion is particular institutional structures that might greatly influence party-interactions. Most democracies in Europe adhere to a proportional representation system with a rather low electoral threshold, in turn facilitating the entrenchment of new political parties. Its counterpart, the single-winner electoral system (in place in France, the UK and the USA) favors established political players to a far greater extent and therefore adheres to a different logic of party competition (Lijphart 1984). This study will therefore focus on Western European countries that were not home to an entrenched PRRP at the end of the 1980s and are currently using a proportional representation system.

Finally, the prime *inclusive* criterion is the possibility of established parties discussing immigration issues. In order to do so, a substantial level of immigration needs to be a given over a longer period of time. Therefore, only those countries that have embraced a similarly stable and high level of immigration are included. This study will therefore focus on Western European countries that were not home to an entrenched PRRP at the end of the 1980s, are using a proportional representation system, and which are exposed to a high and constant inflow of migrants.

In 1990, seven Western European countries using proportional representation systems had no entrenched PRRP: Finland, Germany, Ireland, the Netherlands, Portugal, Spain and Sweden (Table 4.2). Of these, Germany, the Netherlands and Sweden have experienced considerable levels of immigration since 1980. While Finland has never seen high immigration, Ireland, Portugal and Spain have mainly experienced a rapid increase over the last 15 years. Germany, the Netherlands and Sweden, on the other hand, have been exposed to a constant inflow of migrants since the 1980s (Table 4.2 and Fig. 4.2).

Therefore, conditions for the mobilization on immigration-related topics in party discourses in Germany, the Netherlands and Sweden are similar. They compellingly fit the conditions of a similar systems design.

## 4.3   Validity of the Data: A Political Claims Analysis Based on Media Reports

The immigration debate amongst established parties in Germany, the Netherlands and Sweden is scrutinized to understand the variation in PRRP advances. These debates can be operationalized in accessing their salience (how often parties talk about the matter) and what position parties take in the debate. Studies trying to assess the salience and positions devoted to political topics have, to date, relied on two data sources: the Comparative Party Manifesto Program (CMP) and data obtained via a media analysis before pivotal federal election campaigns. Both data sources are rather poorly suited to explaining how party positioning affects the voter, or for assessing reasons for varying party conduct. The CMP-data (used for example by Meguid 2005; Alonso and Claro da Fonseca 2011) is based on the evaluation of party programs and allows comparisons over time and across countries; in so doing, it is limited by the lack of information and difference regarding party conduct between manifesto publications and what parties write and the issues around which they actually campaign. Therefore, the *validity* of the data is rather low, if not absent. This leads Marc Helbling and Anke Tresch to conclude that, instead of relying on CMP-data, 'party-voter linkages are best studied with media data' (Helbling and Tresch 2011, 181). Adhering to these remarks, large comparative research projects such as 'West European Politics in

**Table 4.2** Net-migration of foreigners (immigration minus emigration) in Western European democracies using proportional representation systems not home to a PRRP in the 1980s

|  | 1981–1990 | | 1991–2000 | | 2001–2010 | |
|---|---|---|---|---|---|---|
|  | Incomings (yearly average) | Incomings in % of entire population (1981) | Incomings (yearly average) | Incomings in % of entire population (1991) | Incomings (yearly average) | Incomings in % of entire population (2001) |
| Finland | 3900 | 0.08 | 6000 | 0.12 | 10,200 | 0.20 |
| Germany | 184,300 | 0.30 | 334,700 | 0.41 | 109,500 | 0.13 |
| Ireland | – | – | 8600 | 0.25 | 40,700 | 1.04 |
| Netherlands | 26,600 | 0.18 | 53,600 | 0.36 | 40,000 | 0.25 |
| Portugal | – | – | 8900 | 0.09 | 49,500 | 0.47 |
| Spain | – | – | 62,300 | 0.16 | 495,600 | 1.23 |
| Sweden | 17,300 | 0.21 | 20,100 | 0.23 | 41,500 | 0.46 |

Source: own calculations based on OECD data

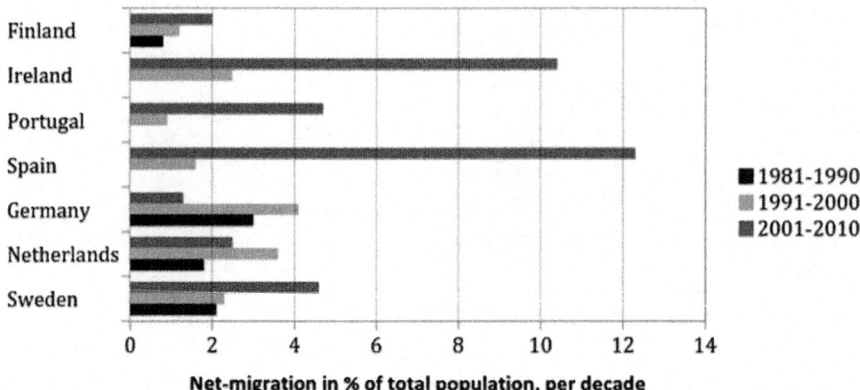

**Fig. 4.2** Percentage of net-migration of foreigners in percent of total population per decade (source: own calculations)

the Age of Globalization' (Kriesi et al. 2008) define party positions based on political claims reported in quality media before federal elections in order to obtain data with high *validity*. The prime limitation relevant here is that only snapshots of party positions are taken (for example for Germany the 2 months before the federal elections of 1974, 1994, 1998 and 2002)—therefore, the *validity* of the party discourse between electoral campaigns is extremely low, if not almost absent; therefore, neither a precise development of party positions and their salience over time, nor the reasons for their respective changes, can be assessed.

Considering the pros and cons of these two approaches, the strengths of both attempts need to be boosted and their shortcomings avoided; this is achieved by obtaining the party salience and position on immigration-related matters via a political claim analysis of political statements as reported in quality media for each separate year.

Studies working with this approach limit themselves to one quality medium because comparative studies have shown that neither the salience, nor the reported party positions (save the evaluation of editors) vary significantly between various quality media sources or even tabloids (Koopmans et al. 2005, 261/2). Consequently, data derived from one quality newspaper can function as a proxy mirroring salience and party positions on immigration-related issues, as long as only political claims of politicians are listed and coded.

Hence, the next question is which newspapers to analyze in order to grasp the party discourse to solve the research puzzle at hand. The liberal-conservative VVD (Volkspartij voor Vrijheid en Democratie) put the immigration issue on the political map of the Netherlands in the early 1990s, while Pim Fortuyn's PRRP LPF (Ljist Pim Fortuyn) succeeded in the federal election campaign in 2002 (Muis 2012). Accordingly, this study relies on the online archives of the liberal-conservative

NRC Handelsblad that are accessible via the database Lexis-Nexis from 1990 to 2002.

The Swedish Liberal Party FP (Folkpartiet Liberalerna) was the first to break the consensus of not politicizing immigration-related issues in Sweden during the rally for the federal election in 2002 (Rydgren and Ruth 2011).[1] The PRRP SD (Sverigedemokraterna) rose steadily in the polls from 2002 and eventually gained parliamentary representation in 2010. The conservative-liberal Svenska Dagbladet is covered by the online archives of Atekst from the late 1990s on and can thus be used for the claim analysis for Sweden.

The immigration issue entered Germany's political discourse with Helmut Kohl's chancellorship in 1982/83, accompanying the Christian Democrats' call for a moral turn in German politics, termed the 'geistig-moralische Wende' (Thränhardt 1995). Only 1989 saw electoral advances of the PRRP Die Republikaner at the federal election, while no right contender could entrench itself in the political system of Germany until the AfD rose in 2013. Thus, this study relies on the Frankfurter Allgemeine Zeitung (FAZ) to obtain political claims on immigration-related issues in Germany because their online archives cover the entire period under scrutiny (1982–2012). The euro crises, which at that time dominated the cultural axis of conflict in German politics, led to the Alternative for Germany (AfD) forming as an anti-Euro party that could not be referred to as a PRRP. However, as the migration topic has resurfaced with force following the refugee crisis in 2015, the AfD has become a full-fledged PRRP. These developments will be covered in detail in Chap. 9.

To mirror the discourse as closely as possible, this study obtains the salience and position of the two largest parties of the center-left and the center-right spectrum in each country; these taken together account for 90–95% of the entire vote-share in each country and allow a comparative perspective between parties in the same party family. Every claim in all articles is coded in which any combination of key words and party names or abbreviations occur in the headlines or first paragraph of the politics section of the daily newspaper (see Tables 4.3 and 4.4).

Claims from these articles were coded using the method of 'core sentences.' It is an inductive approach that captures the relationship between the political actor and a political issue that appears in the newspaper article (also used by Kriesi et al. 2008).

---

[1]Sweden saw the rise of the protest party Ny Demokrati (NyD) in Sweden in the early 1990s, however. Ny Demokrati ran its campaign on a broad anti-establishment agenda; neither in its campaigns nor for its voters were immigration issues of major importance for their electoral breakthrough in the federal election in 1991. Before their breakthrough, immigration issues were not salient in the Swedish party discourse or in the public perception. After accessing the parliament in 1991, it was Ny Demokrati that put the immigration issue on the political agenda, not established political players. The party failed to regain parliamentary representation in the federal election in 1994 and has been absent from the political scene since. Dahlström, C. and P. Esaiasson (2009). The Immigration Issue and Anti-Immigrant Party Success. Is Sweden the Odd Case Out? QoG WORKING PAPER SERIES. The Quality of Government Institute.

**Table 4.3** Political claims and political actors under scrutiny

| | English | Dutch case | Swedish case | German case |
|---|---|---|---|---|
| Newspaper | | NRC Handelblad | Svenska Dagbladet | Frankfurter Allgemeine Zeitung |
| Online archive | | Lexis Nexis | Atekst | FAZ Archiv |
| Keywords (with truncation) | | | | |
| | Immigrant Immigration Foreigner | Immigratie/Migrant/Immigrant (*migr*) Allochtoon (allocht*) Vreemdeling (vreemdel*) | Invandrare/Invandring (invandr*) Migration (*migration*) Utlänning* (utlänning*) Främling (främling*) | Einwanderer/Einwanderung (einwand*) Zuwanderer/Zuwanderung (zuwander*) Migrant/Immigrant/Migration (*migr*) Auslaender (auslaender*) |
| | Asylum | Asiel (asiel*) | Asyl* (asyl*) | Asyl (Asyl*) |
| | Naturalization Citizenship | Inburgering (inburger*) Naturalisatie (naturalisat*) Staatsburgerschap (staatsburgerschap*) | Naturalisering (naturaliser*) Medborgarskap (medborgarskap*) | Einbuergerung (Einbürger*) Staatsbuergerschaft (Staatsbürgerschaft*) |
| | Multiculturalism Integration Assimilation Racism | Multiculturalisme (multicultu*) Integration (integr*) Assimilatie (assimil*) Racisme (racis*) | Mångkulturell (mångkulturell*) Multikulturell (multikulturell*) Integration (integr*) Assimilation (assimil*) Rasism (rasis*) | Multikulturalismus (Multikult*) Integration (Integr*) Assimilation (Assimil*) Rassismus (Rassis*) |
| Four most important parties | | | | |
| Center-right political spectrum | Conservatives/ Moderates | Christen-Democratisch Appèl (CDA) | Moderata samlingspartiet (M)[a] | Christlich-Soziale Union/Christlich Demokratische Union Deutschlands (CDU/CSU)[b] |
| | Liberals | Volkspartij voor Vrijheid en Democratie (VVD) | Folkpartiet liberalerna (FP) | Freie Demokratische Partei (FDP) |

| Center-left politi-cal spectrum | Social-Democrats | Partij van de Arbeid (PvdA) | Sveriges socialdemokratiska arbetareparti (SAP) | Sozialdemokratische Partei Deutschlands (SPD) |
|---|---|---|---|---|
| | Greens/Left | Democraten 66 (D66)[c] | Vänsterpartiet (V)[d] | Bündnis 90/Die Grünen (B90/Gruene)[e] |

[a]Various smaller parties belonging to the mid-right (KD, C), but too small to be included in the study

[b]The CSU only exists in Bavaria. The CDU never stood for election there, while the CSU refrains from reaching out to other states. The CSU is often described as the CDU's "conservative wing"

[c]The Dutch D66 is a left-liberal party whose characteristics do not exactly fit the Green/Left categorization. It is included for two reasons, though. First because, based on electoral advances from 1989 to 2002, the D66 is the fourth largest Dutch party and clearly outreaches the Dutch Green/Left in the period under scrutiny (D66 gathered 9.4% in federal elections in 1989, 1994, 1998, 2002, on average, in contrast to only 5.5% of the votes for the Green/Left); second, because the party clearly has a left-liberal profile (in clear contrast to the right-liberal VVD), and campaigns on positions close to those of the European green parties such as increasing public spending for education, sustainable energy and calls for a democratization of parliamentary decision-making

[d]The Swedish Vänsterpartiet is one of the two smaller parties of the Swedish mid-left. During the period under examination the Swedish Vänsterpartiet gathered significantly more voter support than the Swedish Greens and is therefore included in the study (V gathered 8.0% of the votes in the federal elections of 1998, 2002, 2006 and 2010, on average, in contrast to only 5.4% for the Green party)

[e]The contemporary German party system comprises of two smaller parties of the German mid-left. The Green party is of greater importance than the left party (PDS/Die Linke) because it is present in parliament during the entire period under scrutiny and gathered more voter support than the PDS/Die Linke. (During the federal elections from 1983 to 2009 the Greens collected 7.5% of votes on average, while the PDS/Die Linke only obtained 4.6%. If one focuses on the elections in Reunified Germany from 1990 only, the German Greens still outreach the PDS/Die Linke with 7.8–6.1% on average)

**Table 4.4** Search-strings for online search engines

| Dutch case, Lexis-Nexis | (multicult! ODER integr! ODER assimil! ODER naturalisat! ODER inburger! ODER staatsburgerschap! ODER asiel! ODER racis! ODER immigr! ODER alloch! ODER vreemdel!) UND (PvDA ODER VVD ODER CDA ODER D66 van de arbeid ODER Volkspartij ODER Christen-Democratisch ODER Democraten) |
|---|---|
| Swedish case, Atekst | (mångkulturell* OR multikulturell* OR integr* OR assimil* OR naturaliser* OR medborgarskap* OR asyl* OR rasis* OR invandr* OR *migration* OR främling* OR utlänning*) AND (arbetareparti* OR socialdemokrat* OR moderat* OR folkpartiet* OR vänsterpartiet* OR 'SAP' OR 'S' OR 'M' OR 'FP' OR 'V') |
| German case, FAZ Archiv | (multikult* ODER integr* ODER assimil* ODER einwand* ODER rassis* ODER asyl* ODER zuwander* ODER ausländer* ODER *migr* ODER staatsbürger*) UND (SPD ODER CDU ODER CSU ODER FDP ODER B90 oder grüne ODER sozialdemo* ODER christ* ODER liberal*) |

Each statement is reduced to its core structure, namely the subject (political actor), the object (political issue) and the evaluation. The evaluation uses a five-point scale, ranging from −10 (clearly conservative) to +10 (clearly liberal). −5 and +5 are given if an understated evaluation is given, e.g. if she/he considers support, or support under certain circumstances. 0 is set for an ambivalent position—see codebook (Table 4.5) and examples (Table 4.6) below; this coding technique is close to approaches used in media analysis (Helbling 2012).

A final question of validity concerns the number of claims that are necessary to validly define the party position each year. The adequate sample size can be determined using the split-half method (Krippendorf 2004, 124). Applying this technique to the countries under examination and relying on the coding methods previously outlined, 25–30 claims per year appear necessary (Fig. 4.3).

The party position in all years with fewer than 25 observable claims will be coded according to the last year with more than 25 claims. For example, if the year 2007 hypothetically shows only 13 claims of the conservative party in Sweden, while the year 2006 has 42, the score of the year 2006 will be used for the year 2007 as well. This is for both methodological and logical reasons. First, because a valid assessment of party position is not possible for years with fewer than 25 claims, and second, if a party wants to visibly change its public position, it will consciously make more claims on the issue so that voters will hear and understand the position change. The yearly party position consists of the average of combined individual claims.

This study is based on 53 years of party discourse among the four major established political parties in the three countries under scrutiny. From the search results of the online archives, the political discourse is represented—on average—by 150–160 political claims each year, or around 40 claims for each party each year. This results in the coding of roughly 8000 political claims—approximately 5000 for

**Table 4.5** Codebook of political claim analysis

|  | Clearly conservative (−10) | Nuanced conservative (−5) | Neutral/ambivalent (0) | Nuanced liberal (+5) | Clearly liberal (+10) |
|---|---|---|---|---|---|
| Immigration | Party rejects immigration and means pertaining to it | Party rejects immigration and means pertaining to it—save exception x or under condition y | Party neither supports nor rejects immigration | Party supports immigration and means pertaining to it—save exception x or under condition y | Party supports immigration and means pertaining to it |
| Asylum | Party rejects asylum-seekers and wants to take legal actions to reduce their numbers; party rejects any means to integrate asylum-seekers into the receiving society | Party rejects asylum-seekers and wants to take legal actions to reduce their numbers; party rejects any means to integrate asylum-seekers into the receiving society—save exception x or under condition y | Party neither rejects nor supports asylum-seekers; party neither rejects nor supports means to integrate asylum-seekers into the receiving society | Party calls for low legal barriers for asylum-seekers; party supports any means to integrate asylum-seekers into the receiving society—save exception x or under condition y | Party calls for low legal barriers for asylum-seekers; party supports any means to integrate asylum-seekers into the receiving society |
| Integration | Party conceives the host society's culture as rightfully dominating the integration-process; party supports assimilation; party perceives responsibility of integration to lie mainly with the migrant | Party conceives the host society's culture as rightfully dominating the integration-process; party supports assimilation; party perceives responsibility of integration to lie mainly with the migrant—save exception x or under condition y | Party undecided about integration-process; party neither supporting assimilationist nor multicultural integration; party not perceiving the responsibility of integration to lie only with one side | Party conceives a plurality of cultural strains on equal footing in processes of integration; party supports multiculturalism; party perceives responsibility of integration to lie mainly with the receiving society—save exception x or under condition y | Party conceives a plurality of cultural strains on equal footing in processes of integration; party supports multiculturalism; party perceives responsibility of integration to lie mainly with the receiving society |
| Citizenship | Party rejects (easier) access to citizenship for migrants (e.g. dual citizenship) | Party rejects (easier) access to citizenship for migrants (e.g. dual citizenship)—save exception x or under condition y | Party neither rejects nor supports (easier) access to citizenship for migrants | Party favors (easier) access to citizenship for migrants (e.g. dual citizenship)—save exception x or under condition y | Party favors (easier) access to citizenship for migrants (e.g. dual citizenship) |

**Table 4.6** Examples of political claims and their coding

| Quote | Date | Subject | Object | Evaluation |
|---|---|---|---|---|
| Der SPD-Abgeordnete Schröer sagte: 'Wir wollen eine multikulturelle Gesellschaft. Kulturelle Vielfalt bedroht uns nicht, sondern sie bereichert' | 2.12.1988 | SPD (GER) | Integration | +10 |
| Gerhard (FDP) sagte, diese Jahresquote sei 'ein vernünftiger Kompromiß' zwischen der Aufrechterhaltung des Anwerbestopps (…) und einer gesteuerten Zuwanderung, wie sie die Regierung in ihrer Gesetzesnovelle vorschlägt | 12.03.2003 | FDP (GER) | Immigration | ±0 |
| Het PvdA vindt dat vreemdelingen naast het Nederlandschap hun oorspronkelijke nationaliteit moeten kunnen behouden | 17.2.1995 | PvdA (NL) | Citizenship | +10 |
| De VVD wil alle alleenstaande, minderjarige asielzoekers direct terugsturen naar hun land van herkomst. Alleen in uitzonderlijke gevallen kan een asielaanvraag nader worden onderzocht | 13.06.2001 | VVD (NL) | Asylum | −5 |
| Moderaterna säger ja till att öppna Sverige för arbetskraftsinvandring | 04.08.2002 | M (SE) | Immigration | +5 |
| Stoppa avvisningen av 13 apatiska barn och deras familjer. Det kräver 29 riksdagsledamöter från V, MP och KD i ett gemensamt upprop till migrationsminister Tobias Billström (M) och Migrationsverkets generaldirektör Dan Eliasson | 13.06.2009 | V, MP, KD (SE) | Asylum | +10 |

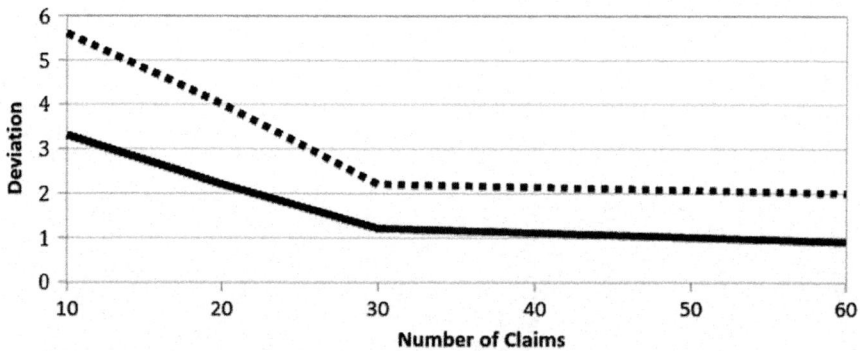

　　■■　max. deviation of calculated party position in five randomly drawn samples with half the size in comparison to the full sample

　　■　average deviation of calculated party position in five randomly drawn samples with half the size in comparison to the sample with full the size

**Fig. 4.3** Assessing the necessary number of claims per year

the German case, covering 31 years, and around 1500 for the Swedish and the Dutch cases—each covering 11 years of party competition.

## 4.4   Reliability of the Data: Inter-Coder-Reliability-Tests

Party positions are obtained using qualitative data in order to ensure a high degree of validity. However, the question is then how to ensure a high degree of *reliability*—independent of the personal political preferences of the coder. In order to guarantee the sufficiency of coding rules and a high level of *reliability*, the author conducted tests of inter-coder-reliability. As the author is the prime coder, randomly drawn samples were used to identify the reliability of his assessment by comparing his answers to those of two scholars of political science from the three countries under scrutiny.

Reliability measures widely used in media studies call for re-evaluating at least 50 randomly selected units; to do so, this study uses Cohen's Kappa—a very conservative index defining values of >0.8 as extremely reliable and values of >0.6 as sufficiently reliable, and values of <0.4 as hardly reliable (Lombard et al. 2002, 593). A randomly drawn sample of ten articles with 156–254 possible claims (depending on the country) is used to test the agreement of the salience-indicator between two scholars of the domestic politics of each country and the author of the study. The party positioning is checked by re-evaluating 50 randomly drawn claims.

Save the precise evaluation of the party position, all indicators score close to and above 0.8, and can therefore be treated as *highly reliable*. The precise evaluation scores significantly lower than all other indicators. Two reasons could explain these outliers. First, the precise evaluation of party statements is highly influenced by political preferences even though the codebook tries to provide clear-cut benchmarks. In addition, the slightly higher values of agreement in the German case might be due to the fact that it is the native tongue of the prime coder. Still, given both these hypotheses, the high Cohen's Kappa for the rough evaluation (all close to or higher than 0.8), as well as the sufficient scores for the precise evaluation (all close to or higher than 0.6), both also indicate a reliable assessment of the parties' precise position (Table 4.7).

**Table 4.7**   Results of inter-coder-reliability-tests

|                                       | NL 1/2 | NL 2/2 | SE 1/2 | SE 2/2 | GER 1/2 | GER 2/2 |
|---------------------------------------|--------|--------|--------|--------|---------|---------|
| Detection of claims                   | 0.91   | 0.86   | 0.71   | 0.75   | 0.85    | 0.84    |
| Detection of parties                  | 0.98   | 0.98   | 0.88   | 0.83   | 0.92    | 0.92    |
| Detection of topic                    | 0.75   | 0.89   | 0.85   | 0.70   | 0.83    | 0.87    |
| Evaluation of position, tri-polar     | 0.87   | 0.83   | 0.71   | 0.76   | 0.82    | 0.84    |
| Evaluation of position, precise       | 0.65   | 0.56   | 0.56   | 0.56   | 0.67    | 0.71    |

## 4.5   The Model of Analysis: Aiming for High Validity and Reliability

The guiding hypothesis of this book assumes that the interaction of established parties' debates on immigration explain the varying electoral advances of PRRP. Revisiting the literature review, this study assumes that the conduct of the established parties is in turn influenced by the perceived social structures moderate political actors observe. These perceived social structures are the 'causes of the causes' (Goertz and Mahoney 2006, 241). This hints at a two-level theory. The first level defines the main causal variables and outcome variable of the theory as a whole. The second level describes the variables causing the main causal variables—the 'causes of the causes'. The 'third level' consists of the operationalization of variables and is of no theoretical value to the theory (Goertz and Mahoney 2006, 247–266).

While the assumed prime causal variables—salience and party position—have been theoretically derived, gathered and operationalized with care, how debates unfold, in turn, seems dependent on how established parties perceive the social structures around them. Established political actors observe two social structures: the society at large (1) and the party political competition (2).

The prime variables departing from society at large can be operationalized as the actual and perceived cultural and economic threat of immigrants to the receiving society (Lucassen and Lubbers 2011). Variation in threat-perceptions on the part of voters might, then, explain the variable conduct of the established parties in the Netherlands, Sweden and Germany. Once more repeating the important theoretical values of perceived structures, this study relies on variables/conditions that mirror actual *and* perceived threat perceptions separately.

Regarding patterns of stratification in party competition that might affect parties' salience and position, party competition is measured by two prime variables: the condition of the conservative party (which mobilizes on the immigration topic) alone, and the polling of the political camps taken together. This leaves up to 13 variables/conditions that might account for variation in the polling of PRRPs and variation in established political parties' salience and position on immigration-related matters (Table 4.8).

This study examines possible reasons for variation in party conduct using a triangulation, working with two different mathematical methods, adhering to both a deterministic and a probabilistic foundation. The deterministic logic is followed in using Qualitative Comparative Analysis (QCA), while probabilistic logic is adhered to in using correlational models. This study draws on the particular strength of QCA in checking whether a combination of various conditions is necessary and/or sufficient for the occurrence of a certain outcome, e.g. the varying positioning of an established party on immigration-related matters or polling changes. QCA works according to a Boolean logic and defines social phenomena in terms of set-theory (Ragin 2008; Schneider and Wagemann 2010a, b). In doing so, its explanatory logic is rather *deterministic* and must not be confused with the

**Table 4.8**  List of variables/conditions and their operationalization

| Concept | Condition/variable | Operationalization, data source | Remarks |
|---|---|---|---|
| Real and perceived threat potential | Real cultural threat potential | Inflows of foreign born per year per Capita, OECD | |
| | Real economic threat potential | Internationally standardized unemployment rate, International Labour Office | |
| | Perceived cultural threat potential | Percentage of voters (very) concerned with immigration/integration /asylum seekers, national surveys (Dutch Election Survey, Swedish Trends, German Politbarometer) | |
| | Perceived economic threat potential | Percentage of voters (very) concerned with economic situation, national surveys (Dutch Election Survey, Swedish Trends, German Politbarometer) | |
| Party descriptive | Salience attributed by mid-right party | Number of claims each year | Referring to conservative agenda-setter in each country (VVD in NL, FP in SE, CDU/CSU in GER) |
| | Salience attributed by mid-left party | Number of claims each year | Referring to largest mid-left party in each country (PvdA in NL, SAP in SE, SPD in GER) |
| | Salience attributed by both major parties | Number of claims each year | Referring to the two party-families listed above |
| | Position of mid-right party | Party position based on coding elaborated in Sects. 4.3 and 4.4 | In binary coding the mid-right party's position is referred to as conservative (or not-conservative) |
| | Position of mid-left party | Party position based on coding elaborated in Sects. 4.3 and 4.4 | In binary coding the mid-left party's position is referred to as liberal (or not-liberal) |
| | General Party Discourse | Combined party positions based on coding elaborated in Sects. 4.3 and 4.4 | In binary coding the combined parties' position is referred to as presence of liberal discourse yes/no (comprising of combined positions of the two major parties) |

(continued)

**Table 4.8** (continued)

| Concept | Condition/variable | Operationalization, data source | Remarks |
|---------|--------------------|---------------------------------|---------|
| Party interaction | Polling of right populist anti-multiculturalism party | Polling based on national election surveys (Dutch Election Survey, Swedish Trends/YouGovSweden, German Politbarometer) | |
| | Crisis of conservative agenda setter | Polling based on national election surveys (Dutch Election Survey, Swedish Trends/YouGovSweden, German Politbarometer) | A crisis is defined as the conservative party polling below the yearly average during period under scrutiny (binary); given that the CDU/CSU and the SPD compete for chancellorship, a CDU/CSU crisis is calculated based on the polling difference between both parties |
| | Which political camp is leading in the polls? Mid-left or mid-right? | Polling based on national election surveys (Dutch Election Survey, Swedish Trends/YouGovSweden, German Politbarometer) | In binary coding operationalized as power option for the mid-left, yes or no |

*probabilistic* reasoning of classic algebra and quantitative research methods. The principal proponent of set theory, Charles Ragin, lists five key features of social research according to Boolean logic:

> To summarize, set relations in social research (1) involve causal or other integral connections linking social phenomena (i.e., are not merely definitional), (2) are theory and knowledge dependent (i.e., require explication), (3) are central to social science theorizing (because theory is primarily verbal in nature, and verbal statements are often set-theoretic), (4) are asymmetric (and thus should not be reformulated as correlational arguments), and (5) can be very strong despite relatively modest correlations (Ragin 2008, 17).

Consequently, instead of measuring the strength of a relation between independent and dependent variables, set-theoretic approaches are concerned with revealing if and to what extent a set of conditions can be seen as a necessary and/or sufficient condition for an outcome. It is crucial to distinguish between necessary and sufficient conditions; the differences between the two can be neatly illustrated using Venn diagrams (Fig. 4.4).

According to standard logic, the assumption that condition A is *necessary* for outcome B to occur is the same as stating that 'B cannot be true unless A is true', or 'if A is false then B is false.' By contraposition, this is the same as saying that 'whenever B is true, so is A.' A good example is the age-constraint in electing the German Bundespräsident: the candidate has to be at least 40 years old in order to become Bundespräsident (Art. 54, Abs. 1, GG). In turn, the person who is Bundespräsident is at least 40 years old. Being at least 40 years old is a *necessary*

**Fig. 4.4** Venn diagrams on
necessary and sufficient
conditions

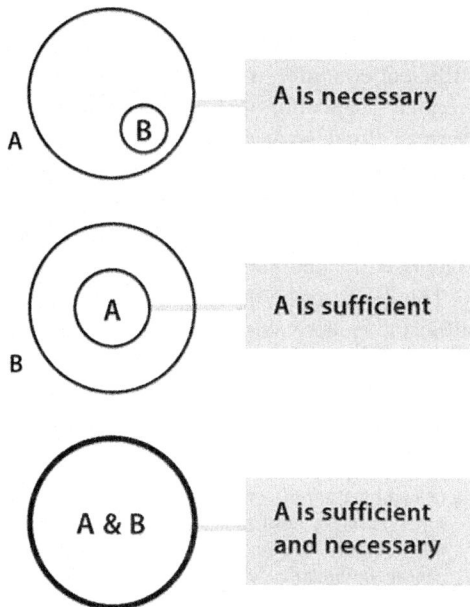

A is necessary

A is sufficient

A is sufficient
and necessary

condition for being elected German Bundespräsident. Using the Venn diagrams, one can say that all Bundespräsidents are part of the group of German citizens above 40. However, this is not a sufficient condition because being 40 years old does not automatically make you German Bundespräsident. The group aged above 40 lists approximately 75,000,000 German citizens with different jobs.

To say that C is a *sufficient* condition for D is to say that whenever D is present, C is also present. In contrast, D being absent does not imply the absence of C as well; D can be present despite the absence of C.

I will stay with the German Bundespräsident to provide an example. Given that the German President must hold German citizenship (Art. 54, Abs. 1, GG) and one acquires German citizenship by having German parents, having German parents is a sufficient condition for acquiring German citizenship, and thus, in turn, for running for office as Bundespräsident. Therefore, all German Bundespräsidents have German citizenship. To recall the Venn diagrams, the group of all people that can become German Bundespräsident is part of the group with German citizenship. It is important to note that one can also obtain German citizenship without having German parents, however (Art. 10, Art. 11, Art. 12, StaG). Thus, having German parents is not a necessary condition for becoming Bundespräsident, nor is being Bundespräsident a sufficient condition for having German parents. The group of German Bundespräsidents does not have to be part of the group of people with German parents (even though that has been the case up to now).

The stronger set-relations between (sets of) conditions, because of their more restrictive nature, are those that are both *necessary and sufficient* conditions for an outcome. This means: if A then B; conversely, if not A, then not B either. Revisiting the example of the German Bundespräsident, it is both a necessary and sufficient condition to be the German Bundespräsident in order to propose a new German Chancellor after a federal election has been cast (Art. 63, GG). Only the German Bundespräesident can do so, therefore it is a necessary condition; if the federal election is cast, the Bundespräsident will propose a German chancellor—a sufficient condition. Revisiting the Venn diagrams, the group of people who can and will propose a new German Chancellor after a federal election is cast is comprised of one person, the German Bundespräesident.

This leads to the question of how to assess the 'usefulness' of an approximated sufficient or necessary condition. Charles Ragin proposes two central descriptive measures to evaluate set-theoretic relationships in this vein: consistency and coverage. Consistency shows the degree to which a subset-relation has been approximated, while coverage indicates the empirical relevance of the subset. To quote Ragin once more:

> *Set-theoretic consistency* assesses the degree to which the cases sharing a given condition or combination of conditions (e.g. democratic dyad) agree in displaying the outcome in question (e.g. nonwarring). That is, consistency indicates how closely the subset relation is approximated. *Set-theoretic coverage*, by contrast, assesses the degree to which a cause or causal combination "accounts for" instances of an outcome (Ragin 2008, 292).

Highly simplified, consistency could be defined simply as the sum of consistent membership scores in a causal condition divided by the sum of all membership scores in a cause or a causal combination; as the causal conditions in fuzzy sets usually do not embrace a value of 1, the consistency drops accordingly. For example, if three children who like to play football score 100% correct answers in a math test—coded as 1—but a fourth child who also likes to play football scores 60%—coded as 0.6—the consistency of the set-relation between 'like to play football' and 'good in math' drops to $(3 \times 1 + 1 \times 0.6)/4 = 0.9$. For a detailed discussion of the calculation of scores of consistency and coverage, see Charles Ragin's elaborations (Ragin 2008). For this project, the 'standards of good practice' in using QCA (Schneider and Wagemann 2010a) are applied. Finally, this study uses very conservative benchmarks for each calculation to ensure the high validity of the findings. Sufficient conditions must score 0.75 or above and necessary conditions 0.90 or above in consistency values in order be treated as liable findings.

In order to check the plausibility of any findings, this study relies on triangulation, testing the hypothesis using deterministic reasoning (QCA) and relying on statistical methods of well-known probabilistic logic. However, the rather low number of cases (max. 53 country-years) and the rather high number of variables (up to 11) result in a very low number of degrees of freedom, which in turn decreases the levels of significance to a large extent. Therefore, the common methods of choice—time-series or structural equation models—face clear limitations and are therefore unsuitable. Consequently, this study relies on simple in-block correlations in order to check whether the causal chains are supported by correlations. Correlations do not imply causations. Still, under their auspices it can be judged whether the argument derived from a deterministic logic is supported or rejected by probabilistic reasoning.

## 4.6   Data Sources and Recoding

QCA analysis calls for recoding the data to a binary logic. The data must be recoded according to a membership in a fuzzy set; 0 implying no membership, 1 implying full membership. For the concepts previously introduced, this requires recoding data, for example as constituting an economic threat (yes/no), indicating a liberal position of the center-left (yes/no) or whether the center-left spectrum is leading in the polls (yes/no). The state of the populist radical right party is measured via polling figures on their support at the federal level. The data is recoded according to an established procedure: extreme outliers are excluded from the recoding, given a 0 or a 1, respectively, while the rest is recoded using the following formula. Extreme outliers are defined as those that score higher or lower than one standard deviation from the mean, and are coded accordingly—with the same value as one standard deviation from the mean (Table 4.9).

The following formula is used for the data-transforming (Verkuilen 2005, 479–489):

$$\text{Membership in fuzzy set} = (\text{data point} - \text{goalpost low})/$$

$$(\text{goalpost high} - \text{goalpost low})$$

The study begins by scrutinizing the immigration debate in the respective countries when the issue became salient; the period under scrutiny ends when the populist radical right party attracted enough seats to influence the public debate (2001 in the Netherlands and 2010/2012 in Sweden), and when the euro-topic replaced immigration matters as key on the cultural axis (2012 in Germany). From 2012 onwards, the developments in German party politics are dealt with in the separate Chap. 9.

**Table 4.9**  Recoding of QCA conditions

| Condition | Recoding | Explaining recoding, data source | Mean Standard deviation High threshold Low threshold | Cases exceeding thresholds and possible explanation |
|---|---|---|---|---|
| Real cultural threat potential | Cross-nationally | Immigration recoded according to per Capita, OECD | 0.75 0.22 0.52 0.97 | 1. Low immigration in the Netherlands 1994–1999 due to lack of EU border 2. High immigration in Germany 1988–1993 due to unchanged asylum-law and reunification |
| Real economic threat potential | Cross-nationally | Unemployment figures harmonized by International Labor Office | 8.1 2.4 5.7 10.5 | 1. Extremely decent economics in the Netherlands 1997–2001 2. Extremely dire economics in Germany 1994–2000 and 2003–2006 |

(continued)

**Table 4.9**  (continued)

| Condition | Recoding | Explaining recoding, data source | Mean Standard deviation High threshold Low threshold | Cases exceeding thresholds and possible explanation |
|---|---|---|---|---|
| Perceived cultural threat potential | Cross-nationally | Similar survey questions, national election surveys | 13.1 10.7 2.6 23.8 | 1. Extremely contested migration topics in the Netherlands 1994–1995 2. Almost no migration topics in (West-)German party discourse 1982–1987 3. Extremely contested migration topics in Germany 1991–1993 |
| Perceived economic threat potential | Cross-nationally | Similar survey questions, national election surveys | 20.7 14.2 6.5 34.9 | 1. Extremely decent economics in the Netherlands 1999–2001 2. Extremely decent economics in (West-)Germany 1986, 1989 and 1990 3. Extremely dire economics in Germany 1993, 1996–1997 and 2002–2005 4. Extremely decent economics in Sweden 2005–2006 |
| General salience | Based on national data | Different newspaper styles | NL 71 35 106 36 | Extremely high salience 1993 (asylum-debates), very low salience in 1996 and 1998 |
|  |  |  | SE 34 21 55 13 | Extremely high salience 2002 (election) and 2005 (asylum debates), very low salience in 2009 |
|  |  |  | GER 104 150 254 0 | Extremely high salience 1992 (asylum debates) |

(continued)

**Table 4.9**   (continued)

| Condition | Recoding | Explaining recoding, data source | Mean Standard deviation High threshold Low threshold | Cases exceeding thresholds and possible explanation |
|---|---|---|---|---|
| Liberal party discourse | Cross-nationally | Same coding rules for all countries | −1.1<br>4.7<br>3.6<br>−5.8 | 1. Extremely conservative discourse in Germany 1982–1983, 1993, 1998–1999 and 2004–2008<br>2. Very liberal discourse in Netherlands 1995 and 2000, Germany 1988 and 1989, and in Sweden 2006–2010 |
| Polling of populist radical right party (PRRP) | Cross-nationally | Similar institutional circumstances, national pollings | 2.1<br>2.9<br>5.0<br>0.0 | Extremely high polling in the Netherlands 2002 (Ljist Pim Fortyn), in Germany 1989 (Die Republikaner) and in Sweden in 2010 (Sverigedemokraterna) |
| Crisis of conservative agenda-setter | Based on national data | Conservative parties embedded in different party dynamics, national pollings, for NL and SE regular party pollings taken, given the size of the CDU/CSU and claim for chancellorship the difference to its major competitor SPD is taken | NL<br>16.4<br>3.7<br>12.7<br>30.1 | Extremely low polling figures of the VVD 1991, very high pollings 1995–1998 |
| | | | SE<br>7.2<br>2.1<br>5.1<br>9.3 | Extremely low pollings of the FP in 2002, very high pollings 2003–2004 and 2007 |
| | | | GER<br>2.5<br>3.6<br>5.1<br>0 | CDU/CSU extremely behind SPD in 1988–1989, 1992, 1997 and 2000 (Difference SPD-CDU/CSU) |
| Mid-left ahead | Cross-nationally | Mid-left and Mid-right camps in all countries NL (PvdA+D66 +GL) − (VVD+CDA) SE (SAP+V+MP) − (FP+M +KC+C) GER (SPD +Gruene) − (CDU/CSU +FDP) | 0,5<br>9.5<br>10<br>0 | Mid-Left Camp extremely successful in the Netherlands 1997–1998 and 2000; in Germany 1988–1989, 1997 and 2000; in Sweden in 2002 and 2008 |

# References

Alonso S, Claro da Fonseca S (2011) Immigration, left and right. Party Polit:1–20

Bornschier S (2010) The new cultural divide and the two-dimensional political space in Western Europe. West Eur Polit 33(3):419–444

Di Tella TS (1997) Populism into the twenty-first century. Gov Oppos 32(2):191–193

Goertz G, Mahoney J (2006) Social science concepts: a user's guide. Princeton University Press, Princeton

Helbling M (2012) Public debates, integration models and transnationalism in Western Europe. J Immigrants Refug Stud 10(3):241–259

Helbling M, Tresch A (2011) Measuring party positions and issue salience from media coverage: discussing and cross-validating new indicators. Elect Stud 30:174–183

Koopmans R et al (2005) Contested citizenship: immigration and cultural diversity in Europe. University of Minnesota Press, Minneapolis

Kriesi H et al (2008) West European politics in the age of globalization. Cambridge University Press, Cambridge

Krippendorf K (2004) Content analysis: an introduction to its methodology. Sage Publication, Thousand Oaks

Lijphart A (1984) Electoral systems and party systems. Oxford University Press, Oxford

Lombard M et al (2002) Content analysis in mass communication: assessment and reporting of intercoder reliability. Hum Commun Res 28(4):587–604

Lucassen G, Lubbers M (2011) Who fears what? Explaining Far-right-wing preference in Europe by distinguishing perceived cultural and economic ethnic threats. Comp Polit Stud 20(10):1–28

Meguid BM (2005) Competition between unequals: The role of mainstream party strategy in niche party success. Am Polit Sci Rev 99(3):347–359

Mudde C (2016) The study of populist radical right parties: towards a fourth wave. C-Rex Working Paper Series 1/2016. Available at: https://www.sv.uio.no/c-rex/english/publications/c-rex-working-paper-series/Cas%20Mudde:%20The%20Study%20of%20Populist%20Radical%20Right%20Parties.pdf. Last accessed 7 May 2017

Muis J (2012) Pim Fortuyn: the evolution of a media phenomenon. Ridderkerk

Przeworski A, Teune H (1970) The logic of comparative social inquiry. Krieger, Malabar

Ragin C (2008) Redesigning social inquiry: fuzzy sets and beyond. University of Chicago Press, Chicago

Rydgren J, Ruth P (2011) Contextual explanations of radical right-wing support in Sweden: socioeconomic marginalization, group threat, and the halo effect. Ethn Racial Stud 36(4):711–728

Schneider C, Wagemann C (2010a) Standards of good practise in qualitative comparative analysis (QCA) and fuzzy-sets. Compa Sociol 9:397–418

Schneider C, Wagemann C (2010b) Qualitative comparative analysis (QCA) and fuzzy-sets: agenda for a research approach and a data analysis technique. Comp Sociol 9:376–396

Thränhardt D (1995) The political uses of xenophobia in England, France and Germany. Party Polit 1(1):323–345

Tilly C (1984) Big structures, large processes, huge comparisons. Sage Foundation, New York

Verkuilen J (2005) Assigning membership in a fuzzy set analysis. Sociol Methods Res 33:462–496

# Chapter 5
# Empirical Results: Why Populists Win or Lose—A Two-Level Theory

## 5.1 Salience: When Are Parties Talking About Immigration?

Conservative parties (VVD, FP and CDU/CSU) are the clear agenda setters in matters of immigration. Comparing the salience values of all countries indicates that conservative parties indeed put far more emphasis on immigration-related topics than all other established political actors. Taking the salience peak of each party in each country as point of reference (therefore, in contrast with the QCA-recoding, including the extreme outliers), the mean score of conservative parties over all years is 0.46, while it ranges, remarkably similarly, from 0.30 to 0.33 for all other parties; the standard deviation is, however, remarkably similar across *all* parties—indicating that party rationales are *comparably volatile* across party families (Table 5.1).

In the Netherlands, the Social Democrats (PvdA) and the Conservative Liberals (VVD) were the prime agenda setters in immigration-related matters between 1990 and 2001. The VVD politicized the issue from 1991 on and—save 1998—dropped its attention to the matter significantly after 1995 (Fig. 5.1).

The Swedish case shows a similar picture: the Social Democrats (SAP) and the conservative Liberals (FP) are the prime agenda setters in Sweden, too. The highest salience scores can be seen for the years 2002, 2005 and 2012 (see Fig. 5.2). Interestingly, the Swedish Social Democrats (SAP) put more emphasis (0.48 mean salience score) on immigration matters than their Dutch (0.34) and German (0.26) counterparts.

The descriptive statistics from Germany fit the comparative picture, with one striking outlier: the German Social Democrats (SPD). With a mean of 0.26 on the ratio of claims per year, they put remarkably less emphasis on immigration-related matters than their Dutch (0.34) or Swedish (0.48) counterparts. Except for 1992, the German case reveals one prime agenda setter on immigration-related topics: the

© Springer International Publishing AG 2018
T. Lochocki, *The Rise of Populism in Western Europe*,
DOI 10.1007/978-3-319-62855-4_5

**Table 5.1** Descriptive statistics on party salience, comparatively

|  | Mean | Standard deviation | Minimum | Maximum |
|---|---|---|---|---|
| Conservatives (VVD, FP, CDU/CSU) | 0.46 | 0.28 | 0 | 1 |
| Social Democrats (PvdA, SAP, SPD) | 0.33 | 0.29 | 0 | 1 |
| Left-Liberals (D66, MP, Gruene) | 0.31 | 0.28 | 0 | 1 |
| Liberal-Moderates (CDA, M, FDP) | 0.30 | 0.30 | 0 | 1 |

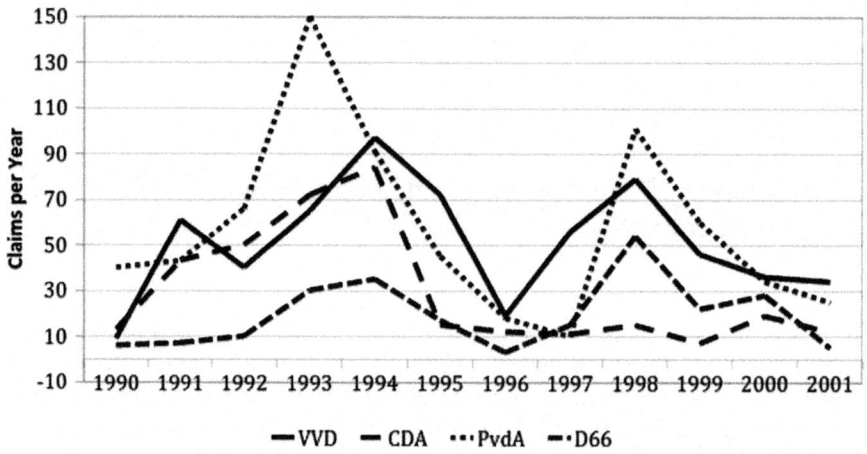

**Fig. 5.1**  Salience of immigration-related topics in the Netherlands 1990–2001

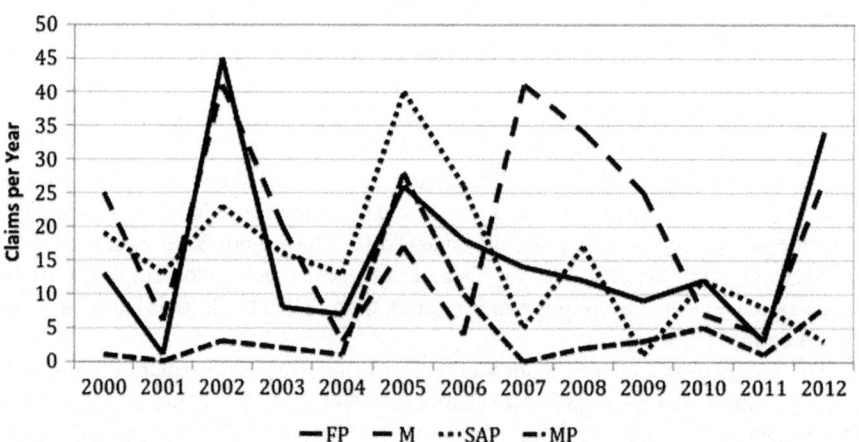

**Fig. 5.2**  Salience of immigration-related topics in Sweden 2000–2012

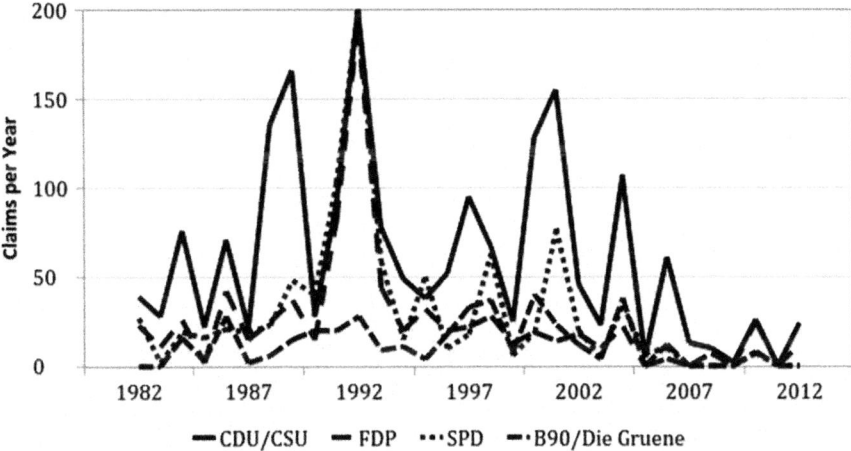

**Fig. 5.3** Salience of immigration-related topics in Germany 1982–2012 (The salience values of the CDU/CSU and SPD for the year 1992 were set to 200 because they define extreme outliers. In fact, they score at 377 and 464, respectively)

conservative CDU/CSU. Highest salience is visible in the late 1980s and early 1990s and around the year 2000 (Fig. 5.3).

The salience-scores show remarkable variation, both within countries and across party-families in the countries under examination. Still, conservative parties are clearly the prime agenda setters in matters of immigration and integration. Given the presumed necessity of periods of high salience preceding advances of PRRPs, this finding is very important. It also raises the question: given that conservative parties are the prime agenda setters and operate in similar scope conditions across all three countries, why are they far more inclined to discuss immigration-related topics at different points in time? And regarding the center-left of the political spectrum, the question arises: why is the German SPD far less inclined to talk about immigration and integration topics than its counterparts in the Netherlands and Sweden?

## 5.2   Positioning: When Do Established Parties Open the Niche for PRRPs?

As with the salience of immigration-related topics in party discourse, striking variation in the positions of established parties on the matter can also be seen, both between party positions in the same country and within party families across the Netherlands, Sweden and Germany. While the standard deviation is comparable across party families, again indicating a comparable volatility across party family and country, the mean values show an expected pattern: the conservatives take the most restrictive position, while the liberal-moderates and the social democrats campaign on rather liberal positions and the left-liberals take clear-cut liberal standpoints (Table 5.2).

**Table 5.2** Descriptive statistics on party positions, comparatively

|  | Mean | Standard deviation | Minimum | Maximum |
|---|---|---|---|---|
| Conservatives (VVD, FP, CDU/CSU) | −3.0 | 3.0 | −8.0 | 2.7 |
| Social Democrats (PvdA, SAP, SPD) | 1.9 | 2.5 | −4.4 | 7.1 |
| Left-Liberals (D66, MP, Gruene) | 6.0 | 3.0 | 1.2 | 9.8 |
| Liberal-Moderates (CDA, M, FDP) | 0.6 | 2.0 | −4.6 | 5.0 |

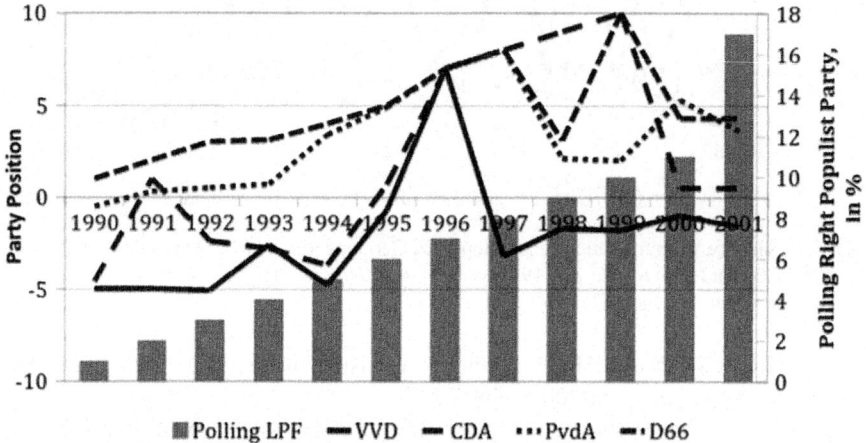

**Fig. 5.4** Party positions on immigration-related topics in the Netherlands

The position-changes of the established conservative parties are of particular interest. The hypothesis suggests that the parties once introduced the topic and the position PRRPs later campaign on. The data backs this assumption 100%. The VVD in the Netherlands dropped its conservative profile over the course of the 1990s and saw the breakthrough of the Ljist Pim Fortuyn (LPF) in 2001 with 17.0% in the election in 2002, followed by the rise of Geert Wilders' Partij voor die Vrijheid (PVV) (Fig. 5.4). This party has been present in Dutch politics ever since, with a steady voter base of around 15–25%. The Swedish Liberals only took a conservative position in 2002 and have faced the steady rise of the Sweden Democrats (SD) since that year—they entered the Swedish Parliament with 5.7% in 2010 and poll around 20% in 2017 (Fig. 5.5). In contrast, the German Conservatives (CDU/CSU) campaigned on centrist positions only at the end of the 1980s and after 2011. At nearly all other times in between the CDU/CSU took very conservative positions on immigration matters, presumably keeping the electoral niche for PRRPs closed. The CDU/CSU only withdrew from its conservative position once, in the late 1980s. The first federal advances of a PRRP (until the AfD entered the German scene) swiftly followed this programmatic turn: at the election for the European Parliament in 1989, Die Republikaner (REP) attracted 7.1% voter support (Fig. 5.6).

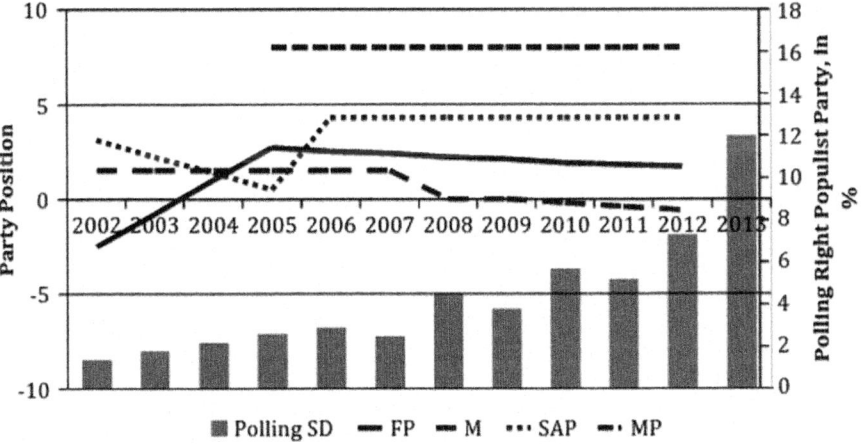

**Fig. 5.5**  Party positions on immigration-related topics in Sweden

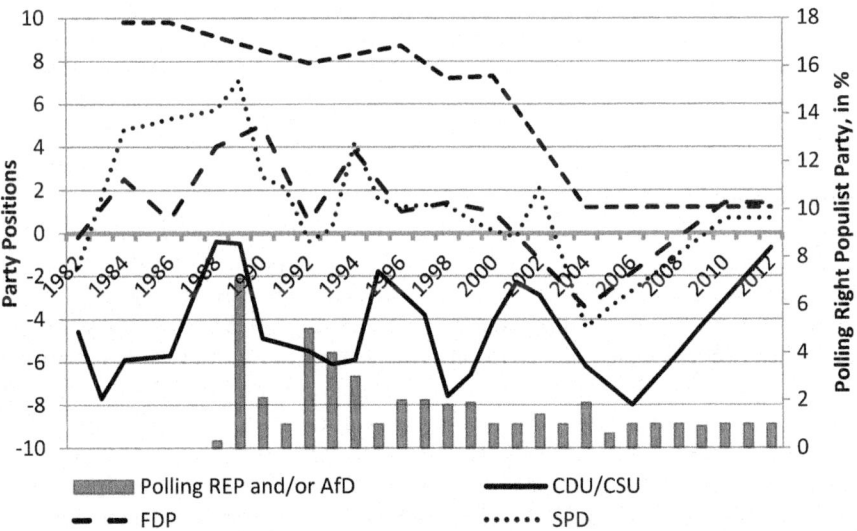

**Fig. 5.6**  Party positions on immigration-related topics in Germany

## 5.3   QCA Results: Ultimately, It Is Not About Immigration at All

The descriptive results show striking variation with the salience of the immigration topic and the respective party positions on the matter; even though all conservative parties increased the salience of immigration-related matters significantly at various points in time, the German Conservatives (CDU/CSU) seem to be the only party that

**Table 5.3** Concepts and their operationalization for the QCA analysis

| Concept | Condition/variable |
|---|---|
| Real and perceived structural threat potential | Objective cultural threat potential |
| | Objective economic threat potential |
| | Perceived cultural threat potential |
| | Perceived economic threat potential |
| Party descriptive | Salience in the party discourse (comprising combined salience of Social Democrats and Conservatives) |
| | Discourse amongst established parties: liberal (liberal position of the Social-Democrats and centrist of Conservatives) or not (centrist position of Social Democrats and conservative position of the Conservatives) |
| Party interaction | Polling of populist radical right party (PRRP) |
| | Crisis of conservative agenda-setter |
| | Which political camp is leading in the polls |

only rarely dropped its very conservative profile in a salient debate, thus presumably keeping the electoral niche for a PRRP closed. Hence, the prime research question comes back to the fore: is the salience of immigration topics and the respective positioning by established parties key in explaining the electoral advances of PRRPs?

To check this question under the auspices of a QCA analysis, the variables and conditions were operationalized according to the theoretical considerations in the literature review and methodical sensitivities as discussed in the chapter on research design (Table 5.3).

Populist radical right parties poll successfully when established parties discuss immigration at length, but do not offer a conservative position on the subject (1). They drop in the polls when established parties drop the liberal discourse, offering conservative messages and discussing immigration less (2). Mirroring these results are PRRPs polling well when a liberal discourse prevails while the conservative party is undergoing a crisis (3); their polling goes down if the liberal discourse vanishes and the conservative party is recovering from its crisis (4). PRRPs also poll well if voters perceive a massive cultural threat (5); they lose support if voters neither feel a cultural, nor an economic threat (6). These necessary conditions with very high coverage values show that PRRPs are clearly dependent on the political messaging of other parties on immigration matters. The high coverage values of the conditions that explain dropping popular support for PRRPs indicate that established parties' messaging *alone* enables them to reclaim voters from populist radical right parties. The lower coverage values with factors enabling electoral advances of PRRPs points to other factors aiding the advances of populist radical right parties—for example media access and organizational capacity. However, these factors seem of lesser importance in explaining the loses of PRRPs: if established parties offer conservative positions on immigration matters, voters seem to turn their backs on PRRPs even if the populists have solid media access and are well organized (Table 5.4).

5.3 QCA Results: Ultimately, It Is Not About Immigration at All

**Table 5.4** QCA results accounting for variation in the polling of PRRPs

| | Successful populist radical right party (stable or increasing polling figures) | | | Unsuccessful populist radical right party (decreasing polling figures) | | |
|---|---|---|---|---|---|---|
| | Term | Coverage | Consistency | Term | Coverage | Consistency |
| Necessary conditions | Liberal discourse AND High salience (1) | 0.56 | 0.95 | No liberal discourse AND No high salience (2) | 0.73 | 0.90 |
| | Liberal discourse AND Crisis conservative party (3) | 0.56 | 0.91 | No liberal discourse AND No crisis conservative party (4) | 0.70 | 0.91 |
| | Perceived cultural threat (5) | 0.70 | 0.90 | No perceived cultural threat AND No perceived economic threat (6) | 0.75 | 0.92 |

The descriptive findings and these QCA outcomes show a clear political mechanism: public support for populist radical right parties increases when conservative parties have mobilized on the immigration topic (increasing the salience) and have dropped their conservative position over the course of the debate (liberal discourse). This begs two questions: firstly, why have conservative parties mobilized on the immigration issue in the first place? And secondly, why have they dropped the conservative position they introduced?

The immigration topic is salient amongst established parties if the conservative party undergoes a crisis. Neither an objective, nor a perceived cultural threat can account for high salience. That means that conservative parties base their decision on when to talk about immigration almost entirely on their own condition; based on the QCA results, how many immigrants are arriving (real cultural threat), and what voters think (perceived cultural threat) does not seem to influence the decision of conservative parties. The salience of immigration matters increases when conservative parties face a strong center-left camp while immigration figures rise (1), when they poll well behind the center-left camp while voters are concerned about economics (2) or unemployment rates have risen (3). While here at least some factors other than observing the prime electoral competitor come into play, these factors are entirely unimportant in understanding when conservative parties *stop* talking about immigration. Conservative parties stop talking about the matter when they emerge from their crisis (4) and when the entire bourgeois camp is surpassing the center-left spectrum in the polls (5). The only sufficient condition explaining the increasing salience of immigration topics is again the crisis of the conservatives; similarly, the only sufficient condition explaining the low salience of immigration debates is the absence of a crisis in the conservative party. Thus, the QCA results speak a very clear language: the condition of the conservative party is the only jointly necessary and sufficient condition to explain the salience or absence of immigration topics in the public debate. Conservatives talk about immigration when they undergo a crisis; they drop the issue when they have recovered and improved in the polls. It is neither about immigration numbers, nor about public concerns; it is about the condition of the conservative party (Table 5.5).

But if conservative parties increase the salience of migration topics in beginning a debate with a conservative position, why do they drop it over the course of the debate, eventually opening the electoral niche for a populist radical right party?

The conservatives drop their conservative messages, moving towards the liberal social democrats, when they face a successful center-left camp while the electorate is freed of economic concerns (1). In turn, conservatives 'convince' social democrats to move closer to their conservative positions when the center-left camp is polling badly and the voters feel culturally and economically threatened (2). In contrast to the two previous QCA calculations, here voters' feelings seem to play a major role. However, not as one might expect regarding immigration matters; instead, the conservatives seem inclined to follow the liberal social democrat messages only when the conflict between both parties occurs in a time where voters are not concerned about economics (3) or any form of objective threat (4). How important voters' feelings are in this respect is further illustrated by the only

**Table 5.5** QCA results accounting for variation with the salience of immigration-related topics

| | High salience of immigration topics | | | Low salience of immigration topics | | |
|---|---|---|---|---|---|---|
| | Term | Coverage | Consistency | Term | Coverage | Consistency |
| Necessary conditions | Left camp ahead AND Objective cultural threat (1) | 0.48 | 0.91 | No crisis conservative party (4) | 0.80 | 0.89 |
| | Crisis conservative party AND Left camp ahead AND Perceived economic threat (2) | 0.46 | 0.94 | No crisis conservative party AND No left camp ahead (5) | 0.74 | 0.91 |
| | Crisis conservative party AND Left camp ahead AND Real economic threat (3) | 0.45 | 0.94 | | | |
| Sufficient conditions | Crisis conservative party (6) | 0.64 | 0.76 | No crisis conservative party (7) | 0.87 | 0.80 |

**Table 5.6** QCA results accounting for variation in a liberal discourse on immigration-related topics

| | Liberal discourse on migration matters | | | No liberal discourse on migration matters | | |
|---|---|---|---|---|---|---|
| | Term | Coverage | Consistency | Term | Coverage | Consistency |
| Necessary conditions | Center-left camp leading in the polls AND No perceived economic threat (1) | 0.68 | 0.94 | No center-left camp leading in the polls AND Perceived economic threat AND Perceived cultural threat (2) | 0.60 | 0.90 |
| | Crisis conservative party AND No perceived economic threat (3) | 0.56 | 0.97 | | | |
| | Center-left camp leading in the polls AND No real economic threat AND No real cultural threat (4) | 0.61 | 0.93 | | | |
| Sufficient conditions | | | | Perceived economic threat (5) | 0.71 | 0.82 |

sufficient condition explaining when social democrats accommodate to the conservative messaging of the conservatives—when voters feel threatened economically (5). Conservatives drop their conservative messages on immigration—opening the niche for a PRRP—when they face a successful center-right camp in a society freed of economic concerns (Table 5.6).

These mechanisms perfectly account for the why the German Die Republikaner failed to enter the Bundestag despite polling very well over substantial periods in the late 1980s and early 1990s. This PRRP won 7.1% at the election for the European Parliament in 1989, failed to enter the Bundestag in 1990, again polled near 10% through the early 1990s, but still failed to enter the Bundestag in 1994. Applying the QCA analysis to the years 1988–1994 (using 3-months quarters as units of analysis instead of years) proves the deciphered mechanisms. The REP polled well exactly in the quarters where the CDU/CSU dropped their conservative messages and accommodated the liberal messages from the SPD, while the center-left camp (SPD and Greens) polled ahead of the bourgeois camp (CDU/CSU and FDP) (1). Once the SPD dropped their liberal messages and echoed the conservative messages from the CDU/CSU and the bourgeois camp recovered, the REP dropped in the polls (2). When the bourgeois camp is not surpassing the center-left camp, a conservative turn of the SPD also hurts the REP if voters feel no economic threat (3) and if immigration numbers decrease (4). However, the strongest necessary conditions—as mutually reconfirming—are the liberal debates on immigration and the strength of the respective political camps. The REP loses voter support when voters see the CDU/CSU and the SPD campaigning on a conservative compromise while the bourgeois camp leads in the polls. These developments are further proof that voters pay a high degree of attention to political messaging (Table 5.7).

A possible explanation for why salience no longer has an impact might be that immigration topics have been heated since the late 1980s and therefore present in German voters' minds throughout the period. Bearing in mind that this QCA calculation relies on 3-months quarters, it appears logical that these time periods might be too short for political issues to vanish from voters' calculations.

**Table 5.7** QCA results accounting for variation with voters' support for Die Republikaner (REP) in Germany 1988–1994

| | Polling REP | | | ~Polling REP | | |
|---|---|---|---|---|---|---|
| | Term | Coverage | Consistency | Term | Coverage | Consistency |
| Necessary conditions | Liberal discourse AND Center-left camp leading in the polls (1) | 0.67 | 0.89 | No liberal discourse AND No center-left camp leading in the polls (2) | 0.68 | 0.90 |
| | | | | No liberal discourse AND No perceived economic threat (3) | 0.64 | 0.91 |
| | | | | No liberal discourse AND No real cultural threat (4) | 0.70 | 0.94 |

German voters turned their back on the REP because they observed a conservative compromise between the CDU/CSU and the SPD. However, the positions of both established parties were again largely dependent on German voters evaluating the state of the economy (not the immigrant situation). The CDU/CSU moved closer to the liberal messages of the SPD when the center-left camp led in the polls while Germany was freed of objective cultural and economic threats (1), including perceived economic threats (2). In turn, the SPD dropped their liberal messages and accommodated the conservative messages of the CDU/CSU when neither the center-left camp led, nor the CDU/CSU was weathering a crisis (3); and especially when the bourgeois camp gained voters' sympathies while unemployment figures rose (4). The SPD seems to have been especially inclined to take over CDU/CSU's positions, in turn closing the electoral niche for the REP, as immigration figures dropped (5); as illustrated by the only sufficient condition explaining a conservative compromise (Table 5.8).

**Table 5.8** QCA results accounting for variation positions of the CDU/CSU and the SPD on immigration-related matters in Germany 1988–1994

|  | Liberal discourse | | | No liberal discourse | | |
|---|---|---|---|---|---|---|
|  | Term | Coverage | Consistency | Term | Coverage | Consistency |
| Necessary conditions | Center-left camp leading in the polls AND No real economic threat AND No real cultural threat (1) | 0.37 | 0.89 | No center-left camp leading in the polls AND Crisis conservative party (3) | 0.73 | 0.90 |
|  | Center-left camp leading in the polls AND No real economic threat AND No perceived economic threat (2) | 0.39 | 0.89 | No center-left camp leading in the polls AND Real economic threat (4) | 0.78 | 0.90 |
| Sufficient conditions |  |  |  | No real cultural threat | 0.73 | 0.78 |

Save the impact of issue-salience, the primary conditions that account for electoral variation for PRRPs across several decades in Germany, the Netherlands and Sweden, can also explain the rise and fall of Germany's Die Republikaner (REP) between 1988 and 1994 in detail: once immigration topics have been heatedly discussed, the crucial door-opener for the PRRP is the embracing of a liberal discourse by all established parties—if the CDU/CSU drops the conservative position they have introduced themselves. In turn, this electoral niche opens only if the left camp, led by the SPD, is leading in the polls while the society is freed of economic concerns. As German voters felt threatened economically (not culturally), the SPD joined a conservative compromise with the messaging of the CDU/CSU, in turn closing the electoral niche for the REP.

## 5.4    Supporting the Plausibility of the Argument with Probabilistic Measures

To test the validity of the argument, a triangulation is called for. The findings derived from Boolean QCA logic must be tested under the auspices of probabilistic reasoning. However, this triangulation cannot rely on time-series or structural equation models. The rather small number of cases (53 country-years) and the rather high number of variables (between 5 and 11) would result in a very low number of degrees of freedom, which, in turn, would greatly decrease the levels of significance. Consequently, simple in-block correlations are required in order to determine whether causal chains are supported by correlations. Correlation does not imply causation—it must be theoretically derived. But if the QCA-results were supported by probabilistic statistics, this would support the argument substantially. Therefore, the components of the two-level theory are tested for correlation and their respective significance—the key factors of the argument are highlighted (Table 5.9).

The correlational model clearly supports the QCA-results with one main caveat: in contrast with QCA, the real rate of immigration is indicated to be a strong factor explaining electoral advances of populist radical right parties.

Save this small limitation, the probabilistic model supports all deterministic findings: PRRPs poll well in times of high salience (corr. 0.27; sig. 0,09) and in the presence of liberal discourse (corr. 0.36; sig. 0.02). In turn, the likelihood of salience increases as a result of a real cultural threat (corr. 0.14; sig. 0.35), and first and foremost when the conservative party undergoes a crisis (corr. 0.66; sig. 0.00). Finally, a liberal discourse occurs in times of no perceived economic threat (corr. −0.63; sig. 0.00) and if the center-left camp is polling well ahead of the bourgeois camp (corr. 0.50, sig. 0.00). The in-block correlations are the highest with the respected conditions that have been hypothesized under the auspices of the QCA results. The in-block correlations can be summarized as supporting the findings of the QCA analysis (Table 5.10).

**Table 5.9** Using probabilistic measures: correlations and levels of significance of all conditions

| | | Perceived economic threat | Left camp polling ahead | Liberal discourse | Real cultural threat | Crisis conservative party | Salience | Advances PRRP |
|---|---|---|---|---|---|---|---|---|
| Perceived economic threat | Corr. | 1.00 | | | | | | |
| | Sig. | | | | | | | |
| Left camp polling ahead | Corr. | −0.49 | 1.00 | | | | | |
| | Sig. | 0.00 | | | | | | |
| Liberal discourse | Corr. | −0.63 | 0.50 | 1.00 | | | | |
| | Sig. | 0.00 | 0.00 | | | | | |
| Real cultural threat | Corr. | 0.10 | −0.23 | 0.00 | 1.00 | | | |
| | Sig. | 0.49 | 0.13 | 0.98 | | | | |
| Crisis conservative party | Corr. | −0.11 | 0.34 | 0.09 | 0.30 | 1.00 | | |
| | Sig. | 0.45 | 0.02 | 0.54 | 0.04 | | | |
| Salience | Corr. | −0.11 | 0.11 | 0.08 | 0.14 | 0.66 | 1.00 | |
| | Sig. | 0.43 | 0.44 | 0.60 | 0.35 | 0.00 | | |
| Advances PRRP | Corr. | −0.32 | 0.21 | 0.36 | 0.52 | 0.25 | 0.27 | 1.00 |
| | Sig. | 0.04 | 0.21 | 0.02 | 0.00 | 0.13 | 0.09 | |

**Table 5.10** Using probabilistic measures: correlations and levels of significance for conditions of the two-level theory

|  |  | Salience | Liberal discourse |
|---|---|---|---|
| Advances PRRP | Corr. | 0.27 | 0.36 |
|  | Sig. | 0.09 | 0.02 |
|  |  | Crisis conservative party | Real cultural threat |
| Salience | Corr. | 0.66 | 0.14 |
|  | Sig. | 0.00 | 0.35 |
|  |  | Left camp polling ahead | Perceived economic threat |
| Liberal discourse | Corr. | 0.55 | −0.63 |
|  | Sig. | 0.00 | 0.00 |

## 5.5   A Two-Level Theory of PRRPs' Varying Electoral Support

These findings support studies arguing for the crucial role of established parties in PRRP successes or failures (Ellinas 2010; Meguid 2005; Muis 2012). However, in addition to the high validity and reliability of the data and the calculations, this study extends these findings in two important respects.

Populist radical right parties gather electoral support if conservative parties drop their conservative profile—joining a liberal discourse—in salient immigration debates (Fig. 5.7). However, though the salience of immigration topics and the positing of the established actors are necessary conditions, they are not simultaneously necessary and sufficient (compare Table 5.4). This means that these factors need to be given in order for a PRRP to rise and fall, but other sufficient factors then eventually also come into play. However, the different coverage scores (0.56 for explaining PRRP successes and 0.73 for explaining their losses) for these necessary conditions show that established parties' political messages are extremely important in explaining *when PRRPs lose voter support*. The organizational capacity (Art 2011) and the media access of PRRPs (Ellinas 2010; Muis 2012) are important factors explaining their rise. However, when established parties campaign on a conservative profile in salient immigration debates, none of these factors seem to come to the rescue of PRRPs. This is news to party political researchers, and especially interesting for party strategists. Thought-through political messaging seems very well suited to reclaiming voters from populist radical right parties.

Additionally, this study explains varying party conduct on behalf of established, moderate political actors. It shows why center parties trigger the various steps leading to the advances of populist radical right parties. It explains the 'causes of the causes' (Goertz and Mahoney 2006, 241).

Three points are crucial in using the two-level theory. Firstly, the graphical display of the two-level theory might suggest a strictly parallel occurrence of high salience of immigration issues and a liberal discourse. But this is not the case. At the point that conservatives heat up the immigration issue in political discourse,

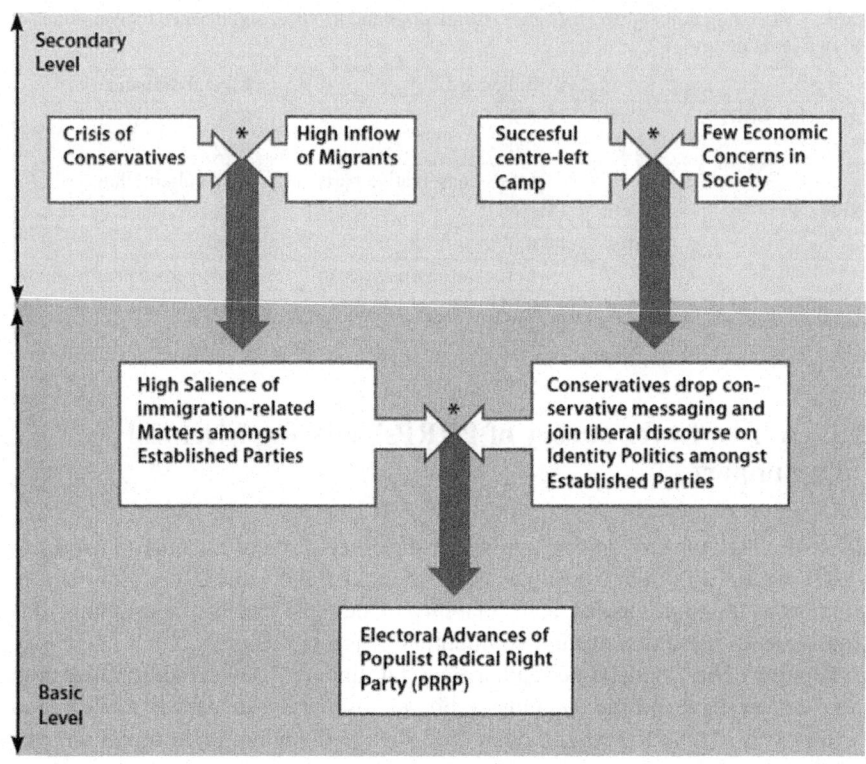

necessary cause 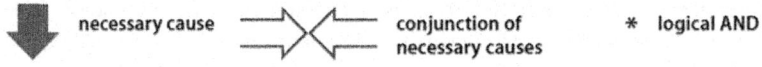 conjunction of necessary causes    * logical AND

**Fig. 5.7** A two-level theory explaining PRRPs' varying electoral support

increasing its salience, the conservative party will *not* join the liberal discourse. The prime aim of this strategic move seems to be the mobilization of voters to ameliorate a crisis, indicated by massively dropping polling figures. *If or when* the conservative party then joins the liberal discourse—or the social democrats accommodate the conservative's demands—depends on the mechanism outlined. Hence, high salience is not accompanied by a liberal discourse for at least a few months. The conservatives maintain their conservative profile for a certain period to mobilize their electorate.

Secondly, it is the *actual* cultural threat that influences the salience of immigration-related topics in political discourse. Conservatives mobilize on the immigration topic only if immigration numbers are really at a high level. If the immigration numbers are low, a conservative party crisis rarely leads to them turning to immigration topics to mobilize voters. However, it is the *perceived* economic threat that influences the position of established parties on the matter. Social democrats and conservatives far more easily reach a conservative compromise, closing the electoral niche for a populist radical right party, when voters are concerned about economics. If voters feel freed of economic worries, established actors are far more inclined to drop conservative messaging on immigration and join a liberal discourse, opening the electoral niche for a PRRP.

Finally, the sensitivity to the difference between *actual* immigration numbers and *perceived* economic concerns is credit to the extensive literature review on social conflict. The lack of these theoretical considerations in various studies in comparative politics might explain why research focusing on actual economic conditions (for example unemployment rates or economic growth) struggle to explain the polling of PRRPs or the conduct of established political parties. As much as it is the discourse on, the perception of, immigration that explains PRRP polling, it is the perception of economics that explains the varying political messaging of established political parties. Established political parties observe what their voters think about economics, and the voters observe what these parties say about immigration. It is about feelings and debates, not about fact and figures. Eventually, populist radical right parties succeed when established parties work with counterproductive political messaging in salient immigration debates.

## References

Art D (2011) Inside the radical right. Cambridge Publishing, Cambridge
Ellinas A (2010) The media and the far right in Western Europe: playing the nationalist card. University Press, Cambridge
Goertz G, Mahoney J (2006) Social science concepts. A user's guide. Princeton University Press, Princeton
Meguid BM (2005) Competition between unequals: the role of mainstream party strategy in niche party success. Am Polit Sci Rev 99(3):347–359
Muis J (2012) Pim Fortuyn: the evolution of a media phenomenon. Ridderkerk

# Chapter 6
# The Netherlands: The PvdA's Pyrrhic Victories or, Waiting for Pim Fortuyn

## 6.1 Frits Bolkestein's Agenda in the Early 1990s: Saving the Netherlands and, First and Foremost, His Volkspartij voor Vrijheid en Democratie (VVD)

The Dutch case illustrates the basic argument over the reasons why a significant increase in the salience of immigration is neatly related to party rationale, and not to actual immigration matters. The salience of immigration-related topics is strongly dependent on the condition of the right-liberal conservative party, the Volkspartij voor Vrijheid en Democratie (VVD). As long as it is faring well in the polls, the salience of the issue decreases; conversely, once the conservative party is in crisis, the issue is heated up in order to mobilize conservative voters.

As previous studies have shown, the leader of the VVD in the 1990s—Frits Bolkestein—was the first Dutch politician to put the immigration issue on the political agenda in the Netherlands, in 1991 (Aarts and Thomassen 2008; Van Kersbergen and Krouwel 2008). This study confirms these findings, showing an increase in VVD-claims reported by NRC Handelblad regarding immigration-related matters, from only nine claims in 1990 to 61 claims in 1991 (six times more). This high salience remained in place until the mid-1990s. NRC Handelblad reports an average of around 60 VVD-claims each year up to 1995; from 1996 on, the average salience attributed to immigration-related matters by the VVD is halved: from 1996 to 2001 only 36 VVD-claims were reported per year (Figs. 6.1 and 6.2).

But why did the VVD politicize the issue in 1991, and why did the salience decrease so sharply from 1996 on? A first thought might be that it is related to a rising *actual cultural threat*, brought on by the increasing number of asylum-seekers to which Western Europe was exposed in the early 1990s. Curiously—according to OECD statistics—the number of asylum-seekers in the Netherlands rose significantly in 1988 (from 6000 in 1987 to 13,500 in 1988) and then again in 1990 (from 14,000 in 1989 to 21,000 in 1990), while their figures remained rather stable at 21,000 in the pivotal year of 1991, and remained high over the course of the 1990s.

© Springer International Publishing AG 2018
T. Lochocki, *The Rise of Populism in Western Europe*,
DOI 10.1007/978-3-319-62855-4_6

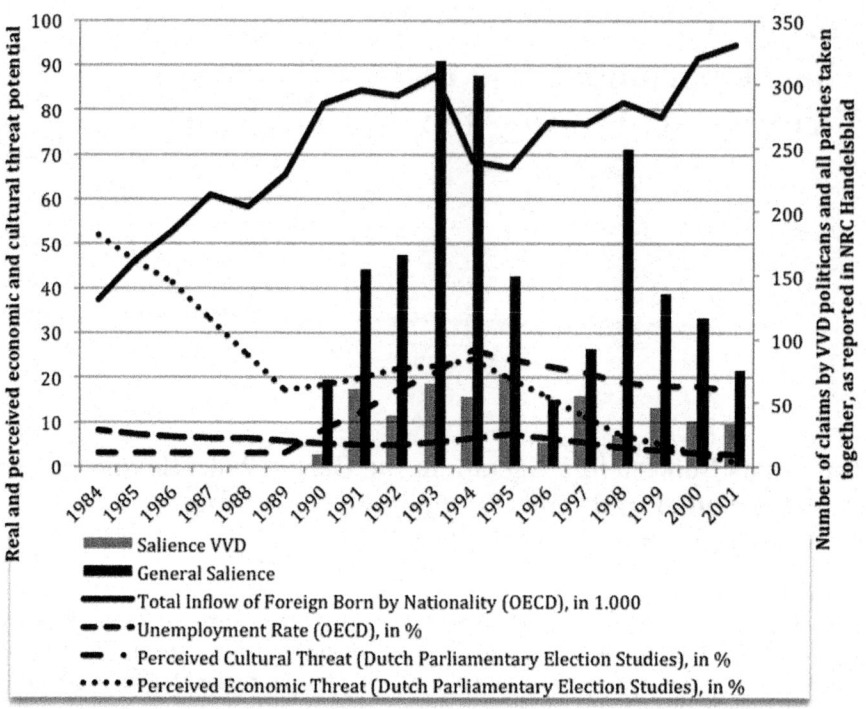

**Fig. 6.1** Real cultural and economic threat potential in the Netherlands: Dutch voters' perceptions and salience of immigration-related topics 1990–2001

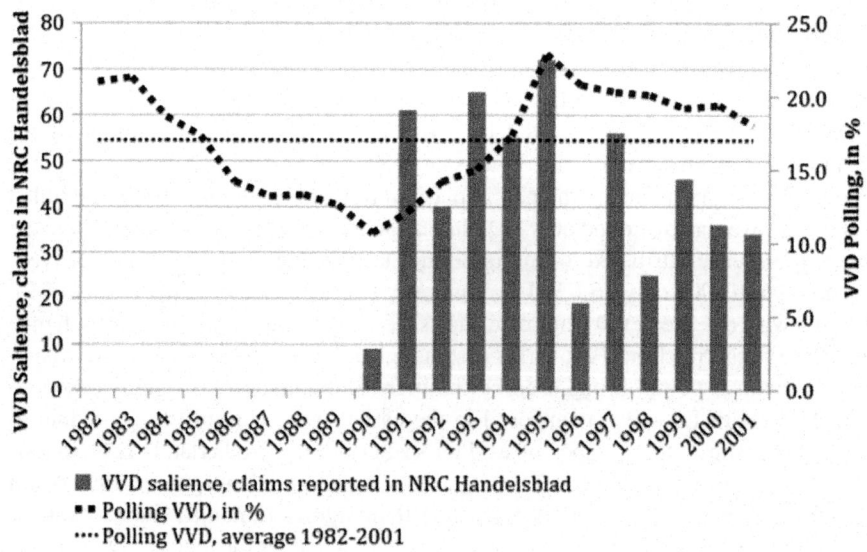

**Fig. 6.2** VVD polling and salience 1990–2001

Foreign-born immigration reached its peak in 1990 and remained at that high level until 2001 (Fig. 6.1). So why not politicize rising numbers of asylum-seekers in 1988 or 1990? And why not talk about the substantial immigration rates after the mid-1990s? Even more striking, as the salience increased significantly in 1991, Frits Bolkestein rarely talked about asylum-seekers at all. Out of 61 VVD-claims reported in 1991 only 10 referred to asylum-seekers, while 84% were concerned with the integration of migrants in general. The same pattern holds in 1992 (90% of 40 claims referring to integration). Only from 1993 on, *after* the integration topic had already been salient for 2 years, did the VVD also put an emphasis on the asylum-seeker issue (65% claims on asylum issues in 1993, 84% in 1994).

Further, the *conceived cultural threat*—the assumption that Dutch voters were concerned about immigration and integration—rose over the course of the early 1990s (possibly correlating with the increase in salience on the part the VVD) but has remained at high levels since then. The integration of migrants was an issue of substantial concern for Dutch voters for ten subsequent years, from 1991 until 2001 on. Therefore, the opinions of Dutch voters cannot be held responsible for the sharp decrease in the salience of immigration-related topics on the part of the VVD from the mid-1990s on.

If the possible increase of an actual and perceived cultural threat cannot explain the increase in salience, maybe the increase of an *actual economic threat* is more telling? Perhaps the unemployment rate peaked in 1991, so the VVD was eager to scapegoat migrants or to divert voters' attention by calling for tougher integration policies? Curiously, the unemployment rate—the *actual economic threat*—fell in the early 1990s, remaining stable between 1987 and 1994 at around 5–6%, and remained low over the course of the 1990s. Dutch voters' concerns regarding economic conditions—the *perceived economic threat*—decreased after 1989. Therefore, the year 1991 and the early 1990s did not constitute a situation of economic threat potential either (Fig. 6.1).

Because the economic and cultural threat potential and the conceived threats in the early 1990s did not differ from previous or later periods, they eliminate any particularities for the year 1991 and the years following that could explain the change in the salience of immigration-related topics (Fig. 6.1). Perhaps party rationale could offer an explanation for the VVD's emphasis on the immigration issue between 1991 and 1995?

Indeed, the VVD was caught in a very peculiar situation in 1991. After dropping out of the governing coalition with the moderate CDA (Christen Democratisch Appèl), which lasted from 1982 to 1989, the VVD was in opposition to a coalition of the CDA and the social-democratic PvdA (Partij van de Arbeid) for the first time in almost 10 years (Aeerts et al. 1999). Even worse, while the VVD polled steadily at around 13–21% in the 1980s, it dropped to 10.7% in annual polls in the early 1990s (own calculations based on NIPO week surveys[1]); the right-liberal VVD

---

[1] https://easy.dans.knaw.nl/ui/datasets/id/easy-dataset:33017/tab/1;jsessionid=3B8F6075DDF6288 A2637B6CDFA211247 (last accessed May 7, 2017).

quickly lost ground compared to the Dutch Christian-Democrats (CDA) and first and foremost to its left-liberal counterpart, the D66 (Democraten 66). Both parties relied on a highly pragmatic political style, lacking any strong ideological foundations or religious affiliations. These classic postmodern, post-material developments benefitted the un-ideological catch-all parties—the CDA and D66—and likewise hit the workers' party (PvdA) and the conservative VVD very hard in the early 1990s: 'De twee belangrijkste ideologische tegenvoeters van het CDA, het liberalisme en het socialisme, bevinden zich beide nog steeds in en diepe en misschien zelfs wel fatale identiteitscrisis' (Righart 1992, 41).[2]

Thus, the VVD experienced a substantial crisis in the early 1990s: it had become an opposition party, without any fair chance of re-entering the governing coalition it had been part of over the last 10 years, rating roughly 50% lower in the polls than in previous years, while competing with two highly successful political contenders for their center-right electorate: the CDA's conservative program and D66's liberal program. Hence, the integration-issue might have been a highly appreciated topic around which to mobilize conservative voters in order to revitalize a conservative party in peril. This argument is strongly supported in looking at the decrease of the salience of immigration issues from 1995 on (Fig. 6.2). While the salience of immigration-related topics discussed by the VVD dropped significantly from 1995 on, the cultural threat potential and feelings of estrangement on the part of Dutch voters remained consistently high (Fig. 6.1). What changed from 1995 onwards was nothing but the polling of the VVD.

Not only did the VVD's polling increase, but so too did its strategic standing in Dutch politics: after 1994 the party was part of the so-called 'purple coalition' among PvdA, D66 and VVD and consistently polled between 17 and 23%. The party occupied a very convenient position: part of the governing coalition, with

---

[2]The identity crisis even concerned Dutch society as a whole in the early 1990s. A side-effect of these postmodern politics and the crisis of proponents of classic social-democratic or liberal ideas was a craving for clear-cut answers to highly complex issues—first and foremost concerning the question of community and *vivre ensemble*: 'Er is momenteel in het publieke domein een inmiskenbaar zoeken naar niewewe zingevingen, moreel houvast, ethische fundamenten. Dit verlangen naar samenhang en betekenisgeving, kortom naar ideologie, wordt gestimuleerd door nieuwe problemen zoals de voortgang van de medische technologie, die confrontatie met nieuwe vormen van fundamentalisme, de milieuvervuiling en de veranderde internationale verhoudingen' (Righart 1992).

The Dutch Sociologist Herman Pleij devoted an entire book to the 'onbehagen' of the Dutch society in the early 1990s, which means the craving for symbols of national reassurance. He complains about 'lelijk Nederland' which—according to him—would be as boring as Denmark, but Denmark is still far more dear to the Danes than the Netherlands is to the Dutch. He further complains about the lack of manners on the part of Dutch students as well as the lack of street names based on important Dutch writers. Finally, travelling to 'Neurenberg' (he means: Nürnberg) relieves him from these pressures; at least the infamous 'Moffenhaat' (a word only existing in Dutch, best translated as 'Germanophobia') finally makes him aware of the 'beauty' of the Netherlands: still better than Germany! (Pleij 1991).

**Table 6.1** VVD polling and salience 1991–2001

|  | Annual average 1991–2001 | VVD crisis (below annual polling average) | No VVD crisis (above annual polling average) |
|---|---|---|---|
| VVD polling | 18.1% | 14.7% | 20.1% |
| Claims on immigration-related matters by VVD | 46.3 | 55.3 | 41.1 |

stable backup support in the polls; therefore, it saw no need to mobilize conservative voters by putting greater emphasis on immigration issues.

The high salience of immigration issues on the part of the VVD in the early 1990s and the lower salience in the following years cannot be accounted for by particular threat-perceptions, but primarily by considering the crisis of the Dutch conservative party—the VVD—in the early 1990s, and its later stabilization at a high level of electoral support. While the VVD polled an annual average of 18.1% between 1991 and 2001, the polling figures during the high salience periods (1991–1994) only showed 14.7% electoral support, while the low-salience years (1995–2001) saw an average VVD-polling of 20.1% (the year 1995 does not fit the pattern, however, with high salience values in spite of polling success). While the salience average from 1991 to 2001 comprised 46.3 annual VVD claims, the years in which the VVD received less than 18.1% support had 58.3 claims, and the years with high VVD polling only 36 claims (Table 6.1).

## 6.2  Waiting for Pim Fortuyn: The Liberal Turn in Dutch Politics in 1995

The salience of immigration-related matters was a given in Dutch party discourse because of the crisis of the conservative VVD in the early 1990s. And with this salience, the conservative position, clearly rejecting multiculturalism, was occupied by the VVD itself. For a populist radical right party to benefit from the salient debates, the niche on the right had to open. And exactly that happened in the mid-1990s. The salient Dutch debates had been characterized by a liberal debate climate since the mid-1990s; no established party offered a conservative program in matters of immigration and integration after 1995. The electoral niche for PRRP was open from the mid-1990s on—it took until the winter of 2001–2002 for Pim Fortuyn to seize the niche in the Dutch party spectrum (Fig. 6.3).

While the VVD stood firm with a conservative position on immigration-related matters from 1991 to 1994 (average party position: −4.5), the party formulated far more liberal positions from 1995 to 2001 (average party position: −1.6, save the year 1997: −1.2—compare with Fig. 6.3). From 1995 onwards, the Dutch party

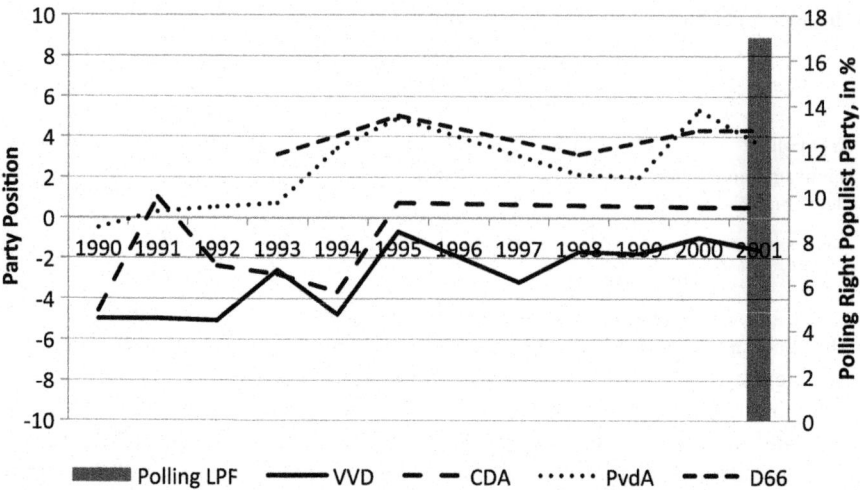

**Fig. 6.3**  Dutch party positions on immigration-related matters 1991–2001

discourse was defined by a liberal discourse on matters of immigration and integration, while the salience of and voters' concerns about the integration of migrants remained high. Therefore, the data shows—similarly to other studies focusing on the Dutch case (Koopmans and Muis 2009)—that the political space for a new contender on the right had already opened in the mid-1990s, at the latest in 1997–1998. However, as long as it was only extremist parties trying to fill the niche accompanied by anti-democratic sentiments, conservative, pro-democratic Dutch voters had to wait for Pim Fortuyn to express their dissatisfaction with the agenda of established parties.

But how did this change to liberal discourse, which characterized the Netherlands between 1995 and 2001, become palpable to the Dutch voter? In order to illustrate changing party positions, examples of the positions of the two most crucial Dutch parties in immigration-related matters are given: the conservative agenda-setter, VVD, and the governing social democratic PvdA. This study will highlight the immigration debates for the year 1991 (when the issue entered the debate in the first place), 1994 (the last year in which the VVD took a clearly conservative position), 1995 (the year in which the substantial shift occurred), 1998 (the year of the last federal election before Pim Fortuyn's party broke through) and 2001 (the year in which the populist radical right party of Pim Fortuyn entered the political scene).

In September 1991, Frits Bolkestein—the party leader of the right-liberal VVD—introduced his ideas for how migrants should have to integrate into Dutch society. It is important to note that he consciously used the word 'aanpassen'—best translated as 'assimilate'. He demanded 'loyalty' on the part of Dutch Muslims to the Dutch state, pointed to an inevitable tension between Islam and Western culture and criticized the Dutch government's policy, which was calling for migrants to keep their own identity, as a failure.[3] In 1991, as the issue first entered the political scene, the social-democratic PvdA was one of the few parties that did not position itself clearly in opposition to Bolkestein's conservative claims.[4] Furthermore, the PvdA's Staatssekretaris Kosto with the Department of Justice *joined ranks* with Bolkestein and passionately vindicated the (at that time) restrictive Dutch asylum-seekers policy.[5] During the year of the 1994 federal election, which saw the VVD rejoining government after 5 years in opposition, the VVD kept its conservative profile on matters of integration: it called for a 'naturalization-contract' between the migrant and the Dutch state, requiring integration and language courses and stronger legal measures to enforce these demands if necessary.[6] In addition, party leader Bolkestein called for tighter asylum laws, a European harmonization of the asylum procedures and for sending asylum-seekers back far sooner than Dutch regulations required at the time.[7]

Like in 1991, the Dutch social democrats now campaigned on clearly liberal positions in the 1994 federal election year: the PvdA's program rejected the infamous claim that 'the Netherlands are full' and called for state-run programs to facilitate the integration of migrants.[8] Therefore, in 1994 the VVD's highly conservative positions clashed with the highly liberal positions of the PvdA. It comes as no surprise that as the new 'purple coalition' was formed after the federal election in May 1994 between the largest party, the Social Democratic PvdA, the left-liberal D66 and the right-liberal VVD, the question of handling the asylum issue remained highly contested until a compromise was reached after 6 months (!) of negotiations at the end of 1994. This compromise could be understood as a clear rejection of the VVD's conservative demands. At the end of 1994, the coalition between the PvdA, the VVD and the D66 changed the previously restrictive asylum law and facilitated significantly greater access for refugees into the Dutch asylum system.[9] This was a watershed. The clear turn in Dutch asylum policy in 1994 was the first policy area in which a general liberal turn in integration policies became visible.

---

[3]Derk-Jan Eppink (1991, September 12). VVD-leider vindt dat moslims zich moeten aanpassen; Bolkestein: compromis met rechtsstaat is niet mogelijk. *NRC Handelsblad*. Retrieved November 11, 2012, from lexisnexis.com.

[4](1991, October 10) Lubbers: soepelheid bij integratie minderheden. Retrieved November 9, 2012, from lexisnexis.com.

[5](1991, December 17) Kosto bereid tot uitstel uitwijzing hongerstakers. Retrieved November 9, 2012, from lexisnexis.com.

[6](1994, April 26). Programmas' Vergeleken; Immigratie. *NRC Handelsblad*. Retrieved November 9, 2012, from lexisnexis.com.

[7](1994, March 14) 'Asielbeleid Europese Unie harmoniseren'. *NRC Handelsblad*. Retrieved November 9, 2012, from lexisnexis.com. Also see: (1994, March 14) CDA, PvdA en D66 fel tegen; VVD: alleen asielzoekers uit Europa. Retrieved November 9, 2012, from lexisnexis.com.

[8](1994, April 26). Programmas' Vergeleken; Immigratie. *NRC Handelsblad*. Retrieved November 9, 2012, from lexisnexis.com.

[9](1994, November 30) Asieldebat: opnieuw neuzen tellen in verdeelde Kamer. *NRC Handelsblad*. Retrieved November 9, 2012, from lexisnexis.com.

This ongoing liberal turn in Dutch asylum policy is nicely illustrated by the VVD's revoking of conservative positions from 1994 to 1995. While the VVD ran its 1994 electoral campaigns on strictly anti-multicultural agendas, from 1995 the VVD officially proclaimed the Netherlands to be a country of immigration,[10] apologized for linking immigration with an increase in criminality,[11] and supported legal measures to aid migrants' integration through strong state assistance. This all stood in stark contrast to earlier VVD statements, which had placed a strong emphasis on the individual responsibility of the migrant. In May[12] and parts of June[13] and August[14] 1995 the VVD supported legal matters to force enterprises to employ a certain amount of 'allochtonen'—a quota for migrants.[15]

In this vein, the VVD was still outflanked by the highly liberal social-democratic PvdA. At the beginning of 1995, the PvdA pushed for a change in Dutch citizenship law, enabling the general acceptance of dual citizenship and conceiving of the handing out of Dutch citizenship as the *beginning* of and incentive for the integration process.[16] The PvdA further backed up various NGOs that aimed to support a multicultural understanding of Dutch society[17]; it moreover advocated a series of legal measures that aided the integration of migrants into the Dutch economy under the auspices of various quota legislations, best referred to as 'affirmative action'.[18]

Therefore, the two most influential Dutch parties throughout the 1990s, which governed the Netherlands hand-in-hand after 1994—the social-democratic PvdA and the liberal-conservative VVD—spearheaded a multicultural and liberal discourse on matters of immigration and integration from 1995 on. While the VVD's prime electoral agendas of the early 1990s were characterized by a rejection of

---

[10]Frank Vermeulen (1995, March 15). 'Nederland de facto immigratieland'; VVD wil migranten verplicht spreiden. *NRC Handelsblad*. Retrieved November 9, 2012, from lexisnexis.com.

[11](1995, March 22) Partijblad VVD maakt 'vreselijke fout' voor minderhedendebat. *NRC Handelsblad*. Retrieved October 15, 2012, from lexisnexis.com.

[12](1995, May 12) Bolkestein steunt Dijkstals plan allochtone werknemers. *NRC Handelsblad*. Retrieved October 15, 2012, from lexisnexis.com.

[13](1995, June 9) Geen overheidsorders; Kamer: straf schenders wet allochtonen. *NRC Handelsblad*. Retrieved October 15, 2012, from lexisnexis.com.

[14](1995, August 1) Alle ministeries voldoen nu aan 'allochtonenwet'. *NRC Handelsblad*. Retrieved October 15, 2012, from lexisnexis.com.

[15](1995, May 12) Bolkestein steunt Dijkstals plan allochtone werknemers. *NRC Handelsblad*. Retrieved October 15, 2012, from lexisnexis.com.

[16](1995, February 17) Naturalisatie vreemdelingen verdeelt Kamer. *NRC Handelsblad*. Retrieved October 15, 2012, from lexisnexis.com.

[17](1995, April 6) Kamer eens met minderhedenorganisatie. *NRC Handelsblad*. Retrieved November 9, 2012, from lexisnexis.com.

[18](1995, August 1) Alle ministeries voldoen nu aan 'allochtonenwet'. *NRC Handelsblad*. Retrieved October 15, 2012, from lexisnexis.com. Also see: (1995, June 9) Geen overheidsorders; Kamer: straf schenders wet allochtonen. *NRC Handelsblad*. Retrieved October 15, 2012, from lexisnexis.com.

multiculturalism, it joined ranks with the social democrats' portrayal of the Netherlands as a highly tolerant and liberal country of immigration beginning in the mid-1990s. The election year of 1998 further exemplifies the centrist course of the once conservative VVD. At first, Frits Bolkestein called for tighter asylum laws to lower the number of incoming refugees before the federal election in May 1998.[19] But Bolkestein was quick to withdraw these demands after the election was held and the purple coalition was confirmed.[20] Facing fierce resistance from the strong PvdA—which was calling for a liberal asylum policy and the acceptance of more refugees in yet to be built shelters—the VVD largely agreed with the asylum legislation as proposed by the liberal politicians of the PvdA and D66.[21]

In November 2001—the exact time during which Pim Fortuyn entered the federal political scene as chairman of the party 'Leefbaar Nederland'—parts of the VVD criticized the liberal asylum regime again controlled by the PvdA-Staatssecretatris Karlsbeek, but the VVD could not break the phalanx of liberal coalition partners, consisting of PvdA and the D66.[22] PvdA's Staatssekretaris Karlsbeek rejected a special control of asylum-seekers for criminal activities.[23] The PvdA further stood firm with a liberal asylum regime and rejected any stricter demands on the part of the VVD.[24] And even further, the asylum regime and Karlsbeek (PvdA) was strongly supported by the *VVD* (!) minister Korthals (Department of Justice).[25]

At the beginning of 2002, facing the rising support for Pim Fortuyn's newly founded party 'Ljist Pim Fortuyn' (LPF), the PvdA continued campaigning on liberal asylum legislation and called for a general amnesty and a handing out of regular residence permits for all asylum-seekers who stayed in the country for longer than 5 years.[26] Parts of the VVD reaffirmed their calls for tighter asylum legislation in the beginning of 2002, but the party as a whole was split over the

---

[19](1998, April 22) Bolkestein wil asielbeleid ingrijpend aanscherpen. *NRC Handelsblad.* Retrieved November 9, 2012, from lexisnexis.com.

[20](1998, June 23) Strijdig met VN-verdrag; VVD ziet af van quotering asielzoekers. *NRC Handelsblad.* Retrieved November 9, 2012, from lexisnexis.com.

[21](1998, June 23) Asielprocedure wordt eenvoudiger. *NRC Handelsblad.* Retrieved November 9, 2012, from lexisnexis.com.

[22](2001, November 9) Asiel en de coalitie, *NRC Handelsblad* Retrieved October 9, 2012, from lexisnexis.com. Also see: Kalsbeek wijkt niet voor VVD. Retrieved October 9, 2012, from lexisnexis.com.

[23]Brams Pols (2001, February 8) VVD: Kalsbeek negeert rapporten asielzoekers. *NRC Handelsblad.* Retrieved November 9, 2012, from lexisnexis.com.

[24](2001, November 7) Asielbeleid van Kalsbeek onder vuur van VVD. *NRC Handelsblad.* Retrieved October 9, 2012, from lexisnexis.com.

[25](2001, November 7) Asielbeleid van Kalsbeek onder vuur van VVD. Retrieved October 9, 2012, from lexisnexis.com.

[26](2001, March 21) PvdA: geef asielzoeker na 5 jaar pardon. NRC Handelsblad. Retrieved October 9, 2012, from lexisnexis.com.

issue.[27] The liberal party discourse, led by the liberal claims of the PvdA and the centrist positions of the formerly conservative VVD, which characterized the Netherlands from 1995 on, accompanied the rise of the populist Pim Fortuyn in the winter of 2001–2002. An opinion piece summarizes the perception Dutch voters must have had of the VVD at the end of 2001; in a coalition with the PvdA and D66, embracing liberal standpoints on matters of integration and asylum, the VVD could not implement conservative policy demands.[28]

The VVD's position on integration and asylum issues was clearly conservative during the early 1990s—calling for assimilation and lower numbers of incoming refugees, and clearly rejecting multiculturalism. After 1995, the VVD was bound to the liberal agendas of its coalition partners PvdA and D66 and therefore conceived as a moderate actor in matters of integration and migration by the Dutch electorate. The major Dutch parties, first and foremost the governing PvdA and the VVD, embraced a liberal agenda on matters of integration and migration from 1995 on. No established party has offered a conservative position since the mid-1990s. This constitutes a void in the electoral market of which the Dutchs voter were very well aware: The high salience of the immigration debates in the 1990s and the stable perception of a high cultural threat of up to a quarter of Dutch voters shows that a substantial part of the Dutch electorate conceived immigration and integration to be a major unsolved political issue throughout the 1990s (Fig. 6.1).

From 1995 onwards the Netherlands was defined by salient immigration debates (though the salience was lower than during 1991–1994), high cultural threat perceptions on the part of the Dutch voters (15–20% considered immigration and integration a prime political problem throughout the 1990s) and a liberal party discourse. No established party catered to the concerns of roughly 1/5 of the Dutch voters by offering a conservative position in matters of immigration and integration, rejecting multiculturalism. All necessary conditions for the electoral advances of a populist radical right party were in place after 1995, especially after 1997–1998: salient immigration debates and a liberal party discourse on the matter after the VVD withdrew the conservative demands it had once introduced itself. Pim Fortuyn seized the electoral void of conservative positions on immigration-related matters, rejecting multiculturalism fiercely, with great success in the winter of 2001–2002, gathering 17.0% of the votes in the federal election in May 2002.

---

[27](2002, January 26) Congres VVD scherper in asielkwestie. Retrieved October 9, 2012, from lexisnexis.com.

(2002, March 21) Blaffen, niet bijten in asieldebat. Retrieved October 9, 2012, from lexisnexis. com.

[28](2001, December 31) Stilstand 2001. *NRC Handelsblad*. Retrieved October 9, 2012, from lexisnexis.com.

## 6.3   The Pyrrhic Victory of the Liberal Dutch Social Democrats

While the increasing salience of immigration issues from the early 1990s can be accounted for by the crisis of the conservative VVD during these years, one question remains: why did the VVD drop their conservative demands after 1995 and join ranks with the liberal discourse proposed by the PvdA? Again, the two-level theory is supported: the VVD joined ranks with the liberal PvdA because the left camp of Dutch politics (PvdA, D66 and GroenLinks) steadily led in the polls and Dutch society had been free of economic concerns since the mid-1990s.

In accounting for the strategic shift of the VVD one might be inclined to point to the constraints imposed by its liberal coalition partners PvdA and D66, which prevented the VVD from implementing more restrictive policies on matters of integration and immigration. Two questions remain, however: why, then, was the VVD campaigning with a tough stance on these matters in the early 1990s at all? And secondly, why didn't it maintain a tough stance on immigration-related matters, rejecting multiculturalism, and eventually leave the coalition? Didn't the VVD have a coalition option with the far less liberal CDA—a centrist, rather than liberal, party, which had governed the country from 1977 until 1994?

The answer is primarily to be found in the varying party positions and the high polling of the left parties. The amelioration of the VVD's position from 1995 on followed a clear turn on the part of the PvdA from a moderate to a clearly liberal proponent in integration debates beginning in 1994 (Fig. 6.3). But why did the VVD follow the PvdA? In stark contrast to the early 1990s, the PvdA left its substantial crisis behind and rose in the polls steadily after 1994. Furthermore, it took over the leading position of Dutch parties that the CDA had occupied in the early 1990s. The PvdA led the purple coalition, as the strongest party, with the Prime Minister Wim Kok from 1994 to 2002; save the years 1948–1958, this was the longest period a social-democratic prime minister governed the Netherlands. While in power, the purple coalition steadily gathered around 60% of voters' support. Because parties are office-seekers and vote-maximizers, the VVD therefore dropped its conservative position after the early 1990s and followed the liberal course of the PvdA and the purple coalition from 1995 on; beginning in 1994, the PvdA was *the* role model of a successful party in the Netherlands, as well as supporting the purple coalition—a safe bet for the VVD to stay in government. A coalition with the more conservative, but low-polling CDA was impossible. While the 1980s showed an open race between the center-right and center-left camps of Dutch politics, after 1994, the center-left always kept the majority of voters' support: the PvdA almost always had the option to exchange the liberal-conservative VVD for the left-liberal GroenLinks (GL) as a coalition partner to form a coalition against the VVD and the CDA. If the VVD wanted to stay in government, it had to compromise with the liberal PvdA and D66; consequently, the VVD dropped its conservative demands in matters of immigration and integration and joined the salient multicultural discourse that

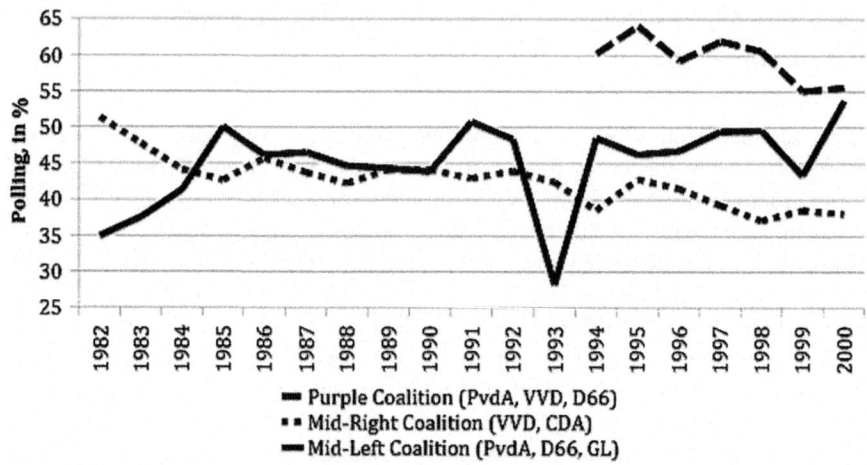

**Fig. 6.4** Polling of PvdA, CDA, VVD and possible coalitions in the Netherlands

had, to a large extent, characterized Dutch politics from 1995 up to Pim Fortuyn's breakthrough in 2002 (Fig. 6.4).

The liberal position of the highly successful PvdA—by far the strongest party in the Netherlands from 1994 to 2002 on and leading a highly successful left camp in Dutch politics in the 1990s—led the right-liberal VVD to moderate its position on immigration-related matters in the 1990s; in so doing, the most conservative Dutch party joined the liberal discourse of the left, opening the electoral niche for a populist radical right party. The high salience of immigration-related matters throughout the 1990s and the void of conservative positions provided by established political players which all supported multiculturalism instead, were the two necessary conditions for Pim Fortuyn's remarkable electoral advances in the winter of 2001–2002.

## 6.4 Tolerance Is Expensive: The Liberal Course of the PvdA After 1994

Finally, the question arises as to why the PvdA had not already adopted this liberal profile in 1991, but waited to do so until 1994, as well as why the Dutch social democrats took a far more liberal position than—for instance—their German counterparts beginning in the 1990s. The two-level theory also proves useful here: the strategic turn of the Dutch social democrats was accompanied by the steady rise of the left camp (PvdA, D66, GL), while Dutch society was free of economic concerns from the beginning of the 1990s.

Controlling for various threat conditions to which the Dutch society was exposed since 1991 (Fig. 6.1), it is visible that the feelings of cultural endangerment on the

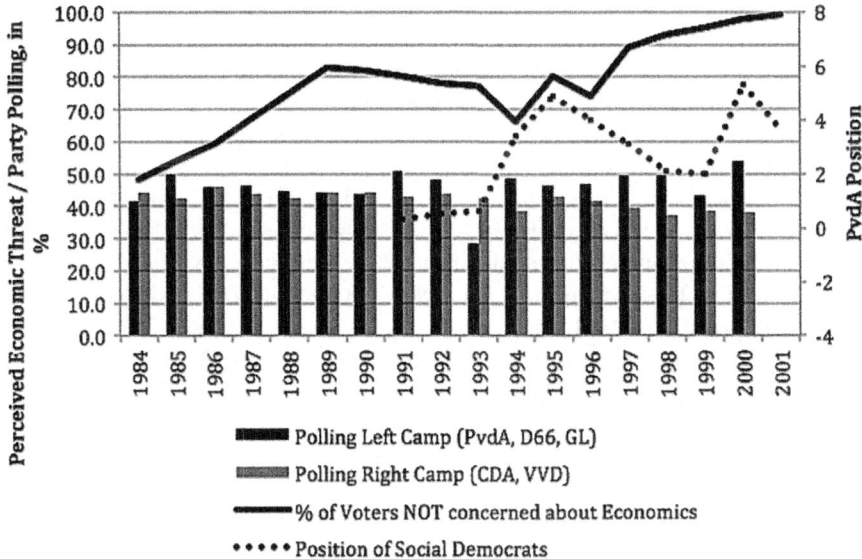

**Fig. 6.5** PvdA-positions, polling of political camps and perceived economic threat

part of the Dutch voters varied little over the course of the 1990s and cannot therefore account for a changing PvdA position in 1994.

However, what Dutch voters thought about economics varied extremely: the Dutch economy had flourished since the early 1990s, unemployment rates had dropped to all-time lows and the Dutch economic reforms became world-renowned as the 'Dutch Miracle'. The feelings of economic endangerment almost dropped to zero in 2001. At the same time, the left side of the Dutch political spectrum (PvdA, D66 and GL) took off in the polls. The PvdA took a clear liberal stance on matters of immigration and integration as the left camp of Dutch politics rose steadily in the polls, while the economic threat potential continued to drop from 1994 on (Fig. 6.5).

## 6.5   Summary: The Delayed Backlash to a Salient Multicultural Discourse

The Dutch case illustrates the mechanism outlined in the two-level theory. The right-liberal VVD put the immigration issue on the agenda in the early 1990s while undergoing a substantial crisis. The VVD lowered the salience in the 1990s, as their polling figures improved massively and it became part of the national government coalition. The VVD moderated its position significantly in these years because it was facing a highly successful (informal) center-left-left coalition (PvdA, D66, GL) campaigning on clearly liberal standpoints. Its spearhead, the PvdA, took these liberal positions from 1994 onwards because the economic threat potential had ceased, while the left camp was polling steadily ahead of the bourgeois spectrum. The VVD joined this liberal discourse, dropped its conservative profile and opened the electoral niche for a populist radical right party in the mid-1990s. Thus, Pim Fortuyn's electoral breakthrough in 2001 did indeed come as a surprise: *surprisingly late*.

This study ends with a detailed investigation of the Dutch case in 2002 as the rise of Pim Fortuyn's LPF was followed shortly after by Geert Wilders' Party for Freedom (PVV). Ultimately, the permanent presence of a PRRP in the Dutch political spectrum altered the political rationale for established Dutch actors in identity politics. The permanent media access and the organizational buildup of an entrenched populist radical right party make it less dependent on the political messaging of established parties. However, the mechanisms revealed seem to hold for contemporary Dutch politics. In the Eurozone debates in 2010–2014, the PVV lost when the Dutch center-right VDD kept its conservative promises; in turn, Geert Wilders' party made gains whenever the VVD overpromised and underdelivered with conservative messaging on Europe (Lochocki 2014). The victory of Mark Rutte's VVD at the Dutch parliamentary election in 2017 seems to follow the same mechanisms: by staying firm on migration matters and especially vis-à-vis Turkish president Recep Erdogan, the VVD could lure back conservative voters from the PVV (O' Leary 2017).

# References

Aarts K, Thomassen J (2008) Dutch voters and the changing party space. Acta Politica 43:203–234
Aeerts R et al (1999) Land van kleine gebaren—een politieke geschiedenis von Nederland 1780–1990, Sun
Koopmans R, Muis J (2009) The rise of right-wing populist Pim Fortuyn in the Netherlands: a discursive opportunity approach. Eur J Polit Res 48:642–664
Lochocki T (2014) The unstoppable far right? How established parties communication strategies and media reporting of European affairs affect the advances of populist radical right parties. GMF Europe Policy Paper 4/2014. Available at: http://www.gmfus.org/publications/unstoppable-far-right. Last accessed 7 May 2017
O'Leary N (2017) How to lose but win. 5 takeaways from the Dutch election. Politico Europe, March 16 2017. Available at: http://www.politico.eu/article/how-to-lose-but-win-5-takeaways-from-the-dutch-election-mark-rutte-geert-wilders/. Last accessed on 7 May 2017
Pleij H (1991) Het Nederlandse Onbehagen. Prometheus, Amsterdam
Righart H (1992) Het einde van Nederland? Kenteringen in politiek, cultuur en milieu, Jan de Boer
Van Kersbergen K, Krouwel A (2008) A double-edged sword! The Dutch centre-right and the 'foreigners issue'. J Eur Publ Policy 15(3):389–414

# Chapter 7
# Sweden: How the Liberals (FP) Gave Birth to the Swedish Democrats (SD)

## 7.1 The Existential Crisis of the FP in the Late 1990s and the Election of 2002

The Swedish case illustrates the basic argument about the reasons for a significant increase in the salience of immigration-related matters in the party discourse as well as elaborating the argument illustrated in the Netherlands: the salience of immigration-related matters is strongly dependent on the condition of the right-liberal party Folkpartiet Liberalerna (FP). As long as it is faring well in the polls, the issue remains rather unpoliticized; conversely, if the liberals are approaching the 4% threshold—preventing access to the federal parliament of Sweden—the issue is used to mobilize conservative voters.

Despite Sweden being a country of immigration at least since the early 1990s, the election campaign for the Riksdagsvalg in 2002 was the first time an established political party put the immigration issue on the political agenda (Rydgren 2002; Dahlström and Esaisson 2009; Rydgren and Ruth 2011).[1] During the entire period under scrutiny (2000–2012) no single party introduced more claims regarding immigration issues to the discourse in 1 year than the Swedish Liberals Folkpartiet Liberalerna (FP) during the election year of 2002. Even the

---

[1] As elaborated in the chapter on case selection the rise of the right populist Ny Demokrati (NyD) in Sweden in the early 1990s was not proceeded by a high salience of immigration issues, neither in the public perception, nor amidst established political parties in Sweden. Ny Demokrati ran its campaign on a broad anti-establishment agenda; neither in its campaigns, nor for their respective voters have immigration issues been of major importance for their electoral breakthrough in the federal election 1991. After accessing the parliament in 1991, Ny Demokrati put the issue on the political agenda, not established political players.

© Springer International Publishing AG 2018
T. Lochocki, *The Rise of Populism in Western Europe*,
DOI 10.1007/978-3-319-62855-4_7

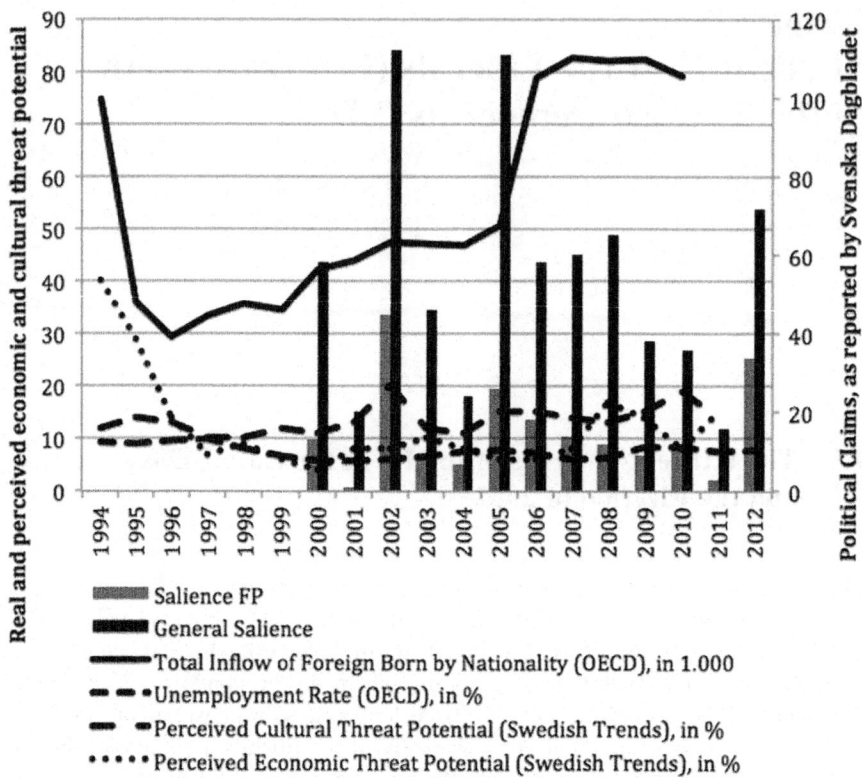

**Fig. 7.1** Real cultural and economic threat potential in Sweden, and Swedish voters' perceptions and salience of immigration-related topics 2000–2012

far larger Swedish conservatives—Moderaterna (M)—and the Swedish Social Democrats—Sveriges Socialdemokratiska Arbetareparti (SAP)—never showed higher salience values. In 2000 and 2001 Svenska Dagbladet reported 13 claims on migration and integration stemming from FP politicians, while in the election year 2002 the salience proxy increased to 45 claims. In 2003, FP put forward only 8 claims, while the salience average from 2003 to 2011 comprised 12 annual claims; only in 2012 did the number of FP claims increase significantly again, to 35 (Figs. 7.1 and 7.2). Hence, the years 2002 and 2012 showed a significant increase in the salience of immigration-related matters introduced by the Swedish Liberals.

But why did the FP politicize the immigration issue in the years 2002 and 2012, and why did the salience decrease so sharply between 2003 and 2011? Considering the total immigration of people with a foreign background, the years 2002 and 2012 do not show critical changes at all: the inflow of migrants to Sweden steadily increased from 1996 on and showed a sharp increase from 2005 to 2006, but not in 2002 or 2012 (Fig. 7.1). According to OECD figures, the number of asylum

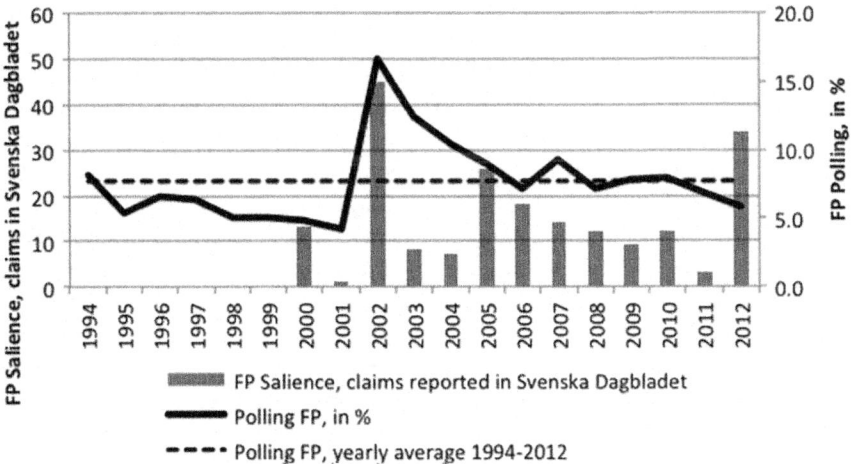

**Fig. 7.2** FP polling and salience 2000–2012

seekers in 2002 (33,000) was significantly higher than in 2001 (23,500) and might explain the particular salience in 2002, but if that increase accounts for the high salience, why did the next peaks of asylum seeker immigration (31,000 in 2003 and 36,000 in 2007) pass by without any acknowledgment by the Swedish Liberals? Even more intriguing, the FP's 2002 election campaign was not concerned with asylum seekers, but primarily with requiring a language test as a precondition for acquiring Swedish citizenship—only one out of 45 claims mentioned asylum seekers.

Maybe not the *actual* cultural threat potential, but *perceptions* of a cultural threat on part of the Swedish voters accounted for FP salience—namely public concerns about matters of immigration and integration? Indeed, the year 2002 shows an increase in voters' concerns about related matters from 13 (2001) to 20% (which might in part be attributed to the increase of salience of immigration-related issues in the party discourse). But assuming that Swedish Liberals talk about migration in response to voters' rising concerns, why wasn't the FP doing so in 2010, as public concern reached its second peak of 19%, or in 2005 or 2006, which had a considerable 15% each?

Neither the increase of the actual cultural threat potential (immigration), nor the increasing concerns of the Swedish electorate—as measured by survey data—can explain the increase in salience of immigration-related matters among the Swedish Liberals in the years 2002 and 2012. Is an increase in an *actual* economic threat more telling? Curiously, Sweden's 6% unemployment rate in 2002 barely differs from the previous or following years: from 1999 until 2008 the figures are equally low—between 5.6 and 7.6%—and this is in stark contrast to the dire years of 1996 and 1997 (which showed 9.6 and 9.9% unemployment rates respectively). Accordingly, *perceptions* of an economic threat on the part of Swedish voters cannot account for the particular salience of immigration issues in 2002 and 2010, either: in clear contrast to the mid-1990s, when around 40% of voters reported being concerned about economics, the years 2002 and 2012 are part of a period of low perceptions of economic threat—7 to 10% between 1997 and 2007 (Fig. 7.1).

Considering that neither the economic nor the cultural threat potential and the respective conceived threats on the part of the Swedish voters for the years 2002 and 2012 show any peculiarities (Fig. 7.1), perhaps party rationale is better suited to account for the high salience of immigration issues in the Folkpartiet Liberalerna in these 2 years? The FP was indeed lingering in a very unpromising situation at the end of the 1990s and in the early 2000s. After the Riksdagsvalg in 1998 the bourgeois Swedish parties could not establish a conservative government and again remained in opposition. Even though the Swedish Social Democrats (SAP) lost by a large amount, the Left (Vaensterpartiet) and Green (Miljoepartiet de Groena) parties gained enough votes to support a minority government of Swedish Social Democrats. This minority government, and the entire center-left block, continued polling well ahead of the respective bourgeois coalition partners after 1998 (Fig. 7.4).

Even worse for the Swedish Liberals, their electoral losses continued. While the FP gained 14.2% in the 1985 elections it lost in all elections to follow; it dropped to 12.2% in 1988, to 9.1% in 1991, to 7.2% in 1994 and eventually to 4.7% in 1998. If this trend were to have persisted, the party was likely to finish below the electoral threshold of 4% in the next election in 2002. This threatened to occur throughout the years 1998–2001; the Swedish Liberals never polled higher than an annual average of 5%. Failing to enter the parliament in 2002 was more likely than ever, and this would have been a major defeat for a party that had been part of the Swedish parliament since its restructuring in 1934.

In brief: before the election campaign in 2002 the Swedish Liberals not only faced a highly successful center-left coalition which was clearly polling well ahead of 50% since the early 1990s (Fig. 7.5), but was also facing an unprecedented defeat at the ballot—failing to gain parliamentary representation for the very first time. Curiously, this is the *exact* situation to which the FP was exposed in only 1 year after their successful campaign in 2002, namely in 2012—the second year in which the Swedish Liberals emphasized matters of integration (Fig. 7.2). 2002 and 2012 were the 2 years in which the FP risked polling below the crucial 4% threshold necessary for parliamentary representation in Sweden, and which indicated by far the highest salience values of immigration issues among the Swedish Liberals; therefore, the politicization of immigration-related topics seems to have been used to mobilize conservative voters to ensure parliamentary representation. The argument is supported by significantly lower salience values between 2003 and 2011 (12 claims were the annual average, in stark contrast to 45 and 34 claims in 2002 and 2012 respectively) as the FP polled between 12.4 (2003) and 6.8% (2011). The 35 claims in 2012 occurred in the year in which the FP was polling below 6% for the first time since 2002 (Table 7.1).

**Table 7.1**  FP polling and salience 2002–2012

|  | Annual average 2002–2012 | FP crisis (2002 and 2012) | No FP crisis (2003–2011) |
|---|---|---|---|
| FP polling | 8.1% | 5.4% | 8.7% |
| Claims on immigration-related matters by FP | 18.4 | 39.5 | 12.1 |

## 7.2   The Break with Swedish Tolerance: The 2002 Election and Its Consequences

The Swedish populist radical right party, Sverige Demokraterna (SD), steadily increased in voters' sympathies from 2002 on; for them to seize the electoral niche, the high salience years of 2002 and 2012 were not sufficient alone, however. The two-level theory indicates a second necessary condition: the dropping of conservative standpoints by the conservative agenda setter, FP, and their joining of the salient liberal, multicultural discourse. And this is exactly what happened in the early 2000s.

With a party position of −2.5 on matters of migration and integration, the election year of 2002 was the only time in which the Swedish Liberals took a clearly conservative position. In 2005, the first time Swedish polls reported a result that would safeguard the access of the populist radical right Swedish Democrats to the parliament (4.1%), the position of Folkpartiet Liberalerna was already clearly liberal, with a score of +2.7; a radical departure from the −2.5 it had received only 3 years before. The election years 2006 and 2010 had too few claims to enable a precise assessment of the FP's positioning, thereby indicating that the leaders of the Swedish Liberals were fine with the Swedish public conceiving the party as a liberal force in matters of migration and integration—as witnessed by the +2.7 position in 2005. The next year in which enough claims are at hand to reliably determine the Liberals' position—2012—shows the populist radical right Swedish Democrats polling above 10% during the winter of 2012–2013 while the Swedish Liberals have boosted their liberal profile with a party position of +1.7.

The year 2002 was not only the first time in which an established Swedish party put immigration-related topics on the political agenda, but also the *only* year during which an established political actor offered a clearly conservative position, rejecting multiculturalism. The supply side of Swedish politics—the programmatic offer of established parties—was fruitful soil for the populist Swedish Democrats from 2003 onwards. From that year all major established parties agreed to a liberal discourse on matters of integration and immigration—even praising multiculturalism.

2002 was the only year in which the Swedish integration debates were not characterized by a liberal discourse. Here, the liberal FP stood with their

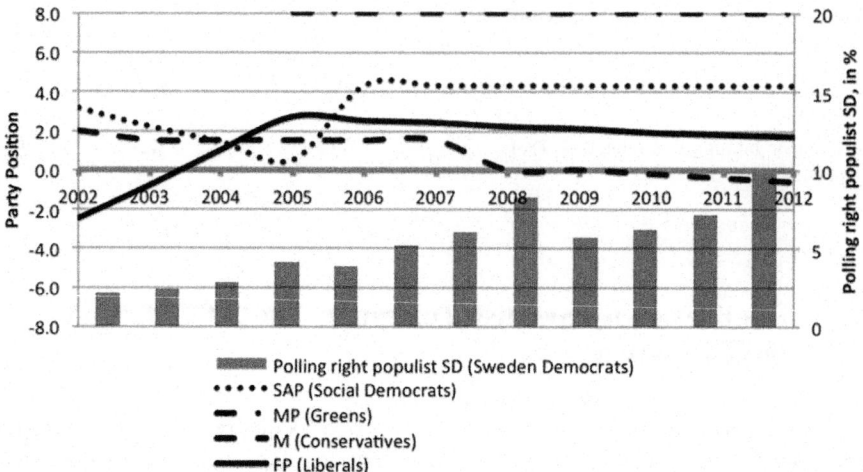

**Fig. 7.3** Party positions on immigration-related topics in Sweden and polling of populist radical right party Sweden Democrats (SD) 2002–2013

conservative claims. But already in 2003 the Swedish Liberals were joining established political parties—and first and foremost the Social Democrats (SAP)—in their liberal standpoints. Thus, the electoral niche for a populist radical right party opened in 2003 and has remained open since (Fig. 7.3).

In order to illustrate the changing party positions, this study will list examples of the conservative agenda setters' and the Social Democrats' (SAP) positions in 2002 (as the issue first entered the political debate), in 2005 (the first year the Swedish Democrats polled above the electoral threshold of 4%), the election years 2006 and 2010 (as the Swedish Democrats eventually entered the parliament) and the high salience period of 2012.

Over half of FP politicians' claims during the 2002 election year were concerned with introducing a new language test as a precondition for acquiring Swedish citizenship. Until that point, Swedish naturalization did not call for any proof of Swedish language proficiency. The leader of the Swedish Liberals, Lars Leijonborg, criticized this policy harshly, calling for a sufficient knowledge of Swedish as a 'natural precondition' for being entitled to Swedish citizenship in the summer of 2002. The language test functioned as a proxy, illustrating the party's interest in harsher enforcement of integration, and clearly putting the responsibility for integration mainly on the migrant.[2] Even though the FP leader would not deny migrants failing the test a residence permit in Sweden, he was adamant in stating that passing the language test was the *sine qua non* to becoming a

---

[2]Mellgren Fredrik (2002, August 6). Leijonborg försvarar språkkrav—Fp's ledare efterlyser högre nivå i debatten om integrationsprogrammet. *Svenska Dagbladet*. Retrieved April 3, 2013, from retriever.no.

full-fledged Swedish citizen, and stood firm on that position throughout the entire election campaign.[3]

Facing the FP's language-test proposal, the Social Democrats (SAP) scored a clear-cut liberal +3.1 in 2002 and could be considered their major liberal counterpart throughout the election campaign. Before the federal election 2002, the Social Democratic party secretary Lars Stjernkvist presented the SAP's integration policy based on anti-discrimination and affirmative action laws.[4] Confronted with the Swedish Liberals' language-test proposal, SAP leader Göran Persson was willing to talk about tighter requirements for naturalization, but considered this a minor issue that did not require emphasis. Instead, he accused the FP's leader Lars Leijonborg of fuelling xenophobic tendencies.[5]

This polarization between the Swedish Liberals' conservative positions and the Social Democrats ended in the following years. The FP dropped its conservative profile right after it introduced it in 2002; already in 2005—the first time the populist radical right party Swedish Democrats (SD) polled above 4%—the Swedish Liberals put far more emphasis on liberal asylum legislation and called for stricter anti-discrimination laws. The FP argued fiercely in favor of granting children of asylum seekers special rights to stay if they were in need of psychological counseling, even though they were deprived of permission to remain in Sweden permanently.[6] The party's spokesperson on matters of integration—Mauricio Rojas—further attacked the conservatives' proposals as lacking clear anti-discrimination laws.[7]

This political statement is particularly important. It illustrates that the Swedish Liberals—which campaigned on a more conservative position than the moderate Swedish conservatives during the 2002 election campaign (comp. Fig. 7.3)—in 2005 accused a *centrist* political force of propagating a *too conservative* agenda. The Swedish Liberals therefore openly positioned themselves as highly tolerant political actors in matters of migration and integration, clearly siding in favor of migrants' interests. The FP propelled a multicultural discourse to which it had objected only a few years before—a striking departure from their previously conservative agenda.

In contrast to 2002, the SAP's position in 2005 was ambivalent. While the Swedish Liberals—among other parties—called for exceptions to grant special residence permits to children of asylum seekers in need of psychological counseling

---

[3]Mellgren Fredrik (2002, September 8). Språktester kan skapa nya klyftor i samhället. *Svenska Dagbladet*. Retrieved April 3, 2013, from retriever.no.

[4]Hennel Lena (2002, April 27). S missar målet om fler invandrare i riksdagen. *Svenska Dagbladet*. Retrieved April 3, 2013, from retriever.no.

[5]Malmström Björn (2002, September 11). Ur debatten Om integrationen. *Svenska Dagbladet*. Retrieved April 3, 2013, from retriever.no.

[6]Engström Annika (2005, February 2). De apatiska flyktingbarnen får inte stanna. *Svenska Dagbladet*. Retrieved April 3, 2013, from retriever.no.

[7]Svenska Dagbladet (2005, May 2). M:s nya invandrarpolitik får kritik Två norrmän omkom utanför Kiruna Frosten tog första betorna i Skåne. *Svenska Dagbladet*. Retrieved April 3, 2013, from retriever.no.

who lacked any legal means to stay in Sweden, the governing SAP clearly opposed these measures.[8] The Social Democrats, however, softened their restrictive stance in the following months, reforming the asylum procedure in a more migrant-friendly fashion, guaranteeing the candidate would receive notification of the decision on his or her case within 6 months' time.[9] The 2006 and 2010 election years (as the Swedish Democrats gained parliamentary representation for the first time) lacked any particular focus on integration debates on the part of FP politicians. Their agenda remained liberal and pro-migration: in 2006 the Swedish Liberals stuck with their call for a language test as a precondition for acquiring Swedish citizenship, but made affirmative action central to their integration agenda.[10]

While the Swedish Social Democrats took an ambivalent position in 2005, the party campaigned on a highly liberal agenda during the federal election in 2006: the party visibly sharpened its pro-migration profile and emphasized means of integration, focusing on affirmative action. While framing the integration process as based on 'rights, responsibilities and opportunities', in August 2006 SAP's integration minister, Jens Orback, offered a financial welcome package for new arrivals and a premium for businesses employing migrants who had been unemployed for longer than 3 months; this was supposed to be complemented by an integration contract signed by both the new arrival and the Swedish state, outlining the responsibilities of the migrant and a decrease in welfare state benefits if the migrant refused to cooperate.[11]

The second part of the integration package, mainly focusing on the responsibilities of the migrants, immediately triggered fierce resistance from other members of the social democratic party and was withdrawn after only a week. The SAP's redrafted proposal put responsibility for a successful integration process onto the receiving society: the SAP cabinet members Jens Orback and Mona Sahlin (who became the SAP's party leader in 2007) presented a new integration program which increased the premium for the employment of migrants and the funding of a Discrimination Ombudsman, announced special job centers designed for migrants only, and emphasized the obligation of Swedish municipalities to aid migrants in their housing search—*no* obligations on the migrants' part were mentioned.[12] Therefore, before the federal election in 2006, the SAP campaigned on a clearly pro-affirmative action and pro-migrant agenda, as it had already done in 2002.

---

[8]Mellgren Fredrik (2005, April 7). Apatiska barn får inte stanna i Sverige. *Svenska Dagbladet*. Retrieved April 3, 2013, from retriever.no.

[9]Olsson Lova (2005, June 9). Inre strid i s om flyktingpolitiken. *Svenska Dagbladet*. Retrieved April 3, 2013, from retriever.no.

[10]El Mahdi Josef (2006, June 28). Fp tar fram gammalt krav om språktest för invandrare. *Svenska Dagbladet*. Retrieved April 3, 2013, from retriever.no.

[11]Wahldén Christina (2006, August 28). S vill ge flyktingar villkorat bidrag—Den som inte vill läsa svenska får lägre ersättning. *Svenska Dagbladet*. Retrieved April 4, 2013, from retriever.no.

[12]Mellgren Fredrik (2006, September 2). Jobbagenter ska öka integrationen. *Svenska Dagbladet*. Retrieved April 4, 2013, from retriever.no.

While the 2002 federal election campaign was defined by a polarization between the conservative positions of the Liberals (FP) and the liberal positions of the Social Democrats (SAP), the 2006 election campaign saw a highly liberal consensus among the major political forces in Sweden on matters of integration and immigration. Therefore, the electoral niche for a political player with a conservative agenda, rejecting multiculturalism, was open from the mid-2000s on.

The established parties used the election campaigns for the federal election in 2010—the first time the populist radical right Swedish Democrats entered the parliament in Stockholm—to reaffirm their liberal profiles: during summer 2010 the only integration-related topic on which FP politicians aired an opinion was concerned with the better integration of students with a foreign background and lacked any particularly conservative positions.[13] In 2010, the Social Democratic party did not emphasize matters of integration and migration in the election for the Riksdag in particular, but stressed the obligation of all municipalities to take in asylum seekers, without exception.[14] The entire center-left spectrum of Swedish politics affirmed this multicultural stance, calling for the right and opportunity for all pupils of a migration background to receive instruction in their mother tongue (e.g. German, Polish or Turkish).[15]

In May 2012, the year with the highest salience of immigration issues among FP politicians since 2002, the minister of integration affairs—the FP politician Erik Ullenhag—proposed a law aimed at cutting welfare benefits to migrants who turned down job offers.[16] These statements were reaffirmed in June 2012 and triggered a heated debate.[17] Note that the FP's claims during the high salience years of 2002 and 2012 were 'reasonable' regardless of actual economic or cultural threats or perceptions—they were concerned with improving migrants' experience of integration in general; therefore, they could be fuelled in party discourse whenever it best suited the Swedish Liberals—whenever they were in need of a topic around which to mobilize voters, as in 2002 and 2012. Despite these conservative demands in 2012, the overall party position of the Swedish Liberals also remained clearly liberal in this year: FP politicians supported full access to the Swedish health care system for all *sans papiers*,[18] and raised awareness about structural racism in

---

[13]Levin David (2010, June 9). Betygsgap skylls på skolan. *Svenska Dagbladet*. Retrieved April 3, 2013, from retriever.no.

[14]Svenska Dagbladet (2010, February 20). Ingen rubrik tilgaenglig. *Svenska Dagbladet*. Retrieved April 4, 2013, from retriever.no.

[15]Levin, David (2010, June 9). Betygsgap skylls på skolan. *Svenska Dagbladet*. Retrieved April 4, 2013, from retriever.no.

[16]Svenska Dagbladet (2012, May 28). *Svenska Dagbladet*. Nej kan minska invandrares stöd. Retrieved April 3, 2013, from retriever.no.

[17]Svenska Dagbladet (2012, June 6). FP:s skräpta krav splittrar alliansen. *Svenska Dagbladet*. Retrieved April 3, 2013, from retriever.no.

[18]Åkerman Mikaela (2012, June 29). Papperslösa får rätt till sjukvård. *Svenska Dagbladet*. Svenska Dagbladet. Retrieved April 3, 2013, from retriever.no.

Sweden[19] throughout 2012. This occurred in the absence of claims of the Social Democrats that would indicate a change in the multicultural and pro-affirmative action agenda on which the party had run since 2002.

Swedish integration debates have been characterized by a highly liberal, multicultural discourse since the year 2003—led by the liberal agenda of the Swedish Social Democrats (SAP). The only point in time during which the Swedish Liberals (FP) put forward a clearly conservative position, rejecting multiculturalism, was the year 2002. Since then, the FP have campaigned with liberal messaging, withdrawing from their earlier conservative profile. Just a year after immigration issues were politicized in Swedish politics for the first time in 2002, no established political actor offered a conservative profile on matters of integration and immigration, rejecting multiculturalism. The populist radical right Sweden Democrats (SD) utilized the salience of the issue over the course of the 2000s and seized their electoral niche as the only political party rejecting multiculturalism. At the end of 2013, they polled between 10 and 12% and thereby became the third-largest Swedish party; in spring 2017, the SDs polled at 20%.

## 7.3   Nothing Is More Convincing than Chances to Gain Votes

Given these descriptive results, one is left with the question: why did the Swedish Liberals (FP) drop their conservative position right after *they themselves* put it forward in 2002? The two-level theory recommends focusing on the polling fortunes of the center-left camp (SAP, V, MP) and the economic concerns of the Swedish voters. And indeed, they offered a series of incentives for the FP to drop their conservative integration agenda right after putting it forward.

Neither the potential of real economic and cultural threat, nor their perceptions indicate any particularities for 2002 and 2012 or the years in between (Fig. 7.1). Party rationale—the aim to mobilize conservative voters—best accounts for the high *salience* in 2002 and 2012; this rationale can also explain FP's change in *positioning*. Save 1991–1994, a social democratic government from 1982 until 2006 ruled Sweden. The Swedish Social Democrats (SAP) was conceived as the 'natural' governing party, while the Swedish Moderates (M) were the 'natural' opposition leader. Only the success of a bourgeois coalition in the federal election in 2006 and their eventual reelection in 2010 brought an end to this 'center-left hegemony', which characterized Swedish politics from the 1980s onwards. The SAP faced considerable setbacks in the polls at times, dropping to around 30% electoral support, but could count on the Left (Vaensterpartiet) and Green (Miljoepartiet de Groena) parties to make up for these losses, guaranteeing a

---

[19]Hellekant Johan (2012, September 4). Förortsidé kritiseras av Rojas. Svenska Dagbladet. Svenska Dagbladet. Retrieved April 3, 2013, from retriever.no.

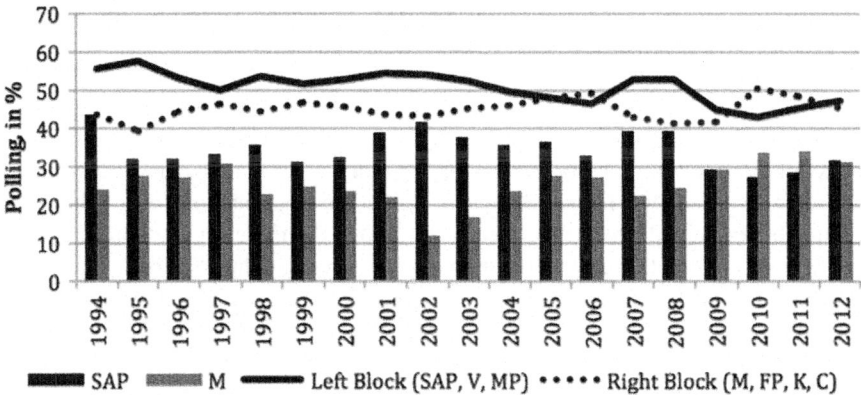

**Fig. 7.4**  Polling of SAP, M and respective coalitions

center-left majority in the polls throughout the 1990s and 2000s up to the 2006 election year (Fig. 7.4).

Given that parties are office-seekers, any Swedish party was therefore wise to orient its position around the most successful Swedish vote-seeker up to 2006: the Swedish Social Democrats (SAP). Recalling the positioning of all Swedish parties on integration matters, the clearly liberal position of the Swedish Social Democrats (except 2005) comes to mind. From 2002 to 2012 the Swedish Greens (MP) scored a highly liberal +8, while the Moderates (M) scored around ±0 and the Swedish Social Democrats an annual average of a considerably liberal position of +4 (Fig. 7.3). Given the strength of the SAP and of the entire center-left spectrum of Swedish politics, the conservative agenda setter in issues of migration and integration—the Swedish Liberals (FP)—was keen to follow the position of the Social Democrats (SAP), who were reaching out to the largest share of centrist Swedish voters. In so doing, the liberal positioning of the SAP led the FP to bolster its liberal and pro-migrant profile over the course of the 2000s and to withdraw from the conservative position it proposed in 2002, when it put the immigration issue on the agenda for the first time. Consequently, the Swedish electorate lost an established political actor that had supplied a conservative position, rejecting multiculturalism; consequently, the political space for the populist radical right Swedish Democrats opened in 2003.

## 7.4   A Multicultural Agenda in a Society Freed of Economic Concerns

Finally, the question arises as to why the SAP embraced this profile in favor of migrants' interests from 2002 to 2012, in contrast to the Dutch social democrats in the early 1990s and their German counterparts from the early

1990s on. Have a strong left camp and few economic concerns also characterized Sweden that led the Dutch social democrats to markedly liberalize their
positions in 1994?

As shown in previous parts of this chapter, the Swedish electorate was exposed
to an increase in potential cultural threat from the mid-2000s onwards and showed
peaks of relatively high cultural threat perceptions in 2002 and 2010. Considering
variation in these two figures, the very stable pro-migrant position of the SAP
cannot be explained with 'objective facts' about immigration. Instead, the economic threat potential and perceptions on the part of the Swedish electorate
remained extremely low throughout the 2000s—this stands in contrast to the dire
early 1990s when roughly three times more Swedish voters conceived an economic
threat potential (33% annual average from 1990 to 1994 and 13% annual average
from 1995 to 1999, in comparison to only 9% annual average from the year 2000
on) (Fig. 7.1). Additionally, a highly successful center-left camp characterized
Swedish politics until the mid-2000s, when the social democratic SAP led a
mid-left coalition (SAP, V, MP) that kept its bourgeois contenders (M, FP, K, C)
out of government until 2006 (Fig. 7.5).

The same conditions, therefore, that account for the liberal positions of the
Dutch social democrats after 1994 explain the liberal position of the Swedish
Social Democrats in the 2000s: a successful center-left camp in combination
with very limited fears of economic threat on the part of Swedish voters. In this
political climate the populist radical right Sweden Democrats (SD) found
the perfect breeding ground for their continuing advances over the past
decade.

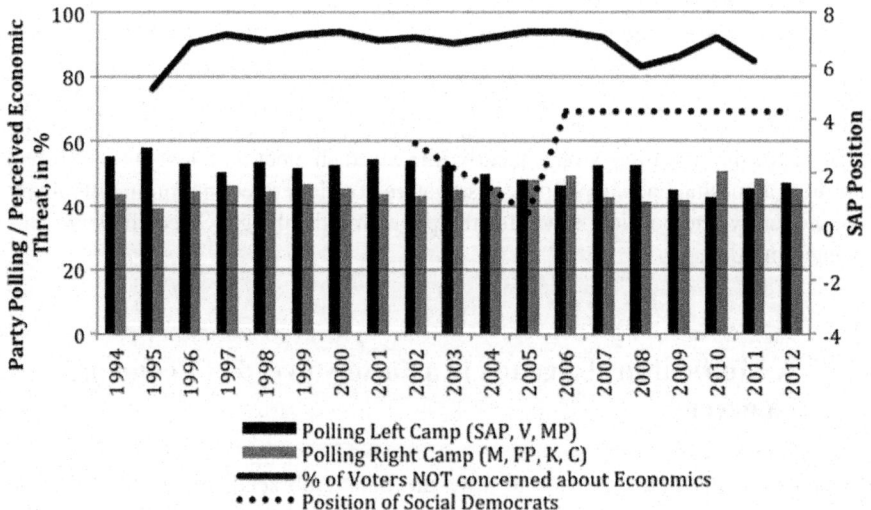

**Fig. 7.5** SAP position, polling political camps and economic threat potential

## 7.5 Summary: The Break from Swedish Tolerance and Its Aftermath

As with the observations on the case in the Netherlands, the Swedish case also illustrates the validity of the previously outlined two-level theory. The Swedish Liberals (FP) broke the tacit consensus among Swedish parties not to campaign on migration topics during the campaign for the federal election in 2002. The prospect of dropping below the federal threshold of 4% and not making it to the Riksdag for the first time since 1934 marked an existential crisis for the FP in these years. The politicization of the immigration issue might have come as a last resort. The FP again increased its salience in 2012 after dropping below 6% in voter support—this further proves the point. However, the FP did not persevere with its conservative messaging. Soon after its successful election campaign in 2002, the FP greatly moderated its positions in matters of immigration and integration. From 2003 onwards, Sweden was again home to a liberal discourse on immigration matters, led by the—by then—most successful Swedish party, the Social Democrats (SAP). Therefore, a political space for the populist radical right Swedish Democrats opened in 2003. The FP moderated its positions because it was facing a highly successful social-democratic party, which had led a hegemonic center-left camp in Swedish politics until 2006, and which was campaigning on clear pro-migrant standpoints. In turn, the Swedish Social Democrats fiercely proclaimed affirmative action measures because the Swedish electorate was freed of economic concerns during the integration debates described, and the center-left camp of Swedish politics (SAP, V, MP) could rely on a stable majority in the polls.

This chapter has considered the case in Sweden in 2012 in detail. Since 2012, the SD's permanent media access and organizational capacity has made it less dependent on the political messaging of established parties. Additionally, the increased salience of immigration topics over the subsequent years has been the perfect setting for the SD. It is very likely that the zigzagging of established Swedish parties on how to handle the refugee crises in 2015–2016 came hand in hand with various cases of overpromising and underdelivering on conservative policies. This would explain why the SD was able to double its support from around 12% in spring 2015 to more than 20% in spring 2017.

## References

Dahlström C, Esaiasson P (2009) The immigration issue and anti-immigrant party success. Is sweden the odd case out? QoG working paper series. The Quality of Government Institute

Rydgren J (2002) Radical right populism in Sweden: still a failure, but for how long? Scand Pol Stud 25(1):27–56

Rydgren J, Ruth P (2011) Voting for the radical right in Swedish municipalities: social marginality and ethnic competition? Scand Pol Stud 34(3):202–224

# Chapter 8
# Germany: How a Conservative Compromise Between CDU/CSU and SPD Blocked the Populist Radical Right Parties REP and Schill

## 8.1 Last Resort Identity Politics: The CDU/CSU's Conservative Agenda

The German case also illustrates the basic reasons for a significant increase in the salience of immigration-related matters in party discourse according to the proposed two-level theory. The salience in the German party discourse is strongly dependent on the condition of the German conservatives CDU/CSU[1]: as long as they are faring well in the polls, there remains silence around the issue; conversely, if the CDU/CSU drops in the polls—in particular in comparison to its direct competitor for the German chancellorship, the Social Democrats (SPD)—the issue is used to mobilize conservative voters.

The data shows a slight increase in the salience of immigration-related topics in the German party discourse over the 1980s. The issue is not particularly salient in any federal election campaign (neither in 1983 nor in 1987). Rather, it is a key component of the conservatives' plea for a general moral turn in German politics ('Geistig-moralische Wende'), which has characterized the CDU/CSU campaigns since the early 1980s, in particular after they took over the chancellorship in 1982 (Thränhardt 1995).

The annual average number of party statements reported by the FAZ between 1982 and 2012 adds up to 66 claims per year—or 51, if 1992, a year of extraordinarily high salience, is excluded. Regardless of these two measures, 1984 and 1986 are the first years in which the average was toppled with 76 and 71 annual claims, respectively. 1988 and 1989 saw 135 and 166 claims by the CDU/CSU, respectively, and mark the highest salience values in the 'Bonner Republik' before reunification in 1989–1990.

---

[1]The CSU only exists in Bavaria. The CDU never stood for election there, while the CSU refrains from reaching out to other states. The CSU is often described as the CDU's "conservative wing."

© Springer International Publishing AG 2018
T. Lochocki, *The Rise of Populism in Western Europe*,
DOI 10.1007/978-3-319-62855-4_8

The CDU/CSU salience drops sharply in 1990, but increases in 1991 and peaks at an all-time high with 377 claims in 1992. Save 1997, the number of political claims then dropped below average and remained there until 1999. The highest salience values in the 'Berliner Republik' were reached in the years 2000 and 2001. While 1999 only saw 25 claims, the CDU/CSU channeled 128 and 155 claims into the discourse in 2000 and 2001 respectively. While the salience increased remarkably from 1999 to 2000, it dropped dramatically from 2001 to 2002: the 155 claims from 2001 were followed by only 46 in 2002. Save the year 2004, immigration-related topics have ceased to be important issues on the political agenda of German conservatives ever since; the annual average of CDU/CSU claims dropped to 21 (!) from 2002 to 2012—excluding the year 2004.

How to account for this striking variation? Why has the immigration issue been off the political agenda in Germany since 2004? And what do the high-salience years 1984, 1986, 1988, 1989, 1992, 1997, 2000, 2001 and 2004 have in common? Are they an indicator of the increasing cultural threat *potential* to which (West) Germany was exposed in these years? Indeed, the inflow of migrants to (West) Germany rose steadily over the 1980s, but stabilized at the very high level of around 800,000 immigrants per year from 1989 to 1997. How then to account for the decreasing salience between 1993 and 1996? Further, while the salience approached zero from 2003 on, the annual immigration rate remained stable with an average of 600,000 new migrants to Germany per year until 2012.

Asylum figures might account for the particular salience of the year 1992, as—according to OECD statistics—Germany took in 440,000 asylum seekers (more than 0.54% of its entire population of 80.6 million, at the time, and the highest ratio ever recorded by OECD reports). Still, the *first* years in which the salience increased significantly, namely in 1984 and 1986, lacked a remarkable increase in the number of asylum seekers—their figures remain rather low at 36,000 and 100,000 per year respectively. Later high-salience periods—1997, 2000, 2001 and 2004—were years in which Germany accepted even fewer refugees than in low-salience years. Even more curiously, only 8% of the CDU/CSU claims in 1984 and just 13% in 1988 concerned asylum-related issues. Therefore, neither the general inflow of migrants, nor of asylum-seekers in particular, can explain the high salience periods—the *actual cultural threat* potential cannot account for the politicization of immigration-related issues in (West) Germany.

Considering these results, perhaps not the actual cultural threat potential, but the *perceived cultural threat* on the part of German voters was the reason for the increasing salience of immigration-related issues among the German conservatives? For lack of a better indicator, I rely here on the 'Politbarometer' questions regarding the most important challenges facing the country, and this poses a challenge in itself: the first year the answer category migrant/integration/asylum-seekers was included was 1987. This means there is an absence of precise information for the early and mid-1980s, but gives reason to assume that if experienced social researchers omitted this categorization for 5 years during which the salience in the party discourse steadily increased, the public might not have been too wary of

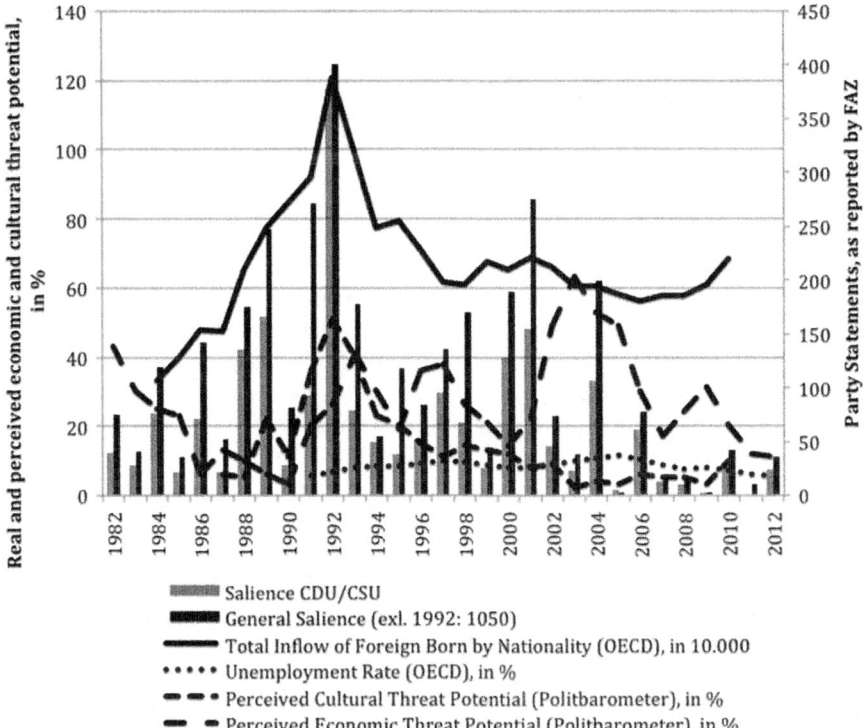

**Fig. 8.1** Real cultural and economic threat potential in Germany, German voters' perceptions and salience of immigration-related topics 1982–2012 (The general salience of the year 1992 is not comprised of 400, but of 1050 (!) claims; for the sake of readability, the mathematically correct listing is omitted)

immigration-related issues. Not to push this assumption too far, but the empirical data at hand for the following years support this argument.

Considering that the annual average (1987–2012) of German voters troubled by a cultural threat was 14%, public concerns remained significantly high in 1994 and 1995, at more than 20% without any accompanying salience. Conversely—save 1989 and 1992—no high-salience period in the 'Berliner Republik' correlated with an increased cultural threat perception on the part of the German voter. Given the lack of a correlation between remarkable threat perceptions of German voters and high-salience periods in the political debate, cultural perceptions seem not to have resulted in a significant increase of CDU/CSU claims on immigration-related matters (Fig. 8.1).

While neither the actual cultural threat potential nor the cultural threat perception offer any generalizable patterns, perhaps the sphere of economics is more telling? The *actual economic threat* is distributed rather clearly over time: until German reunification in 1989/1990 the unemployment rate in Germany remained rather low, at around 6% per year; from 1993 to 2007 it increased to 9% per year and dropped to around 7% after 2008. The low actual economic threat was accompanied by high salience periods in 1988 and 1989 and years with very low salience after 2008; the dire years 1993–2007 further show a striking variation in the number of CDU/CSU claims. Therefore, the *actual economic threat* can barely account for the salience of immigration-related issues among German conservatives.

A similar picture emerges regarding the *perception of an economic threat*: on annual average, 27% of German citizens portrayed economic challenges as of prime concern between 1982 and 2010. While from 1984 to 1992 only 15% conceived an economic threat on annual average, this figure increased to 27% from 1993 to 2001, peaking at a remarkable annual average of 49% (!) from 2002 to 2006 before dropping to 23% after 2007. Showing a mainly similar pattern to that found with the *actual* economic threat, the economic threat *perception* on the part of the German voters does not suggest a causal mechanism in relation to the salience of the CDU/CSU on immigration-related matters (Fig. 8.1).

Considering that years of high salience in immigration-related topics bear no resemblance to either the economic or cultural threat potential or perceptions on the part of the voters, how to account for the variation here? Would focusing on the condition of the conservative party CDU/CSU offer more insights? Indeed, revisiting polling figures over the last 30 years reveals a striking pattern: all high-salience years correspond with remarkably low polling figures for the CDU/CSU. The first time the conservatives dropped sharply in the polls during the 1980s was the year 1984—the exact year in which immigration-related issues grew in importance for the very first time. The high-salience years 1988 and 1989 correspond with the hitherto lowest polling values of the CDU/CSU; while the conservatives poll around 40% on annual average 1982–2012, they gathered 45% by 1987, and dropped to only 36 and 33% in 1988 and 1989 respectively. The polling figures increased due to the successful management of German reunification by chancellor Helmut Kohl's (CDU) administration—up to 44% on annual average in 1990, safeguarding the reelection of the governing coalition (CDU/CSU and the Liberals, FDP). In 1991 the polls were already beginning to point in the opposite direction; a new low-point was reached in 1992 when only 33% of voters supported the conservatives and there was an all-time high in the salience of immigration-related matters, with 377 (!) claims.

The next year with remarkable salience—1997—goes hand in hand with a dramatic drop in voter support; the CDU/CSU fell from an annual average of 40% throughout the mid-1990s to 34% in 1997. Immigration-related issues become a subject of contestation in 2000 and 2001 as the so-called 'Spendenskandal' hit the CDU/CSU and the conservatives dropped to 35 and 37% in the polls. The year 2004 fits this pattern perfectly, showing a sharp drop in voter support from 50% in 2003 to 44% in 2004. The very first time a considerable polling loss of the CDU/CSU does *not* correspond with increasing salience is the year 2010, but this exception can neatly be explained by focusing on *who* is taking away the votes from the conservatives in this year: it is the Greens, not the SPD. Thus, the CDU/CSU remained the

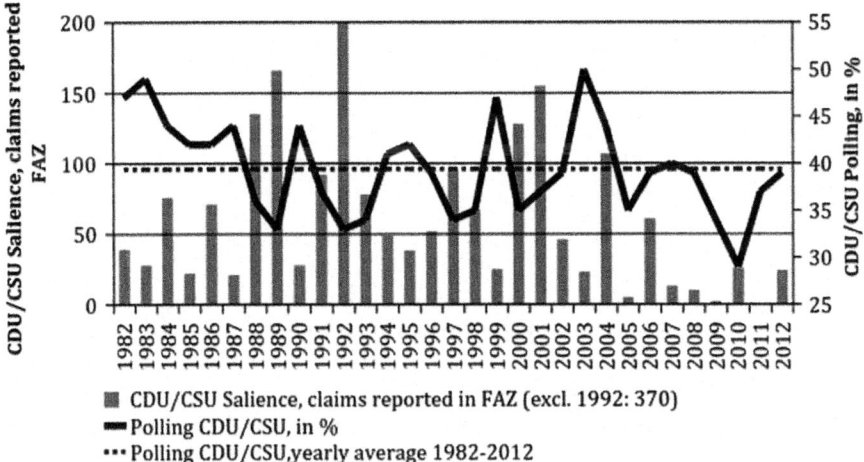

CDU/CSU Salience, claims reported in FAZ (excl. 1992: 370)
Polling CDU/CSU, in %
Polling CDU/CSU,yearly average 1982-2012

**Fig. 8.2**  CDU/CSU polling and salience 1982–2012 (For the sake of readability, the high salience of 370 in the year 1992 is set at 200)

strongest party in spite of dropping in the polls in 2010, and kept issues of immigration off the political agenda (Fig. 8.2).

The German conservatives (CDU/CSU) seem to emphasize issues regarding asylum-seekers, immigration and the integration of migrants mainly in response to dire polling figures in order to mobilize conservative voters. This argument is further supported when focusing on the dramatic decreases in the salience of immigration-related issues in relation to the previous year: be it the year 1990, when German Reunification assured the reelection of chancellor Helmut Kohl (CDU); from 1993 to 1996, after the fierce asylum debates in the early 1990s, while the CDU/CSU was steadily rising in voter support; in the year 1999, while German voters were disappointed in the performance of the first red-green government (SPD and Greens) that took over office following the federal election in 1998; and finally in the year 2002, while all polls indicated a landslide victory of the CDU/CSU at the federal election in autumn in vain. Only the low salience years 2005 and 2007 seem not to have been preceded by a remarkable increase in voter support for the CDU/CSU, and still, they listed the conservatives as strongest party (Fig. 8.2).

The CDU/CSU polled at 39.5% on annual average from 1982 to 2012. The conservatives' voter support during the high salience years 1988, 1989, 1991–1993, 1997, 2000, 2001 and 2004 was down to 34.5%. During low salience years, the CDU/CSU polled substantially higher—at 43%. The average annual number of claims reads 66; the years during which the CDU/CDU polled below its average comprise 102 claims; when the conservatives gathered more than 40%, salience decreased to 40 claims per year. In other words: when the party experienced a crisis it made roughly 53% more claims, and if it was faring well in the polls it made roughly 39% fewer claims than the annual average (Table 8.1).

**Table 8.1**  CDU/CSU polling and salience 1982–2012

|  | Yearly average 1982–2012 | CDU/CSU crisis (below 39%, 13 years) | No CDU/CSU crisis (above 39%, 18 years) |
|---|---|---|---|
| CDU/CSU polling | 39.4% | 34.5% | 42.8% |
| Claims on immigration-related matters by CDU/CSU (excl. 1992) | 66.4 (56.1) | 102.0 (86.3) | 40.1 |

Save for very few years in the late 2000s, the condition of the CDU/CSU is the best indicator of the high salience attributed by the German conservatives to immigration-related matters. Political issues regarding asylum-seekers, immigration and the integration of migrants were mainly emphasized in response to the CDU/CSU's dire polling figures in order to mobilize conservative voters. This explains the very low salience of immigration topics in Germany from 2005 to the historical refugee situation of the year 2015: the CDU/CSU, under Chancellor Angela Merkel, has never been in danger of losing its position as the strongest German party. The party has not conceived an incentive to mobilize conservative voters in politicizing immigration-related topics since 2005.

## 8.2   The Glimpse of a Salient Multicultural Discourse and the First Advances of the Populist Radical Right Party 'Die Republikaner' (REP) in 1989

The remarkable variation in the salience of immigration-related matters in the German party discourse does not correspond with variation in the electoral advances of its populist radical right parties. Before the Alternative for Germany (AfD) entered German politics in 2013, the election for the European Parliament in 1989 was the only time a PRRP could gather remarkable voter support in (West) Germany: 'Die Republikaner' (REP) gathered 7.1% and scored similar figures in federal polls, indicating the political climate in (West) Germany. The party dropped dramatically in voter support thereafter, missing the 5% electoral threshold during the federal election in 1990 by a wide margin and—save the year 1992—it has never polled close to 5% since. According to the two-level theory, the late 1980s were supposedly the only time in which political debate in Germany was characterized by a salient debate about immigration-related topics that was defined by a liberal, multicultural discourse. Indeed, the data affirms these assumptions.

The CDU/CSU put the issue on the agenda in the early 1980s and campaigned on clearly conservative positions throughout the 1980s, but greatly moderated its position in 1988 and 1989. The conservatives' position during 1982 and 1987 was −5.5 on annual average, but the party proclaimed a far more liberal profile in the years 1988 and 1989—scoring an ambivalent −0.4 and −0.5. Thus, 'Die Republikaner' seized the niche the CDU/CSU opened in the late 1980s; a substantial part of the REP's failure to enter the federal parliament in 1990 with only 2.1% of the vote was the CDU/CSU's reclaiming of a conservative position, clearly rejecting multiculturalism, from the 1990 election year on. From 1990 to 1994 the German conservatives scored −5.5 on annual average, while the populist radical right party 'Die Republikaner' dropped in voter support over the same years and also missed the 5% threshold with only 1.9% at the 1994 Bundestagswahl.

Despite some position changes beginning in 1995, the CDU/CSU occupied a clearly conservative position in the salient debates of immigration and integration until 2011. The average annual score from 1995 to 2011 remains conservative, at −4.7 (ranging from −1.8 in 1995 to −8.0 in 2006). The attempts of a new PRRP contender in the early 2000s—for example the PRO Party with its leader Ronald Schill—were bound to fail given the closed electoral niche on the right. A position change is clearly visible from 2012 on, however: while the CDU/CSU's position was clearly conservative in 2010, at −3.1, the year 2012 shows an ambivalent −0.7 (Fig. 8.3). The reason why this change went unaccompanied by the rise of a populist radical right party was the lack of salient multicultural campaigns on the part of the SPD and the *very low salience* of immigration-related matters in the German party discourse in general from 2004 on (Fig. 8.2).

Neither German voters nor conservative politicians may have been as aware of the lack of a clearly conservative position on the part of the CDU/CSU as they were in 1988–1989, but still, the electoral niche for a PRRP party in Germany opened in 2012 for the first time since 1988. However, without any cultural matters being discussed, conservative German voters were not mobilized. This began to change

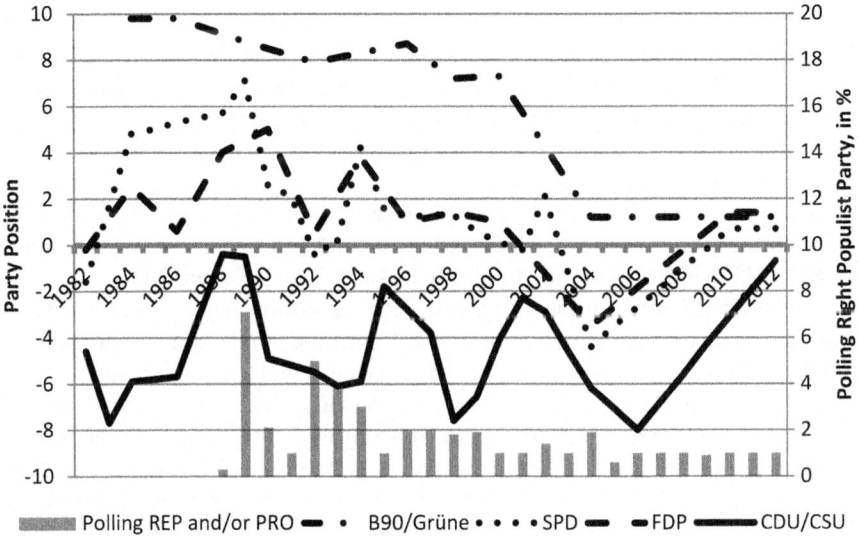

**Fig. 8.3** Party positions on immigration-related topics in Germany and polling of REP/PRO 1982–2012

from 2012 onwards, with Eurozone issues and migration topics debated passionately, eventually benefitting the AfD. However, before the euro crisis in 2012 PRRPs were unable to benefit from the conservative void on immigration issues, because the second necessary condition for their rise was still lacking: the high salience of immigration matters.

The 1989 federal election was the only time in which the CDU/CSU dropped its conservative messaging on migration matters during a highly salient debate in favor of the liberal claims of the SPD. This in turn opened the electoral niche for the REP. Up until the advances of the AfD in 2013, all salient immigration debates were characterized by a clearly conservative position on the part of the CDU/CSU and an ambivalent position by the SPD (Fig. 8.3). The reasons for the rise of the AfD will be explained in detail in Chap. 9.

The data not only shows the striking position change of the CDU/CSU, but also two other remarkable strategic shifts. The first concerns the dropping of the SPD's multicultural agenda beginning in 1990. While the German social democrats campaigned on highly liberal positions throughout the 1980s (a +5.6 annual average from 1984 to 1989), the party took an ambivalent position after 1990 (a +0.2 annual average since 1990). A similar conservative turn can be seen taken by the German Greens. Until the year 2000 their annual average position scored a remarkable +8.5; since 2001, the party has taken a far more nuanced position with a +1.2 (Fig. 8.3).

In order to illustrate changing party positions, the following pages are devoted to examples of the CDU/CSU's and SPD's positions, placing an emphasis on the years 1988–1994 during the rise and fall of the PRRP 'Die Republikaner'.

A coalition between the Social Democrats (SPD) and the Liberals (FDP) governed Germany from 1969 to 1982, first under the leadership of chancellor Willy Brandt, SPD (1969–1974), and then chancellor Helmut Schmidt, SPD (1974–1982). The FDP withdrew from the coalition with the Social Democrats and enabled Helmut Kohl (CDU) to claim chancellorship because of a successful 'Misstrauensvotum' against Helmut Schmidt (SPD) on October 1, 1982, and an affirming 'Vertrauensfrage' in favor of Helmut Kohl (CDU) on December 17, 1982. Helmut Kohl also aimed for affirmation by the voters, and so called for a 'vorgezogene Bundestagswahl' on March 6, 1983. The German population endorsed the coalition between the CDU/CSU and FPD, with 48.8% voting for the CDU/CSU and 7.0% for the FDP (SPD: 38.2%, Die Gruenen: 5.6%).

A significant portion of the CDU/CSU's election campaigns in 1982 and 1983 was concerned with the narrative of a moral turn in German politics—a 'geistig-moralische Wende'. This moral turn emphasized that Germany should be less intimidated by its National-Socialist past, but rather understand itself as a 'normal nation' and stand firmly for its own national interests. A vital part of this theme was to stop the immigration of guest workers and their families and, instead, to encourage them to return to their home countries by offering 'repatriation fees'. The CDU/CSU and FDP announced new policies shortly after assuming control of the government in autumn 1982 that aimed at inducing voluntary return of migrants.[2] The department for domestic affairs, led by Friedrich Zimmermann (CSU), announced increased restrictions on the immigration of the family members of guest workers in the winter of 1983[3] and the beginning of 1984.[4] A key part of this repatriation process was to erect barriers to prevent family members from joining their relatives who were working in Germany, as the CDU/CSU conceived them as a crucial obstacle to integration.[5] During the early 1980s the CDU/CSU portrayed (West) Germany as being incapable of taking in more migrants and as *not* being a country of immigration.[6]

The CDU/CSU began accompanying these demands with calls for more restrictive asylum legislation in 1985.[7] Chancellor Helmut Kohl formulated an ambitious goal in the summer of 1986: the change of Article 16 of the German constitution, which guaranteed a rather generous asylum policy.[8] This paragraph of the German constitution can be understood as departing from a commitment to transforming the perception of German soil, from a country people flee in order to escape political persecution (as in Nazi Germany), to a safe haven for refugees. Because changing the German constitution is only possible with a two-thirds majority in both German chambers—Bundestag and Bundesrat—support from the SPD and FPD was necessary. However, both parties rejected the CDU/CSU's proposal that summer.[9]

---

[2]Frankfurter Allgemeine Zeitung (1982, September 29) Maßnahmen gegen 'soziale Isolation' Was Union und FDP zur Ausländerpolitik vereinbart haben. Retrieved June 19, 2013 from FAZ archive.

[3]Frankfurter Allgemeine Zeitung (1983, November 18) Zimmermanns 'Positionspapier' umstritten. Bonns Ausländerpolitik/Widerstand vor allem aus der FDP. Retrieved June 19, 2013 from FAZ archive.

[4]Frankfurter Allgemeine Zeitung (1984, January 5) Kompromiß in der Ausländerpolitik? Ein Angebot der Unions-Fraktion an die FDP. Keine Beschränkung des Kindernachzugs/ 'Handreichung' für Zimmermann/Der Koalitionspartner verwirrt. Retrieved June 19, 2013 from FAZ archive.

[5]Frankfurter Allgemeine Zeitung (1984, August 29) Neuer Streit in Bonn über die Ausländerpolitik. Änderungswünsche Genschers/Innenministerium: Die FDP ist unberechenbar/ Die Frage der Zuwanderung. Retrieved June 19, 2013 from FAZ archive.

[6]Frankfurter Allgemeine Zeitung (1984, October 6) Die Koalition demonstriert Einvernehmen in der Ausländerpolitik. Die SPD bietet Zusammenarbeit an/Debatte im Bundestag. Retrieved June 19, 2013 from FAZ archive.

[7]Frankfurter Allgemeine Zeitung (1985, February 13) Immer mehr Ausländer suchen Zuflucht in Deutschland Das Asylverfahren wird wieder zum Zankapfel CDU-regierte Länder verlangen befristete Anerkennung/FDP gegen 'Verschärfung'. Retrieved June 19, 2013 from FAZ archive. Frankfurter Allgemeine Zeitung (1985, June 15) Bundesrat beschließt Novelle zum Asylrecht. SPD-Länder lehnen Entwurf ab/'Geltende Regeln ausreichend'. Retrieved June 19, 2013 from FAZ archive.

[8]Frankfurter Allgemeine Zeitung (1986, June 6) Streit um Kohls Äußerungen zum Asylrecht. Grundgesetzänderung notwendig?/SPD: Linie Lummers/Zustimmung aus den Kommunen. Retrieved June 19, 2013 from FAZ archive.

[9]Frankfurter Allgemeine Zeitung (1986, July 28) Kohl nennt den Zustrom von Asylbewerbern einen unerträglichen Zustand. 'Nachdrücklich mit der DDR reden'/Unterstützung aus der SPD/Keine Mehrheit für Grundgesetzänderung. Retrieved June 19, 2013 from FAZ archive.

Until the mid 1980s, the SPD did not clearly position itself against the conservative demands of the CDU/CSU. The salience attributed to immigration-related issues by the SPD was rather low, while its position was clearly liberal; facing the CDU/CSU's proposals of repatriation and putting a strict stop to the immigration of family members of guest workers, the Social Democrats campaigned in favor of a liberal immigration policy in 1984. The party rejected any limits on the immigration of family members, in favor of facilitating naturalization instead.[10] While the CDU/CSU proposed to change Article 16 of the German constitution, which lays out the asylum policy, the SPD stood firm in guaranteeing maximum rights to individuals claiming asylum in Germany in 1985.[11]

While the asylum debate continued after 1986, the CDU/CSU attacked the SPD and the FDP for considering giving non-German residents the right to vote in municipal elections ('Kommunalwahlrecht fuer Auslaender').[12] In 1986 the SPD began to increase the number of immigration-related claims they made to counter those of the CDU/CSU. The salience attributed to the SPD reached an unprecedented peak of 32 claims (the annual average 1982–1985 was 16), and the SPD from the federal states of Hessen and Hamburg proposed clear policy measures for the integration of migrants: the asylum law should remain unchanged,[13] naturalization facilitated, dual citizenship implemented[14] and migrants without German citizenship granted the right to vote in municipal elections ('Auslaenderwahlrecht').[15]

The CDU/CSU fiercely opposed these proposals in 1987, as it considered granting voting rights to non-Germans a breach of the German constitution.[16] In the same year the multicultural campaigns reached the federal SPD and the debate meanwhile created a nationwide echo: after the SPD-led government in the federal

---

[10]Frankfurter Allgemeine Zeitung (1984, September 19) Fest steht nur: Bonns Ausländerpolitik soll 'pragmatisch' sein. Die Details weiter umstritten/Beratungen der Koalitionsführung/Die SPD will eine Debatte erzwingen. Retrieved June 19, 2013 from FAZ archive.

[11]Frankfurter Allgemeine Zeitung (1985, August 27) CDU-Vorschläge zum Asylrecht abgewiesen. Hessens Innenminister sieht darin 'Attacke auf das Grundrecht'. Retrieved June 19, 2013 from FAZ archive.

[12]Frankfurter Allgemeine Zeitung (1987, July 22) Berliner CDU gegen Wahlrecht für Ausländer 'Der Integration nicht förderlich'/Mehrheit im Senat. Retrieved June 19, 2013 from FAZ archive.

[13]Frankfurter Allgemeine Zeitung (1986, July 28) Gewalttaten gegen Asylbewerber in Berlin Senat warnt vor Ausländerfeindlichkeit. Die CDU skeptisch gegenüber einer Verfassungsänderung. Retrieved June 19, 2013 from FAZ archive.

[14]Frankfurter Allgemeine Zeitung (1986, August 21) SPD: Wünschenswert, doch mit dem Grundgesetz unvereinbar. Die Debatte über das Kommunalwahlrecht für Ausländer im Wiesbadener Landtag. Retrieved June 19, 2013 from FAZ archive.

[15]Frankfurter Allgemeine Zeitung (1986, September 23) SPD Hessen-Süd will 'Träume wahrmachen'. Vorreiterrolle in Energie- und Ausländerpolitik beansprucht/Kommunales Wahlrecht für Ausländer. Retrieved June 19, 2013 from FAZ archive.

[16]Frankfurter Allgemeine Zeitung (1987, August 24) Die CDU erwägt Klage gegen Ausländerwahlrecht. Retrieved June 19, 2013 from FAZ archive.

state of Hamburg called for the implementation of the 'Auslaenderwahlrecht',[17] the board of the federal SPD and the SPD faction in the Bundestag called for a general implementation across all of Germany.[18] In the same year the speaker of the SPD's working group on matters of asylum in the German Bundestag—Gerd Wartenberg—demanded a liberalization of the asylum procedure. Applicants should not be checked individually, but granted asylum if they were likely to face political persecution in their home country; applicants who were not entitled to asylum status based on the German constitution should receive a secure residence permit if they were refugees as laid out by the Geneva Convention; and refugees should be entitled to work permits that allowed them to work freely, because a threat to the German job market was seen as unlikely.[19]

In 1986 and 1987 the debate over German integration policy was the most extreme polarization ever measured: the CDU/CSU scored at a highly conservative −5.0/−3.6, fiercely rejecting multiculturalism, while the SPD embraced a clearly liberal, multicultural position with +5.3/+5.5. This polarization quickly came to an end in 1988, however: at the beginning of 1988, the CDU/CSU's conservative claims were accompanied by far more moderate voices, namely coming from members of the faction of the CDU/CSU in the German parliament and Kanzleramtsminister Wolfgang Schaeuble (CDU), arguing in favor of *more* immigration.[20]

And this was only the beginning of a liberal turn on the part of the CDU/CSU. In March 1988, parts of the CDU aimed to grant non-German residents the right to vote in municipal elections.[21] In April 1988, members of the CDU faction of the federal parliament called for anti-discrimination laws and for understanding (West) Germany as a multicultural society.[22] Whereas the CDU/CSU portrayed Germany as not a country of immigration and saw continued immigration as a cause of severe

---

[17]Frankfurter Allgemeine Zeitung (1987, July 15) SPD und FDP wollen in Hamburg ein Wahlrecht für Ausländer einführen. Von Münch: Einigung wahrscheinlich/CDU fürchtet Radikalisierung. Retrieved June 19, 2013 from FAZ archive.

[18]Frankfurter Allgemeine Zeitung (1987, October 9) Die SPD-Fraktion spricht sich für Ausländerwahlrecht aus Penner: Auf Gemeinden begrenzt/'Nicht allein unter rechtlichen Gesichtspunkten betrachten'. Retrieved June 19, 2013 from FAZ archive.

[19]Frankfurter Allgemeine Zeitung (1987, October 15) SPD unzufrieden mit der Asylpolitik. Brandts Büroleiter stellt 'Jahrbuch der Stiftung für Flüchtlingshilfe' vor. Retrieved June 19, 2013 from FAZ archive.

[20]Frankfurter Allgemeine Zeitung (1988, March 2) Heftige Auseinandersetzung über Ausländerpolitik in der CDU. Sozialausschüsse fordern Erleichterung der Zuzugsmöglichkeiten/Kritik der innenpolitischen Arbeitsgruppe. Retrieved June 19, 2013 from FAZ archive.

[21]Frankfurter Allgemeine Zeitung (1988 March 9)Die Vorstellungen der Sozialausschüsse zum Ausländerrecht finden Anklang. Ein Brief von elf CDU-Abgeordneten/Widerspruch der Innenpolitiker. Retrieved June 19, 2013 from FAZ archive.

[22]Bannas, Guenter (1988, April 7) Beim Ausländerrecht langsam voran
    Programmkommission und Sozialausschüsse der CDU und die CSU auf verschiedenen Wegen. Retrieved June 19, 2013 from FAZ archive.

integration problems in 1984, the positions changed in 1988, when the CDU no longer saw multiculturalism as a threat or posing major challenges.[23]

The CDU reformulated substantial parts of its agenda and called for the integration of (former) guest workers and their family members in November 1988.[24] By the end of 1988, the CDU had revised most of its positions on repatriation, citizenship and the immigration of family members of (former) guest workers and proposed centrist, not to say liberal immigration and integration policies.[25]

While the CDU/CSU began to take over parts of the liberal SPD's agenda, the SPD clearly reaffirmed its multicultural profile at the end of the 1980s. The SPD called for a new immigration law based on 'humanitarian grounds', enabling migrants who had returned to their home country to claim a German residence permit and citizenship if they reconsidered their decision.[26] The SPD fraction in the Bundestag called for an 'Auslaenderwahlrecht' for migrants coming from countries that were part of the European Community (EG), while the board of the SPD demanded this right for migrants regardless of their home country[27]—immigration should be allowed in general, right of domicile granted after 8 years, and entitlement to citizenship after 10 years[28]; the asylum procedure should be further liberalized and asylum-seekers who could not return to their countries of origin granted residence permits.[29] A member of the SPD faction deeply involved in the party's multicultural agenda in December 1988 called for fostering and supporting measures to aid Germany's appearance as a multicultural society.[30]

The CDU reaffirmed its recently moderated course, following the SPD's calls, in 1989. The party still aimed for tighter asylum legislation, but now they also portrayed Germany as a multicultural and tolerant society.[31]

---

[23]Ibid.

[24]Frankfurter Allgemeine Zeitung (1988, November 4) Stimmen in der CDU für kommunales Wahlrecht der EG-Ausländer. Ausschuß-Beschluß zur Ausländer- und Asylpolitik/'Wird überarbeitet'. Retrieved June 19, 2013 from FAZ archive.

[25]Ibid.

[26]Frankfurter Allgemeine Zeitung (1988, March 4) SPD will Ausländerkindern Rückkehr erleichtern. Retrieved June 19, 2013 from FAZ archive.

[27]Frankfurter Allgemeine Zeitung (1988, March 10) SPD: Die Union soll Farbe bekennen. Kommunales Wahlrecht für EG-Ausländer?/Das Verfassungsrecht. Retrieved June 19, 2013 from FAZ archive.

[28]Frankfurter Allgemeine Zeitung (1988, June 30) Antrag der SPD zum Ausländerrecht. Retrieved June 19, 2013 from FAZ archive.

[29]Frankfurter Allgemeine Zeitung (1988, October 5) EG-Harmonisierung, aber nicht auf Kosten der Flüchtlinge. SPD-Antrag zum Asylrecht/Materielle Angleichung/Europäisches Flüchtlingsamt. Retrieved June 19, 2013 from FAZ archive.

[30]Frankfurter Allgemeine Zeitung (1988, December 2) Die SPD fordert Recht auf Niederlassung für Ausländer. Retrieved June 19, 2013 from FAZ archive.

[31]Frankfurter Allgemeine Zeitung (1989, January 17) CDU-Fachausschuß lehnt Einführung eines kommunalen Wahlrechts für Ausländer aus EG-Ländern ab Leitlinien zu Ausländer- und Asylpolitik beschlossen/Zuzug soll beschränkt werden. Retrieved June 19, 2013 from FAZ archive.

In January[32] and February 1989[33] the speaker for domestic affairs of the CDU faction in the German Bundestag, Johannes Gerster, accepted dual citizenship status for migrants in Germany. In April 1989, Hessen's CDU called for facilitating naturalization processes.[34] In the same month the proponent of a far more liberal agenda, Wolfgang Schaeuble (CDU), replaced Friedrich Zimmerman (CSU) as the head of the department for interior affairs and spiritus rector of the former repatriation programs. The CDU continued on this multicultural course, dropping its former conservative agenda almost entirely from 1988 on.

Meanwhile, the SPD was reaching its most pro-multicultural score, +7.1, and campaigned on its multicultural agenda with the highest salience score in West Germany until that time: the FAZ reports 48 SPD-claims for 1989 (annual average 1982–1988: 20). The chairperson of Hessen's SPD, Hans Krollmann, reaffirmed the SPD's desire to build a multicultural society in February 1989.[35] SPD factions—stemming both from regional parliaments and the Bundestag—demanded the 'Auslaenderwahlrecht'[36] and the facilitation of naturalization procedures,[37] the acceptance of Dual Citizenship[38] and work-entitlements for asylum-seekers.[39]

In stark contrast to the polarization between the SPD and the CDU/CSU in the years 1986–1987, during which the SPD embraced a clearly liberal and the CDU/CSU a clearly conservative agenda, the CDU/CSU dropped its positions almost entirely and came to share a large number of the SPD's standpoints. The years 1988–1989 were not only comprised of the highest salience values ever measured in West Germany with 175 and 245 annual claims respectively (compared with an annual average 1982–1987 of 78 claims) but also revealed the

---

[32]Ibid.

[33]Frankfurter Allgemeine Zeitung (1989, February 24) Entscheidung über Ausländerrecht vor Ostern Gerster: Einigung ist möglich/CDU-Kommission zum Asylrecht. Retrieved June 19, 2013 from FAZ archive.

[34]Frankfurter Allgemeine Zeitung (1989, April 15) Die hessische CDU will Einbürgerung von Ausländern erleichtern Vorschläge der Landtagsfraktion/Wahlrecht für Bürger der EG-Staaten. Retrieved June 19, 2013 from FAZ archive.

[35]Frankfurter Allgemeine Zeitung (1989, February 2) Hessen will das Aufnahmeverfahren für Asylbewerber beschleunigen. FDP-Minister Gerhardt warnt vor Wahlrecht für Ausländer. Retrieved June 19, 2013 from FAZ archive.

[36]Frankfurter Allgemeine Zeitung (1989, February 15) Kieler Landtag stimmt für Parlamentsreform. CDU gegen Volksinitiative und Volksbefragung/Ausländerwahlrecht. Retrieved June 19, 2013 from FAZ archive.

[37]Frankfurter Allgemeine Zeitung (1989, March 15) SPD legt Entwurf zum Ausländerrecht vor. 'Niederlassungsrecht' nach achtjährigem Aufenthalt. Retrieved June 19, 2013 from FAZ archive.

[38]Frankfurter Allgemeine Zeitung (1989, March 25) Die SPD legt einen Gesetzentwurf zur Einbürgerung von Ausländern vor. Rechtsanspruch auf Staatsbürgerschaft/Doppelstaatsangehörigkeit. Retrieved June 19, 2013 from FAZ archive.

[39]Frankfurter Allgemeine Zeitung (1989, September 7) SPD und CDU über Entwurf zum Ausländergesetz weitgehend einig. Sozialdemokraten wollen höheres 'Nachzugalter'/Abschluß der Haushaltsdebatte im Bundestag. Retrieved June 19, 2013 from FAZ archive.

CDU/CSU's centrist position of −0.4/−0.5 (the annual average 1982–1987 was −5.5) while the SPD retained its highly liberal position of +5.7/+7.1.

The years 1988–1989 showed the highest salience values of the 'Bonner Republik' and were, for the first time, characterized by a liberal, multicultural discourse on the part of the CDU/CSU and the SPD. The first federal election cast in this discursive climate was the election for the European Parliament in 1989. The populist radical right 'Die Republikaner' (REP) celebrated its first major advances, gathering 7.1%, while the CDU/CSU dropped to 37.7% (FDP: 5.6, SPD: 37.3, Die Gruenen: 8.4%). In following the SPD's liberal positions embracing multiculturalism in the salient debates of the years 1988–1989, the CDU/CSU opened the electoral niche the REP seized in 1989.

However, the CDU/CSU quickly dropped this multiculturalist profile entirely from 1990 onwards. Only two out of 28 CDU/CSU claims in 1990 embraced a liberal perspective on migration and integration. Instead, the CDU/CSU sharpened its conservative profile once more; the party secretary of the CSU characterized Germany as *not* a country of migration.[40] In August 1990 the former proponents of liberal asylum policies—Johannes Gerster and Alfons Mueller (both members of the CDU faction in the federal parliament) —openly called for a change of the German constitution to severely restrict the continued influx of asylum-seekers.[41]

Despite these rather limited claims, the CDU/CSU reclaimed its conservative position with a clear −4.5 in the 1990 election year. But it wasn't only the established German conservatives that changed course; so too did the SPD. The SPD dropped its highly liberal profile in 1989 (+7.1) and proclaimed a centrist +2.6 during the 1990 election year. Even more significantly, only half of the 40 SPD claims in this year were defined by a liberal evaluation of matters of immigration and integration while the integration topic almost completely vanished from the agenda: only 5 out of 40 SPD claims (25%) were concerned with integration; instead, 29 statements concerned asylum procedures (73%). Even more intriguingly, while the SPD defended the liberal asylum regime based on Article 16 and campaigned to extend it over the 1980s, the SPD candidate for chancellor in 1990—Oscar Lafontaine—openly pondered the implementation of constraints on asylum procedures.[42]

While the SPD dropped its liberal integration agenda almost entirely from its campaign for the federal elections in December 1990, the CDU/CSU likewise conceived no incentive to respond with liberal claims. In stark contrast to

[40]Frankfurter Allgemeine Zeitung (1990, May 12) Bei der Verabschiedung des Ausländerrechts Streit um das Wort 'Einwanderungsland'. Das Gesetz kann in Kraft treten/Die SPD bis zuletzt dagegen/'Übereilt'/Zweiter Durchgang im Bundesrat. Retrieved June 19, 2013 from FAZ archive.

[41]Frankfurter Allgemeine Zeitung (1990, August 7) In der SPD verschärft sich der Streit um das Asylrecht. Penner widerspricht Lafontaines Vorschlag/Osteuropa und die Dritte Welt. Retrieved June 19, 2013 from FAZ archive.

[42]Frankfurter Allgemeine Zeitung (1990, August 7) In der SPD verschärft sich der Streit um das Asylrecht. Penner widerspricht Lafontaines Vorschlag/Osteuropa und die Dritte Welt. Retrieved June 19, 2013 from FAZ archive.

1988–1989, the salience of immigration topics was remarkably lower in the 1990 election year (only 81 claims) while the liberal discourse of the years 1988–1989 was replaced by a clearly conservative position on the part of the CDU/CSU (−5.5) and centrist campaigning by the SPD (+2.6).

Under these circumstances it was very difficult for the REP to offer a unique selling point to German voters. To make mattes worse for the REP, the election campaign of 1990 stood in the light of German reunification. Helmut Kohl and his CDU fulfilled a decade-long pledge to reunite the country. The CDU could thus deliver on all key matters in which German conservative voters would be interested. The CDU/CSU won the election—despite its dire polling figures in the late 1980s—with 43.5% (FDP: 11.0, SPD: 33.5, Die Gruenen: 5.1%), and the REP only obtained 2.1%. Therefore, the coalition between the CDU/CSU and the FDP was reaffirmed. The conservative voters the CDU/CSU had mobilized over the course of the 1980s with conservative positions on integration matters opted for the REP in 1988–1989 because of the CDU/CSU's multicultural turn, while the SPD ran even more liberal campaigns in these years. These conservative voters rejoined Helmut Kohl's party (and the SPD) in 1990 because the CDU/CSU achieved reunification and again clearly rejected multiculturalism, while the SPD also dropped its multicultural agenda almost entirely.

The CDU/CSU continued on this conservative course in 1991. In stark contrast to 1988 and 1989, the CDU/CSU rejected the right to vote for non-German residents in municipal elections in 1991,[43] and affirmed their desire to change the liberal asylum law guaranteed by article 16 of the German constitution.[44] Dropping issues of integration from its agenda, the CDU/CSU focused almost all its public claims on the change of the asylum article in 1991: 71 out of 92 claims (84%) reported by the FAZ in this year concerned the asylum issue; only 15 dealt with the integration of migrants.

1991 marked the highest measured salience of the SPD until that time, with 103 SPD claims, because the party had a lot to discuss. Yet again, and in stark contrast to the 1980s, integration topics no longer played any role: only 4 out of 103 claims (4%) concerned topics of suffrage or the like. 88 claims (88%) dealt with the challenges of increased numbers of asylum-seekers. The SPD position remained at an ambivalent +2.1 while the party struggled over how to best handle the asylum issue.

With the number of asylum-seekers increasing and the CDU/CSU campaigning to amend article 16 of the German constitution, which safeguards the individual right to asylum in Germany, the SPD's internal struggles were heating up. The left

---

[43]Frankfurter Allgemeine Zeitung (1991, June 24) Die Union gegen Ausländerwahlrecht. Reaktionen auf die Forderungen Kinkels und der SPD. Retrieved June 19, 2013 from FAZ archive.

[44]Frankfurter Allgemeine Zeitung (1991, August 7) Neue Vorschläge der SPD zum Asylrecht. Quotierung/'Vorklärung'/Beschränkungen für Aussiedler. Retrieved June 19, 2013 from FAZ archive.

wing of the SPD wanted to avoid any changes to this paragraph,[45] while Ministerpraesidents of the SPD and representatives of municipalities especially, were calling for a tightening of asylum legislation.[46] Even the former candidate for chancellor and Ministerpraesident of the Saarland, Oscar Lafontaine, took a conservative position, calling for a radical departure from the liberal asylum regime.[47] The board of the SPD tried to reach a compromise between both camps, rejecting a change to the constitution, but calling for a tightening of asylum procedures.[48] The debates continued fiercely in 1992, a year in which the FAZ reports an all-time high of 460 (!) SPD claims. Yet again, integration topics were no longer of concern to the SPD, and least of all a multicultural agenda: only 15 out of 460 claims (3%) concerned matters of integration, while the SPD's overall position dropped to −0.4—the most conservative position measured since 1982. 402 claims (87%) concerned the asylum procedures.

While the debates among the SPD continued, asylum figures peaked at an all-time high in 1992 with 440,000 incoming asylum seekers (more than 0.54% of Germany's entire population of 80.6 million at the time; the highest ratio ever recorded by OECD statistics). The CDU/CSU campaigned on altering paragraph 16 almost exclusively: 322 out of 377 claims (85%) in 1992 concerned the change of the asylum law.

In August 1992, the SPD was nearing an agreement on changes to the asylum law. The so-called 'Turn of Petersberg'—'Petersberger Wende'—led to the SPD beginning negotiations with the CDU/CSU and the FDP in order to alter the German constitution on asylum matters, first and foremost concerning Article 16. Further, the SPD agreed on a limitation of immigration to Germany.[49]

---

[45]Frankfurter Allgemeine Zeitung (1991, August 7) Neue Vorschläge der SPD zum Asylrecht. Quotierung/'Vorklärung'/Beschränkungen für Aussiedler. Retrieved June 19, 2013 from FAZ archive. And Frankfurter Allgemeine Zeitung (1991, September 9) SPD schließt Grundgesetzänderung zur Straffung des Asylverfahrens nicht aus. Vor dem Parteiengespräch/ Lafontaine: Sammelstellen einrichten. Retrieved June 19, 2013 from FAZ archive.

[46]Frankfurter Allgemeine Zeitung (1991, August 24) Die SPD sieht Gemeinsamkeiten mit Schäuble in der Asylfrage. Weiterhin Meinungsverschiedenheiten über Grundgesetz-Änderung. Retrieved June 19, 2013 from FAZ archive. And Frankfurter Allgemeine Zeitung (1991, October 15) SPD und FDP lehnen die Vorschläge Schäubles zum Asylrecht ab. Kritik auch am Veröffentlichungstermin/Ein Brief des Innenministers an die Länder. Retrieved June 19, 2013 from FAZ archive. And Frankfurter Allgemeine Zeitung (1991, October 23) Union will weiter Verfassungsänderung Bohl schlägt SPD und FDP Gespräch über Asylpolitik vor. Retrieved June 19, 2013 from FAZ archive.

[47]Frankfurter Allgemeine Zeitung (1991, September 11) SPD schließt Grandgesetzänderung zur Straffung des Asylverfahrens nicht aus. Vor dem Parteiengespräch/Lafontaine: Sammelstellen einrichten. Retrieved June 19, 2013 from FAZ archive.

[48]Frankfurter Allgemeine Zeitung (1991, September 24) 'Das Grundrecht nicht antasten'. SPD-Präsidium zur Asyldebatte/Übereinstimmungen mit der FDP. Retrieved June 19, 2013 from FAZ archive.

[49]Frankfurter Allgemeine Sonntagszeitung (1992, August 23) Asyl und UN-Einsätze: Die SPD schwenkt um. Zu Gesetzesänderung bereit/CDU begrüßt Einlenken. Retrieved June 19, 2013 from FAZ archive.

The new party course remained highly contested, however. For instance, the SPD from Hessen opposed any changes to article 16.[50] The federal board of the SPD was, however, in support of the conservative turn.[51] Oscar Lafontaine even went one step further, doubting whether the German constitution should guarantee an individual's right to asylum at all.[52]

The negotiations with the CDU/CSU and the FDP ended in December 1992 with two changes to the German constitution reaching beyond the internal SPD agreements: the individual right to asylum was severely constrained and social support for successful applicants cut. The SPD was divided about accepting this agreement.[53] In December 1992, however, the SPD faction of the Bundestag accepted the compromise with a 101 to 64 majority.[54]

After the FDP and the SPD dropped their position and agreed to change the German constitution to reduce the number of asylum-seekers, the 'Asylkompromiss' was supported by the CDU/CSU, FDP and SPD alike on December 6, 1992.[55] Article 16 of the German constitution was changed with the support of more than two-thirds of the votes of the Bundestag and the Bundesrat in May 1993; opportunities to apply for asylum in Germany were significantly limited; and the number of asylum-seekers dropped from 440,000 in 1992 to around 100,000 per year in the subsequent years.

After these agreements, the SPD could have returned to its late 1980s multicultural agenda, but refrained from doing so. In 1993, 44 out of 59 claims (75%) concerned details of the new asylum laws while only 7 (12%) concerned questions of integration. The SPD's position remained centrist, with a score of +0.2. The multicultural SPD agenda from the late 1980s was gone.

Freed of a liberal opponent, the number of CDU/CSU claims dropped to 78 in 1993, with 67 (86%) complimenting the change in the asylum law or clarifying legal details. Matters of integration were not touched upon, save a few small

---

[50]Frankfurter Allgemeine Sonntagszeitung (1992, September 6) Hessens SPD: Absage an Engholm und Eichel. Mehrheit gegen Asylrechts-Änderung/Neuer CDU-Vorschlag. Retrieved June 19, 2013 from FAZ archive.

[51]Frankfurter Allgemeine Zeitung (1992, September 14) SPD-Vorstand zu Grundgesetzänderung beim Asylrecht bereit. Unterstützung für Engholms 'Petersberger Wende'/Klausurtagung/Sonderparteitag im November. Retrieved June 19, 2013 from FAZ archive.

[52]Frankfurter Allgemeine Zeitung (1992, September 17) Lafontaine will das individuelle Grundrecht auf Asyl abschaffen Der stellvertretende SPD Vorsitzende für das Schweizer Modell/Vorbild Genfer Konvention. Retrieved June 19, 2013 from FAZ archive.

[53]Frankfurter Allgemeine Zeitung (1992, December 15) Der SPD-Parteirat billigt den Bonner Asylkompromiß. Zugleich werden Nachbesserungen gefordert/Nach zähen Auseinandersetzungen. Retrieved June 19, 2013 from FAZ archive.

[54]Frankfurter Allgemeine Zeitung (1992, December 16) Die SPD-Fraktion stimmt dem Asylkompromiß zu. Verhandlungen mit Prag und Warschau gefordert/Die Union lehnt Nachbesserungen strikt ab. Retrieved June 19, 2013 from FAZ archive.

[55]Frankfurter Allgemeine Zeitung (1992, December 9) In der SPD zeichnet sich Zustimmung ab. Der Asylkompromiß/Diskussionen wird es noch geben. Retrieved June 19, 2013 from FAZ archive.

proposed changes to the German naturalization law, to enable migrants who had been living in Germany for 15 years, as well as their children (if born in Germany), to apply for German citizenship; the possibility of dual citizenship was fiercely rejected by the CDU/CSU.[56]

The decreasing salience and the conservative consensus between the CDU/CSU and SPD also characterized the 1994 election year. Before the election in October 1994 only 25 CDU/CSU claims were reported by the FAZ and were mainly concerned with the rejection of dual citizenship by the German Conservatives.[57] Before the federal election in 1994 only 15 SPD claims were reported by the FAZ. Again, the SPD did not campaign on a multicultural agenda. The party only very carefully touched upon immigration issues, supporting limited migration dependent on the economic resources at hand, the facilitation of naturalization and the possibilities of dual citizenship.[58]

The populist radical right party REP could only briefly benefit from the struggles between the CDU/CSU and the SPD in the early 1990s: the new party made some substantial advances in various regional elections in the early 1990s and polled at around 6% in the federal polls between the summer of 1992 and the spring of 1993. These few successful months were framed by the same discursive climate as the year 1989–1989: both the CDU/CSU and SPD were embracing a liberal profile in the highly salient debates over the change in the asylum law. However, both major parties dropped their liberal positions over the course of the debate and blocked the electoral niche for the REP beginning in spring 1993 (Fig. 8.4).

While the election for the European Parliament in 1989 was defined by the high salience of immigration-related issues, liberal discourse and significant vote gains for the populist radical right party REP, the federal election campaign in 1994 followed the same pattern as the 1990 campaign: immigration-related topics played little role, while the two most influential parties, the CDU/CSU and SPD, were largely in agreement on their conservative standpoints. As in 1990, the REP could find no niche in the electoral market and again failed to enter the Bundestag in October 1994. While the REP polled at 6.3% support at the end of 1992, the party's share was dropping to 3.7 by the end of 1993, and to only 1.9% at the federal election for the Bundestag in October 1994 (CDU/CSU: 41.4, FDP: 6.9, SPD: 36.4, Die Gruenen: 7.1%). The CDU/CSU and FDP coalition was reelected.

---

[56]Frankfurter Allgemeine Zeitung (1993, January 28) Koalition und SPD einig über Asyl-Gesetzentwurf. Länderlisten noch nicht endgültig/Ghana, Rumänien, Indien und Bulgarien 'verfolgungsfrei'? Retrieved June 19, 2013 from FAZ archive.

[57]Frankfurter Allgemeine Zeitung (1994, April 14) FDP bleibt der Abstimmung fern. Die Koalition uneins über doppelte Staatsbürgerschaft. Retrieved June 19, 2013 from FAZ archive.

[58]Frankfurter Allgemeine Zeitung (1994, July 8) Die SPD kündigt ein Einwanderungsgesetz an. Retrieved June 19, 2013 from FAZ archive.

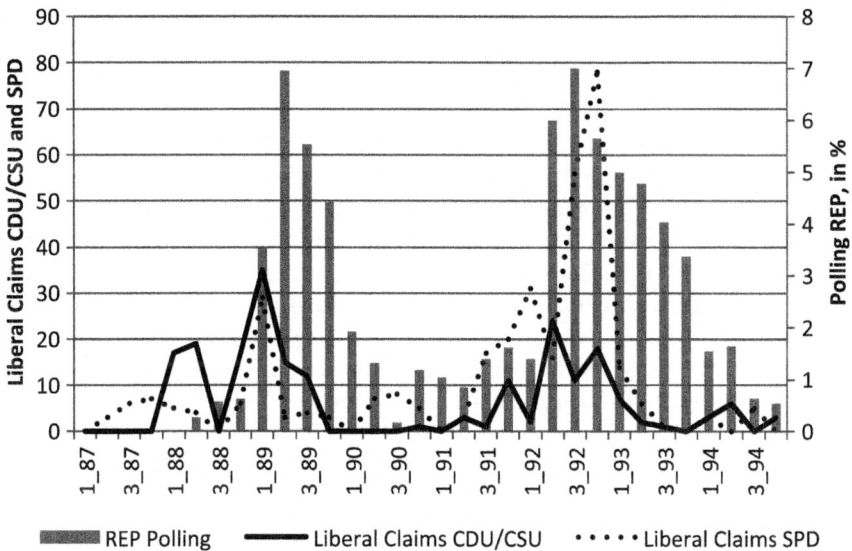

**Fig. 8.4** Liberal claims by CDU/CSU and SPD and polling of REP 1987–1994

The mid-1990s were marked by no major party conflicts over matters of integration and migration. In 1995, a few CDU/CSU politicians argued about the pros and cons of dual citizenship without altering the CDU/CSU's conservative position.[59] Party-internal struggles between liberal opponents and the conservative part of the CDU/CSU—among them the head of the department for domestic affairs, Manfred Kanther (CDU), who succeeded Rudolf Seiters and Wolfgang Schaeuble (both CDU) from 1993 on—persisted in 1996 that Germany is no country of immigration.[60]

The SPD also remained uncertain about its position on matters of immigration and integration. Debates lingered over the question of whether the SPD should call for a new immigration law.[61] In October 1995, the new chairperson of the SPD,

---

[59]Frankfurter Allgemeine Zeitung (1995, September 29) Koalition streitet über Ausländerrecht. Auch in der CDU Meinungsverschiedenheiten über den Kurs Kanthers. Retrieved June 19, 2013 from FAZ archive.

[60]Frankfurter Allgemeine Zeitung (1996, July 11) Begrenzt oder unbegrenzt? CDU-Politiker werben für Einwanderungsgesetz/Staatsbürgerschaft. Retrieved June 19, 2013 from FAZ archive.

[61]Frankfurter Allgemeine Zeitung (1995, September 13) Einwanderungsgesetz oder nicht? Unterschiedliche Haltungen in der SPD/Debatte in Mannheim. Retrieved June 19, 2013 from FAZ archive.

Rudolph Scharping, explained the lack of rigor surrounding the necessity to stop migration into Germany by alluding to the dire economic circumstances.[62]

In the summer of 1996 the CDU dropped the few liberal considerations left over from 1995 and mainly followed the CSU's rejection of dual citizenship.[63] While there were almost no immigration-related SPD claims in 1996, salience increased in 1997 with the SPD calling for immigration under the condition that it served the economic interests of Germany.[64] The party was, however, by no means reclaiming its former liberal position. On the contrary, the new rising star of the SPD—the Ministerpraesident of Niedersachsen, Gerhard Schroeder—even tried to outdo the German conservatives by calling for the expulsion of criminals without German citizenship.[65]

At its annual party meeting at Wildbad Kreuth in January 1997, the CSU reaffirmed its notion of Germany not being a country of immigration.[66] The head of the department for domestic affairs, Manfred Kanther (CDU), reaffirmed this view in April 1997.[67] Debates about dual citizenship among CDU/CSU members of parliament broke out again in the winter of 1997, but were cut off, as they had been in 1995, rejecting dual citizenship.[68]

---

[62]Frankfurter Allgemeine Zeitung (1995, October 6) Kommission verwirft Antrag des SPD-Vorstands Nun doch wieder ein Zuwanderungsgesetz? Nach Kritik aus der Partei/Lafontaine soll Leitantrag zur Beschäftigungspolitik formulieren. Retrieved June 19, 2013 from FAZ archive.

[63]Frankfurter Allgemeine Zeitung (1996, July 18) Die CSU bekräftigt Ablehnung der doppelten Staatsbürgerschaft. Glos: CDU darf wichtige Positionen nicht dem Zeitgeist opfern. Retrieved June 19, 2013 from FAZ archive.

[64]Frankfurter Allgemeine Zeitung (1997, June 6) Das Einwanderungsgesetz bleibt umstritten. Uneinigkeit in der Koalition/Grüne für Niederlassungsgesetz/Debatte im Bundestag. Retrieved June 19, 2013 from FAZ archive.

[65]Frankfurter Allgemeine Zeitung (1997, July 28) Schröder trifft auf Widerstand in der SPD. Streit um Aussagen zur Ausländerkriminalität/Lob der CSU. Retrieved June 19, 2013 from FAZ archive.

[66]Frankfurter Allgemeine Zeitung (1997, January 10) Die CSU will 'Anreize' für die Einwanderung beseitigen. Retrieved June 19, 2013 from FAZ archive.

[67]Frankfurter Allgemeine Zeitung (1997, April 11) FDP für Zuwanderungsgesetz noch in dieser Legislaturperiode. Einführung von Quoten/Union lehnt Vorschlag ab/Grüne befürchten Abschottung. Retrieved June 19, 2013 from FAZ archive.

[68]Frankfurter Allgemeine Zeitung (1997, Oktober 27) Weiterhin Uneinigkeit über doppelte Staatsbürgerschaft. Ablehnung in der Union, Zustimmung aus der FDP/Forderung nach Aufhebung des Fraktionszwangs. Retrieved June 19, 2013 from FAZ archive.

The 1998 election year saw the reaffirmation of these conservative standpoints: the CDU/CSU rejected dual citizenship,[69] cut financial support for asylum-seekers[70] and demanded the deportation of criminal non-German residents[71]—the CDU/CSU position was clearly conservative, scoring −7.6 in 1998.

In contrast with its conduct in the 1980s, the SPD avoided polarization over immigration matters and did not take a clearly liberal position during the 1998 election year. Even though the SPD took a clear position throughout 1998 (35 claims are reported before the Bundestagswahl in September 1998 and 25 after the victory of the red-green coalition between the SPD and Die Gruenen on September 27), the SPD continued to campaign on a centrist agenda, and consciously denied a multicultural profile. The future chancellor, Gerhard Schroeder (SPD), supported cuts in social support for asylum-seekers denied permanent residency before the federal election in summer 1998.[72] Instead of supporting dual citizenship, the party primarily aimed to facilitate naturalization processes.[73] After forming a coalition with Die Gruenen, the SPD aimed for only modest changes in the naturalization process.[74]

Chancellor Gerhard Schroeder (SPD), as well as the new head of the department for interior affairs, Otto Schily (SPD), both clearly rejected increasing immigration.[75] With scores of +2.3 and +1.3, respectively, the SPD held a clearly centrist position before the 1998 election, and throughout the entire year of 1998. With the electoral niche on the right closed (CDU/CSU: −7.6), the REP again failed to enter

---

[69]Frankfurter Allgemeine Zeitung (1998, March 28) Die Koalition lehnt die erleichterte Einbürgerung von Ausländerkindern ab. SPD-Entwurf gescheitert/Westerwelle: Mit der FDP keine wechselnden Mehrheiten/Enthaltungen. Retrieved June 19, 2013 from FAZ archive.

[70]Frankfurter Allgemeine Zeitung (1998, June 22) SPD streitet weiter über Leistungen für Asylbewerber. Retrieved June 19, 2013 from FAZ archive.

[71]Frankfurter Allgemeine Zeitung (1998, August 18) Scholz: Bessere Integration von Einwanderungswilligen erfordert schärfere Bekämpfung der Ausländerkriminalität. CDU-Rechtspolitiker fordert Abschaffung des Grundrechts auf Asyl/'Magnetwirkung' beenden. Retrieved June 19, 2013 from FAZ archive.

[72]Frankfurter Allgemeine Zeitung (1998, June 19) Die Mehrheit der FDP für das Asylbewerberleistungsgesetz. Abstimmung verschoben/SPD-Fraktion gegen den Entwurf/ 'Mißbrauchsvorwurf zum Teil nicht gerechtfertigt' Retrieved June 19, 2013 from FAZ archive. And Frankfurter Allgemeine Zeitung (1998, June 22) SPD streitet weiter über Leistungen für Asylbewerber. Retrieved June 19, 2013 from FAZ archive.

[73]Frankfurter Allgemeine Zeitung (1998, July 16) SPD will nach Wahlsieg in drei Monaten Ausländerrecht ändern. Retrieved June 19, 2013 from FAZ archive.

[74]Frankfurter Allgemeine Zeitung (1998, October 15) Die SPD setzt sich in der Innen- und Rechtspolitik durch. Keine Legalisierung weicher Rauschgifte/Deutscher Paß für Ausländer dritter Generation. Retrieved June 19, 2013 from FAZ archive.

[75]Frankfurter Allgemeine Zeitung (1998, November 18) Schilys Äußerung zur Zuwanderung belebt die Diskussion um eine gesetzliche Regelung. FDP will Gesetzentwurf wieder vorlegen/ Lob und Tadel für den Innenminister aus der Koalition. Retrieved June 19, 2013 from FAZ archive.
And Frankfurter Allgemeine Zeitung (1998, November 26) Gruene kritisieren Schroeders Aeusserungen zur Auslaenderpolitik. Retrieved June 19, 2013 from FAZ archive.

the Bundestag with only 1.8% at the federal election in September 1998. The CDU/CSU could not continue its coalition with the FDP due to the SPD's remarkable vote gains (CDU/CSU: 35.1, FDP: 6.2, SPD: 40.9. Die Gruenen: 6.7, PDS: 5.1%). A red-green coalition was formed and took office for the first time in German history in the autumn of 1998.

The year 1999 was characterized by a very low salience of immigration issues on the part of the CDU/CSU, with 23 out 25 claims (92%) focusing on the rejection of dual citizenship as proposed by the red-green coalition of the SPD and Die Gruenen. The lion's share of these claims came in January and February, accompanying the 'Unterschriftenkampagne gegen Doppelte Staatsbuergeschaft' initiated by the CDU/CSU.[76] This campaign dominated a pivotal election in the federal state of Hessen in 1999; a CDU victory in this state would have deprived the red-green government of a majority in the second German chamber—the Bundesrat—preventing the SPD and Die Gruenen from implementing dual citizenship. The CDU won this election easily and forced the red-green coalition to compromise with the Liberals (FDP) in order to achieve a majority in both German chambers. These consultations resulted in the so-called 'Optionsmodell', significantly constraining the possibility of dual citizenship. It is important to note that immigration-related claims by the SPD were rare in 1999; the attempt to implement dual citizenship was barely mentioned by SPD politicians. The issue, as well as the liberal position the party was forced to drop, seemed of little importance to the SPD.

The picture changed in the year that followed. The salience of immigration topics took off in the year 2000—while 1999 only saw 25 claims, the CDU/CSU placed 128 in the following year. Curiously, this was the first year since the late 1980s in which the CDU/CSU had taken clear positions on a variety of immigration-related issues. The CDU rejected the immigration of highly-skilled migrants proposed by the red-green coalition,[77] pondered another change to the asylum paragraph in the German constitution[78] and outlined its demands for an immigration law. For the first time since 1989, the CDU/CSU clearly defined its position on matters of integration, too. While the CDU/CSU was campaigning on defining Germany as a multicultural and tolerant society in 1988–1989, the conservatives proclaimed a 'Deutsche Leitkultur' ('German Guiding Culture') as the primary principle for the integration of migrants in Germany in November 2001. Integration into German society was supposed to be based on acquiring the language and accepting the constitution, laws and social rules of Germany; particular

---

[76]Frankfurter Allgemeine Zeitung (1999, January 18) CDU wertet Unterschriftenaktion als 'Riesenerfolg'. Auseinandersetzungen über die Ausländerpolitik in hessischen Städten/Kritik der SPD. Retrieved June 19, 2013 from FAZ archive.

[77]Frankfurter Allgemeine Zeitung (2000, April 4) CDU und CSU fordern Beschränkung des Asylrechts. Innenminister der Länder stellen Positionspapier vor/Verfahren sollen beschleunigt werden. Retrieved June 19, 2013 from FAZ archive.

[78]Frankfurter Allgemeine Zeitung (2000, May 16) SPD und CDU sehen Chance für Konsens in Ausländerpolitik. Eine Folge der 'wirkungsmächtigen' Rede des Bundespräsidenten/Gründliche Debatte gefordert. Retrieved June 19, 2013 from FAZ archive.

emphasis was placed on the importance of the Christian heritage on which Germany was assumed to be built.[79]

Salience also increased in 2000 with the SPD, but in accordance with rather than in opposition to the conservative claims of the CDU/CSU. The SPD emphasized the need for a stricter asylum procedure,[80] doubted the necessity of a new immigration law,[81] and stressed the rejection of multiculturalism; according to Chancellor Schroeder migrants were obligated to respect the constitution and laws as much as master the German language.[82] Instead of proposing new legislations, the SPD entrusted to an independent commission the drafting of new legislation on matters of migration and integration, which was led by a member of the Conservatives (!), Rita Suessmuth (CDU).[83] As the commission presented its results during the summer of 2001, the SPD and Die Gruene aimed for a party-spanning consensus.[84]

The head of the department of domestic affairs—Otto Schily (SPD)—appreciated the recommendations of the independent commission, but reformulated them more restrictively. He underscored the necessity of restricting immigration and the conditions that allowed it, while leaving the asylum law basically intact and making language and integration courses compulsory for new migrants.[85]

The newly drafted law passed the Bundestag on March 1, 2002, and the Bundesrat on March 22. Due to unclear voting behavior in the grand coalition between the SPD and the CDU/CSU in the federal state of Brandenburg, the German Constitutional Court rejected the vote in the Bundesrat on December 18, 2002, triggering a renegotiation between the SPD and the CDU/CSU. Before the federal election in September 2002, the SPD did not campaign on immigration-

---

[79]Frankfurter Allgemeine Zeitung (2000, November 7) 'Der Begriff irritiert den Gegner, was schon mal gut ist'. Die CDU-Führung verständigt sich auf Grundaussagen zur Zuwanderung/ 'Leitkultur in Deutschland'. Retrieved June 19, 2013 from FAZ archive.

[80]Frankfurter Allgemeine Zeitung (2000, July 12) Schily: Kommission soll frei von Tabus taetig werden. Aenderung des Asylverfahrens? Bosbach: CDU legt im Fruejahr Vorschlaege zur Einwanderung vor. Retrieved June 19, 2013 from FAZ archive.

[81]Frankfurter Allgemeine Zeitung (2000, October 15) Zu sensibel fuer den Wahlkampf? Die CDU diskutiert ueber den Umgang mit dem Thema Auslaenderpolitik. Retrieved June 19, 2013 from FAZ archive.

[82]Frankfurter Allgemeine Zeitung (2000, November 5) Meyer will Debatte ueber „Nation' und „Patriotismus' Schroeder ermahnt „Eiferer' zu Toleranz/CDU beraet ueber Zuwanderung/Mueller regt Volksabstimmung an. Retrieved June 19, 2013 from FAZ archive.

[83]Frankfurter Allgemeine Zeitung (2000, July 12) Schily: Kommission soll frei von Tabus taetig werden. Aenderung des Asylverfahrens? Bosbach: CDU legt im Fruejahr Vorschlaege zur Einwanderung vor. Retrieved June 19, 2013 from FAZ archive.

[84]Frankfurter Allgemeine Zeitung (2001, May 29) Die Union lehnt eine „Konsensrunde' zur Zuwanderungspolitik ab. Merz: SPD und Gruene sollen zunaechst Gesetzentwurf vorlege/Struck lobt Mueller. Retrieved June 19, 2013 from FAZ archive.

[85]Frankfurter Allgemeine Zeitung (2001, November 5) Nach dem Kompromiss in der Koalition sucht Schily wieder die Stimmen der Union. Zugestaendnisse an Gruene beim Einwanderungsgesetz/CDU und CSU reagieren abweisend. Retrieved June 19, 2013 from FAZ archive.

related issues; the FAZ reports only 17 SPD claims between January and September. Instead, the SPD emphasized its willingness to regulate immigration, mainly in the interests of the German economy, and to aim for a compromise with the German Conservatives.[86]

As the SPD decreased its willingness to mobilize on immigration-related issues in opposition to the CDU/CSU beginning in 2002, the CDU/CSU did the same. While the CDU/CSU used 66 of 128 claims (52%) in 2001 to define its new integration concept of a 'Deutsche Leitkultur', clearly rejecting multiculturalism, these efforts decreased remarkably during the 2002 election year. At the time of the election in September, only 28 claims on matters of immigration and integration were reported by the FAZ, with 47 for the entire year; these focused mainly on the alleged failure and the rejection of multiculturalism.[87]

As in all other elections in reunified Germany, immigration-related issues were not a topic during the election campaigns in 2002, and the salience of immigration issues remained remarkably low throughout the election year. While the CDU/CSU's position scored a clearly conservative $-2.9$, the SPD continued to embrace its centrist profile with a $+2.1$. Again, the niche for a new electoral competitor on the right remained closed; the 2002 election resulted in an unexpected reaffirmation of the red-green coalition that countered its devastating polling figures in the months before the election, while the REP won less than 2.0% voter support (SPD: 38.5, Die Gruenen: 9.4, CDU/CSU: 38.5, FDP: 7.6, PDS: 4.1%)—preventing its entry to the parliament.

Regardless of the loss at the federal election, the salience of immigration issues for the CDU/CSU further decreased significantly in 2003. The CSU gave its annual plea for the limitation of immigration at Wildbad Kreuth in January[88] and the CDU/CSU rejected a draft for a new immigration law proposed by the red-green coalition in March.[89] Debates about this law—the SPD was keen on drafting in agreement with the CDU/CSU—also dominated the spring and summer of 2004:

---

[86]Frankfurter Allgemeine Zeitung (2002, March 1) Der Bundestag stimmt dem Einwanderungsgesetz zu. Drei Abtruennige bei der CDU/„Union verhandlungsbereit'/ Entscheidung am 22. Maerz im Bundesrat. Retrieved June 19, 2013 from FAZ archive.

[87]Frankfurter Allgemeine Zeitung (2002, September 10) CDU nennt 'multikulturelle Harmonie' Selbsttäuschung. Forderungen der Wertekommission: Westen soll seine Werte gegenüber dem Islam offensiv vertreten. Retrieved June 19, 2013 from FAZ archive.

[88]Frankfurter Allgemeine Zeitung (2003, January 6) Wulff: Zuwanderung in den Wahlkampf. Vorschläge der CSU/Rau appelliert an die Parteien.

[89]Frankfurter Allgemeine Zeitung (2003, March 14) Keine Annäherung im Streit über die Einwanderung. Erste Lesung des unveränderten Gesetzentwurfs/Union auch gegen FDP-Kompromiß. Retrieved June 19, 2013 from FAZ archive.

the CDU/CSU demanded clear rules for the deportation of highly criminal migrants, restrictive asylum laws, a security check before naturalization by the German secret services, free language and integration courses for migrants and the possibility of delaying or withdrawing residence permits in case immigrants did not adhere to the outlined legislation.[90]

After negotiation among all German parties, the Bundestag and the Bundesrat accepted a new law in the summer of 2004. The SPD omitted any liberal demands and accepted the conservatives' immigration reforms.[91] Consequently, the position of the SPD on immigration-related matters in 2004 was the most conservative ever measured: −4.4.

After the new law passed the Bundestag in August 2004 with the votes of the CDU/CSU, the conservative party focused on the question of patriotism and national identity in times of migration. The Ministerpraesident of Hessen, Roland Koch (CDU) and the chairperson of the CDU, Angela Merkel, defined the German constitution, the German language and the rejection of multiculturalism as guiding principles of integration into the German society. In 2005, the red-green coalition called for 'vorgezogene Neuwahlen' due to the loss of their majority in the most important federal state, Nordrhein-Westphalen, after the regional election in May 2005. The year 2005 saw very few SPD claims, among them a clear rejection of the general acceptance of dual citizenship.[92] Again, neither a topic nor a liberal discourse was present that would enable a populist radical right party to advance. The federal election resulted in a stalemate between the camps of the SPD and Die Gruenen on one side, and the CDU/CSU and the FDP on the other (SPD: 34.2, Die Gruenen: 8.1, CDU/CSU: 35.2, FDP: 9.8, PDS/Die Linke: 8.7%). A grand coalition between the CDU/CSU and the SPD was formed; Angela Merkel (CDU) was elected chancellor on November 22, 2005.

Immigration-related issues remained off the political agenda in 2005. The topic returned in 2006 in debates about the preconditions for naturalization in general, and the details of a naturalization test in particular. The head of the department of

---

[90]Frankfurter Allgemeine Zeitung (2004, May 26) SPD und Union 'im Grundsatz' einig über ein Einwanderungsgesetz. Schröder: Fortschritt/Merkel: Große Bandbreite/Bis zum 30. Juni im Vermittlungsausschuß. Retrieved June 19, 2013 from FAZ archive.

[91]Frankfurter Allgemeine Zeitung (2004, May 25) SPD und Union „im Grundsatz' einig ueber ein Einwanderungsgesetz. Schroeder: Fortschritt/Merkel: Grosse Bandbreite/Bis zum 30. Juni im Vermittlungsausschuss. Retrieved June 19, 2013 from FAZ archive.

[92]Frankfurter Allgemeine Zeitung (2005, Ferbuary 7) 48,000 Tuerkischstaemmige verlieren deutschen Pass. Illegale doppelte Staatsbuergerschaft/SPD-Politikerin fuer erleichterte Wiedereinbuergerin/Schily dagegen. Retrieved June 19, 2013 from FAZ archive.

domestic affairs—Wolfang Schaeuble (CDU)—emphasized the importance of migration and naturalization if immigrants integrated according to the benchmarks set by German authorities.[93]

The CSU's position was more conservative, and clearly placed the responsibility of integration fully on the migrant.[94] During the grand coalition between the CDU/CSU and SPD from 2005 to 2009, the Social Democrats made no liberal claims, save the call for highly skilled migrants to have easier access to the country in 2006.[95]

In 2007, the CDU formulated a new basic program that was to be a foundation for all future election campaigns. The foundations of the CDU's integration agenda were: the German Leading Culture ('Deutsche Leitkultur'), patriotism, national pride based on German history, rejection of 'parallel societies' ('Parallelgesellschaften') and the dismissal of the right to cultural difference if it constitutes a threat to the basic principles of democracy and human rights.[96] Save an election campaign of the CDU in Hessen, with a discussion of criminal youth with migration backgrounds,[97] 2008 lacked any immigration-related claims, as did 2009.

The SPD experienced dramatic losses in the election for the federal parliament in September 2009, and marked the end of the grand coalition (CDU/CSU: 33.8, FDP: 14.6, SPD: 23.0, Die Gruenen: 10.7, Die Linke: 11.9%); a new government was formed between the CDU/CSU and the FDP.

The integration topic reentered German party discourse in 2010 when a book was published by Thilo Sarrazin claiming that German integration policy was, in general, a failure and that the country was being held back due to the lower educational and 'intelligence' levels of migrants ('Deutschland schafft sich ab. Wie wir unser Land aufs Spiel setzen'). The reaction of the CDU/CSU lacked any direct references to Thilo Sarrazin and consisted of very few statements: only 26 claims were measured in 2010—far fewer than the annual average (1982–2012) of 56. They all shared the same tone concerning migration and integration: future

---

[93]Frankfurter Allgemeine Zeitung (2006, April 10) Die große Koalition streitet über die Integration von Ausländern. Platzeck: Gedankenlose Reflexe/Stoiber: Rot-grüne Fesseln der Vergangenheit. Retrieved June 19, 2013 from FAZ archive.

[94]Ibid.

[95]Frankfurter Allgemeine Zeitung (2006, August 7) Erleichterte Einwanderung fuer „Spitzenkraefte'. Wiefelspuetz: Union und SPD einig/Gesetzentwurf schon im September. Retrieved June 19, 2013 from FAZ archive.

[96]Frankfurter Allgemeine Zeitung (2007, February 28) 'Schwarz-Rot-Gold ohne Überheblichkeit'. Begriff der Leitkultur soll in das neue CDU-Programm/Integration als Zukunftsaufgabe. Retrieved June 19, 2013 from FAZ archive. And Frankfurter Allgemeine Zeitung (2007, May 5) CDU sieht Ehe und Familie weiter als 'Fundament der Gesellschaft'. Pofallas Programmentwurf/'Deutschland ist Integrationsland'. Retrieved June 19, 2013 from FAZ archive.

[97]Holl, Thomas/Lohse, Eckart (2008, January 13) Welche Angst der Bürger wiegt schwerer? Ausländerkriminalität contra Mindestlohn. Roland Koch hat vorerst die Diskussionshoheit an sich gerissen. Doch die SPD holt auf. Retrieved June 19, 2013 from FAZ archive.

migration shall mainly be based on the demands of the German economy, while migrants who refuse to integrate into German society or to acquire sufficient language skills will face harsh sanctions (e.g. cuts in welfare benefits, deprivation of residence permits).[98] The Social Democrats also responded with very few claims (the FAZ reports only 7 SPD claims in 2010) and did not take a clearly liberal position against Thilo Sarrazin's claims. The SPD's chairman Sigmar Gabriel affirmed the party's conservative position in integration matters.[99]

Thus, the Sarrazin debate was characterized by the same conduct on the part of the two largest German parties that had prevented the entrenchment of a PRRP since 1990: the high salience periods 1992–1993 and 2000–2001 showed the CDU/CSU in a clearly conservative position and the SPD lacking a multicultural profile, keeping the electoral niche for a populist radical right party closed. Since 2002, both parties have attributed a very low salience to the matter and kept their conservative profiles. As a result, neither a topic has been substantially politicized, nor an electoral niche opened for a new PRRP contender.

In May 2011, the SPD announced that it was going to try to install a 15% quota for party members with migration backgrounds in all Social Democratic leading bodies.[100] 2012 lacked SPD claims on the federal level. In the same year the CDU/CSU/FDP coalition also granted migrants from non-EU countries easier access to the German job-market—approaching a quota system similar to Canada's.[101]

The conservatives' position in 2012 was rather centrist (−0.7), and only immigration topics were mentioned; their position on integration-related topics remained conservative. In contrast to 1988–1989, multiculturalism was strongly rejected, and the main responsibility for integration placed on the migrants' shoulders. Still, the electoral niche for a populist radical right party in Germany became open from 2011 for the first time since 1988–1989. As outlined by the two-level theory, however, the extremely low salience of immigration-related topics in the German party discourse prevented the electoral advances of a PRRP party up until Eurozone issues were discussed vividly from 2012 onwards (see Chap. 9).

---

[98]Frankfurter Allgemeine Zeitung (2010, October 12) Frau Böhmer schockiert über Seehofer. Kanzlerin stützt CSU-Politiker/'Zuwanderungsstopp'. Retrieved June 19, 2013 from FAZ archive. And Klöckner verlangt 'null Toleranz' gegenüber Integrationsverweigerern. Papier der CDU-Spitzenkandidatin/Für Punktesystem. Retrieved June 19, 2013 from FAZ archive.

[99]Frankfurter Allgemeine Zeitung (2010, September 24) SPD will Integration erzwingen. Retrieved June 19, 2013 from FAZ archive.

[100]Frankfurter Allgemeine Zeitung (2011, May 11) SPD-Vorstand beschliesst Einwanderquote. In allen Fuehrungsgremien der Partei 15 Prozent/Weiter Streit ueber Sarrazin. Retrieved June 19, 2013 from FAZ archive.

[101]Frankfurter Allgemeine Zeitung (2012, March 29) Schwarz-Gelb will Einwanderung von Fachkräften erleichtern. Visum für Arbeitssuche/Niedrigere Verdienstschwellen/FDP: Einstieg in Punktesystem. Retrieved June 19, 2013 from FAZ archive.

## 8.3    Applauding Multiculturalism in Public? Only If the CDU/CSU Has to!

Considering the examples given, the years 1988–1989 are the only ones in which the CDU/CSU campaigned on a centrist position during salient debates on immigration and integration; at the end of the 1980s, the CDU/CSU joined the liberal discourse driven by the SPD, in turn enabling the electoral advances of the populist radical right party 'Die Republikaner' (REP). So how can we account for this unique change in the CDU/CSU's agenda in 1988–1989? According to the two-level theory, and in comparison to party interactions in the Netherlands and Sweden, the years 1988–1989 should have been the only period with a successful left camp in a society free of economic concerns. Does this combination exist only in these 2 years in Germany—despite the 30 years under scrutiny?

As outlined in the section on variation in CDU/CSU salience, the years 1988–1989 were not particularly high ones for threat potential in (West) Germany. The total inflow of migrants and asylum seekers increased throughout the 1980s; therefore, the *actual* cultural threat remained high in 1988–1989, while the German Politbarometer did not indicate any great cultural threat *perception* on the part of German voters in the late 1980s. The unemployment rate remained low throughout the 1980s, with correspondingly low rates of socio-economic concerns. Thus neither the *actual* economic threat nor the economic threat *perception* differed in 1988–1989 from the rest of the 1980s (Fig. 8.1). As with the variation in salience of the CDU/CSU, party rationale is also better suited to account for variation in the conservatives' position, because the years 1988–1989 were a unique situation in German party discourse: they were the only 2 years in which the SPD campaigned on a clearly multicultural agenda *while* polling far ahead of the CDU/CSU (Fig. 8.5).

Considering the CDU/CSU's extremely low polling figures in the late 1980s, when facing a highly successful social democratic contender with a clearly multicultural agenda, it was only logical for the CDU/CSU to embrace parts of the SPD's campaigns as the conservatives fell far behind the center-left parties in 1988–1989. This adoption transformed the CDU/CSU's position from clearly conservative to a centrist agenda with strong multicultural elements; conservative voters the conservatives mobilized in the 1980s therefore opted for the clearly conservative position which—in the late 1980s—was being offered only by the populist REP.

The SPD campaigned on a multicultural agenda after 1984, but only in 1988 and 1989 did the party poll far ahead of the CDU/CSU. Therefore, an earlier liberalization in the conservatives' position did not promise any vote gains. The breakthrough of the populist REP took place in the only federal election in which the CDU/CSU did not campaign on a clearly conservative position in matters of immigration and integration, but joined the liberal discourse, propelled by the liberal SPD: the election for the European Parliament in 1989.

A reasonable explanation of how the CDU/CSU was able to oust the REP from 1990 on was the SPD's dropping of its multicultural agenda over the course of the

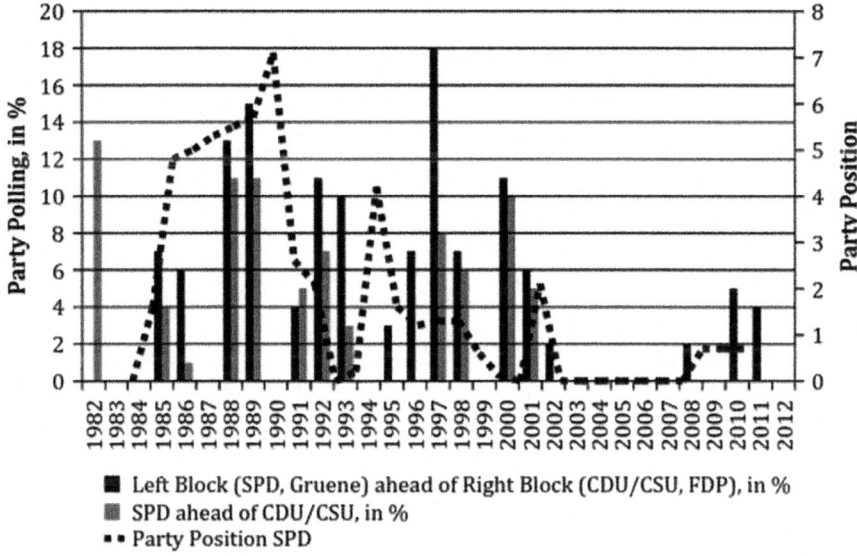

- ■ Left Block (SPD, Gruene) ahead of Right Block (CDU/CSU, FDP), in %
- ▨ SPD ahead of CDU/CSU, in %
- ■ ■ Party Position SPD

**Fig. 8.5**  Polling of SPD and Left block and SPD's position 1982–2012

early 1990s. The CDU/CSU had no motivation to make any multicultural claims in the German discourse; this enabled the party to regain and keep its conservative profile and to reclaim the conservative voters it had previously lost to the REP. By not campaigning on multiculturalism, the SPD could also reclaim conservative voters (Fig. 8.4). The SPD fared well ahead of the CDU/CSU between 1997 and 2000, too—but unlike in the late 1980s, in the late 1990s the SPD was no longer campaigning on multicultural positions. Accordingly, and despite its low polling figures, the CDU/CSU perceived no incentive to alter its conservative position on immigration-related matters. The SPD had refrained from a clear-cut multicultural and liberal agenda after 1989, in turn freeing the CDU/CSU from incentives to alter its agenda on integration and immigration in salient party debates, and keeping the electoral space for a populist radical right party closed from 1990 (Table 8.2).

## 8.4  First the Grub, Then the Morals: The SPD and Multiculturalism

Finally, the question arises as to why the SPD embraced a clearly multicultural profile in favor of migrants' interests from 1983 to 1989. And why did the SPD notably change its agenda from 1990 on, offering no incentives for the CDU/CSU to alter its conservative position, and keeping the electoral niche closed for a PRRP? In revisiting the previous chapters and deciphering CDU/CSU salience and positioning, the question of which factors constituted the prime difference

**Table 8.2** Brief overview of German parties' positions on matters of integration and immigration and advances of populist radical right party (1982–2012)

| | 1982–1987 | 1988–1989 | 1990–2012 |
|---|---|---|---|
| **CDU/CSU** | | | |
| Immigration | Germany no country of immigration | Germany an open, tolerant country | Immigration mainly catering to interests of German economy |
| Integration | Repatriation of guest workers, stop of influx | Multiculturalism | Rejection of multiculturalism, responsibility for integration mainly migrants' obligation |
| Citizenship | Rejection of dual citizenship | Appreciation of dual citizenship | Rejection of dual citizenship |
| Asylum | Change to paragraph 16 | Change to paragraph 16 | Change to paragraph 16, no liberalization of asylum-procedure |
| **SPD** | | | |
| Immigration | Immigration on humanitarian grounds | Immigration on humanitarian grounds | Immigration catering mainly to interests of German economy |
| Integration | Appreciation of multiculturalism, affirmative action in order to integrate guest workers and their families, influx | Appreciation of multiculturalism, affirmative action in order to integrate guest workers and their families, influx | No campaigns on multiculturalism, only limited measures of affirmative action |
| Citizenship | Calling for dual citizenship | Calling for dual citizenship | Calling for dual citizenship, but acceptance of compromise from 1999 on |
| Asylum | No change to paragraph 16, rather extension | No change to paragraph 16, rather extension | Agreeing on change to paragraph 16 |
| Advances of populist radical right party (REP and/or PRO) | | | |
| | – | 7.1% Europawahl 1989 | 1.5–2.0% (annual average) |

between German party discourse in 1983–1989 and 1990–2012 remains. The two-level theory suggests that the strength of the left camp of German politics (SPD and Gruene) and the good economic situation produced a unique combination in the mid- and late 1980s. As described in the chapter on salience, the inflow of migrants and asylum-seekers into Germany steadily increased over the course of the 1980s, and—save for 1991 and 1992—has remained stable since 1987 at around 600,000 arrivals per year. Therefore, *actual* cultural threat cannot explain the SPD's turn from 1990 on. The *perception* of a cultural threat, according to Politbarometer surveys, peaked in the early 1990s with up to 40% of German voters concerned with integration, asylum and immigration to Germany; these numbers have dropped since 1995, however, at an annual average of 5–10%, and can therefore not account for the SPD's lack of a multicultural agenda since the mid-1990s (Fig. 8.1).

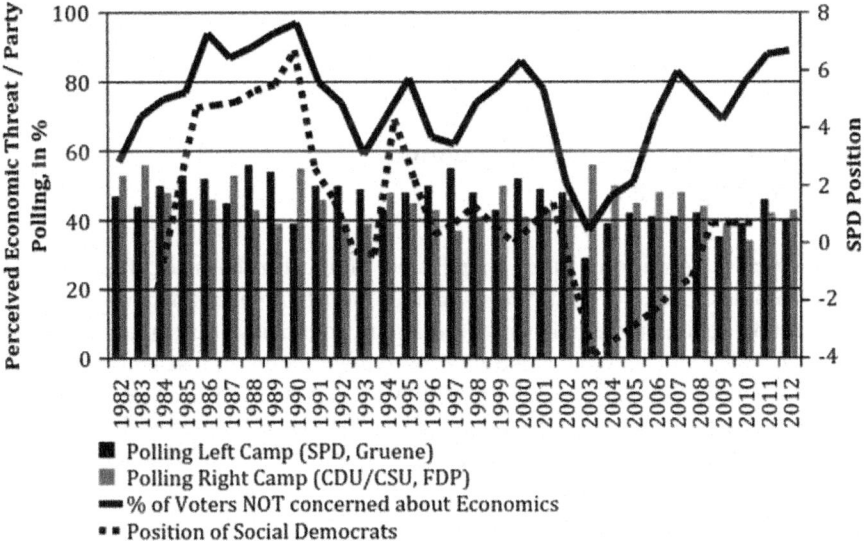

**Fig. 8.6** SPD position and economic threat potential

However, the economic sphere changed dramatically from 1983 to 1989 and 1990 to 2012. The *actual* economic threat increased substantially from the 1990s on; in stark contrast to the 1980s, unemployment rates rose in the 'Berliner Republik'. This change is clearly visible in the perceptions of economic threat: while only 5–10% of German voters conceived an economic threat in the 1980s, these figures rose to around 30% in the 1990s and even 50% in the 2000s. These dire numbers alone could account for the ambivalent SPD positions after 1990, if the German public had not believed the economic climate to be stable since the late 2000s. This change in the perception of the economic situation in Germany has not yet led the SPD to openly campaign on multiculturalism, but how come? The 1980s were not only characterized by a benign economic climate, they were also *the only time* in which the left camp of German politics (SPD, Gruene) steadily polled ahead of the center-right parties (CDU/CSU, FDP). While the economic climate in Germany since 2010 might approximate the benevolence of the 1980s, the weakness of the German mid-left camp still prevents the SPD from openly campaigning with multicultural agendas (Figs. 8.1 and 8.6).

The two necessary conditions the two-level theory outlines for a salient multicultural agenda (first and foremost driven by the Social Democrats)—a successful left camp and a society free of economic concerns—can only be found in Germany up to 1990. This explains the lack of a pronounced multicultural agenda on the part of the SPD since. Either the German voters conceived of a high economic threat, or a strong bourgeois camp dominated politics; each was sufficient to prevent a salient multicultural agenda from being introduced by the strongest German center-left party, the SPD[102] (Fig. 8.6).


## 8.5  Summary: Are Dire Economics Good or Bad for Migrants?

The German case illustrates the generalizable political mechanism. The German conservatives CDU/CSU politicize immigration-related topics whenever they are significantly behind in the polls and need a topic to mobilize conservative voters. The CDU/CSU will only moderate its conservative profile in a salient debate, in turn opening an electoral niche on the right by joining the liberal party discourse, if it conceives of it as an incentive to gain votes. This incentive was visible only in 1988 and 1989, when the German Social Democrats (SPD) polled far ahead of the CDU/CSU while embracing a clearly multicultural agenda regarding matters of integration and immigration. The CDU/CSU adopted substantial parts of this multicultural agenda in 1988 and 1989 and thereby opened the niche on the right; this left the conservative voters, who the CDU/CSU had mobilized over the 1980s, to vote for the sole political party that had clearly rejected multiculturalism during the 1989 elections for the European Parliament: the populist radical right 'Die Republikaner' (REP). The CDU/CSU regained its conservative voters by effectively leading German reunification and through the total lack of multicultural agendas from 1990 on. Because the SPD also stopped campaigning on multicultural positions after 1990, the CDU/CSU was not in danger of losing centrist voters to the SPD if it reclaimed a conservative position. The conservative compromise in political messaging between the CDU/CSU and the SPD ousted the populist radical right 'Die Republikaner' (REP). This mechanism has still largely characterized salient integration debates in the 'Berliner Republik' since 1990: the German conservatives can keep the electoral niche on the far right closed whenever they decide to heat up the topic in order to mobilize conservative voters.

The reason for the German Social Democrats dropping their multicultural agenda almost entirely after 1990 can be found in the high economic threat potential to which the German voter has conceived of being exposed to since 1990 and the weakness of the left camp (SPD and Gruene). Unlike in the 1980s, the SPD has

---

[102]Curiously, the SPD reclaimed its multicultural agenda from the 1980s in the late 2000s (e.g. in demanding dual citizenship), but avoids campaigning openly on these liberal positions (which would increase SPD-salience significantly). Therefore, the benign economic conditions in Germany since the late 2000s seem to have led the SPD to change position, but the strength of the center-right camp seems to prevent the SPD to campaign with these agendas openly. In one sentence: the SPD seems to have adopted a liberal agenda, but does not conceive of this multicultural agenda as promising to gather more voters' sympathies (in stark contrast to the late 1980s, when the SPD openly campaigned on multicultural campaigns while polling up to 15% ahead of the CDU/CSU).

therefore refrained from openly campaigning on liberal, multicultural positions in matters of migration and integration.

The picture changed as debates about German national identity focused on a rather new issue to German party politics: the EU. In 2011–2012 the tacit compromise to refrain from politicizing European issues broke and eventually benefitted the rise of the populist radical right party AfD. These developments are dealt with in detail in Chap. 9.

# Reference

Thränhardt D (1995) The political uses of xenophobia in England, France and Germany. Party Polit 1(1):323–345

# Chapter 9
# Generalizing the Findings: Explaining the Rise of UKIP and the AfD

The findings of this study can be used to explain the varying advances of populist radical right parties across Western Europe. The study relies on a most similar case design in order to scrutinize the politicization of the immigration issue in the immigration societies of Germany, the Netherlands and Sweden. The salience of and political messaging on immigration works as a *proxy* to account for how established parties deal with identity politics. Consequently, the handling of other political issues also affecting the national identity—for instance, European issues—can equally be explained. As such, the mechanisms revealed by this study can account for the ups and down of populist radical right parties in the salient debates about the EU in recent years. Discussing the recent rise of the Alternative for Germany (AfD) and the United Kingdom Independent Party (UKIP) showcases the generalizability of these mechanisms across Western Europe. The outlined mechanisms also serve as a theoretical model to explain the advances of the French Front National over recent decades and their electoral failures too (Michelot et al. 2017).

## 9.1 Remarks: Sartori's Ladder of Generality

Giovanni Sartori's 'ladder of generality' (Sartori 1984) provides the tools to extend this study's findings beyond the cases studied in detail. Sartori is concerned with how the extension (empirical coverage) of a concept varies with its intension (the concept itself): he points out that the more limited the empirical coverage of a concept is, the more precise the concept is, and vice versa. The two-level theory explaining variation in the electoral advances of populist radical right parties is derived from a rather small sample of three countries with similar scope conditions. The cases are 53 years of immigration debates in the respective countries. Recalling the chapter on country selection, this study is concerned with Western European countries that use a proportional representation system, and which were free of an entrenched populist radical right party at the end of the 1980s while being subject to

© Springer International Publishing AG 2018
T. Lochocki, *The Rise of Populism in Western Europe*,
DOI 10.1007/978-3-319-62855-4_9

a high and constant inflow of immigrants: Germany, the Netherlands and Sweden. The main components of the two-level theory are also defined very precisely; electoral advances of populist radical right parties are the result of the conjunction of two necessary causes: high salience of immigration-related topics (1) and a liberal party discourse (2) on these matters. The high salience is a result of a crisis within the conservative parties (1.1) in times of a constant, substantial flow of immigrants (1.2); the liberal party discourse—or in other words, the conservative party having dropped their conservative profile to follow the liberal position of the social democrats—results from the combination of a successful left camp (2.1) and the perception of a good economic climate (2.2). These conditions can be understood as defining a concept with a *high degree of intension* and a *low degree of extension*; a rather precise concept covering relatively few empirical observations.

The question is, therefore, how to alter the concept in order to make it applicable to more countries or to more cases (or social phenomena). Gary Goertz proposes a clear procedure:

> One can increase the coverage (i.e., extension) of a concept by reducing its intension (i.e., number of attributes). More specifically, and more accurately, we can increase the extension by reducing the number of necessary attributes in the intension. 'Conceptual stretching' thus means in operational terms eliminating necessary dimensions. This makes the concept more general and simultaneously increases the distance it can travel. (Goertz and Mahoney 2006, 72)

Or, in more simple terms, the more *broadly* and *less detailed* the definition of the key components of the concept, the *more countries* and *more cases* can be covered.

Recalling the chapter on case selection, this study limited its scope to three exclusive criteria and one inclusive criterion. The most far-reaching exclusive criterion was the focus on Western European countries; the second the focus on countries without an entrenched populist radical right party; the least far-reaching was the focus on states using proportional representation systems. The only inclusive criterion consists of a substantial inflow of immigration, so that established parties have reason to argue about immigration (see Chap. 4).

The two least exclusive criteria (proportional representation system and steady inflow of immigrants) are exactly mirrored by the findings: the two-level theory lists the critical importance of the center-left camp polling ahead; this calculation would be far less decisive in a winner take all system as in France and the UK, as here it is not political camps but parties that compete against each other. In understanding immigration debates as a proxy conflict about national identity, the inflow of migrants—which is listed as a key component—can be ruled out too. When other political issues can be mobilized as allegedly threatening the national identity (e.g. foreign policy or European Union issues), the number of immigrants is no longer so important. This implies that the two-level theory can be applied to all Western European countries free of populist radical right parties in the 1980s if the necessary conditions 'success of center-left political camp' and 'high inflow of immigrants' are dropped from the equation. The two-level theory with higher

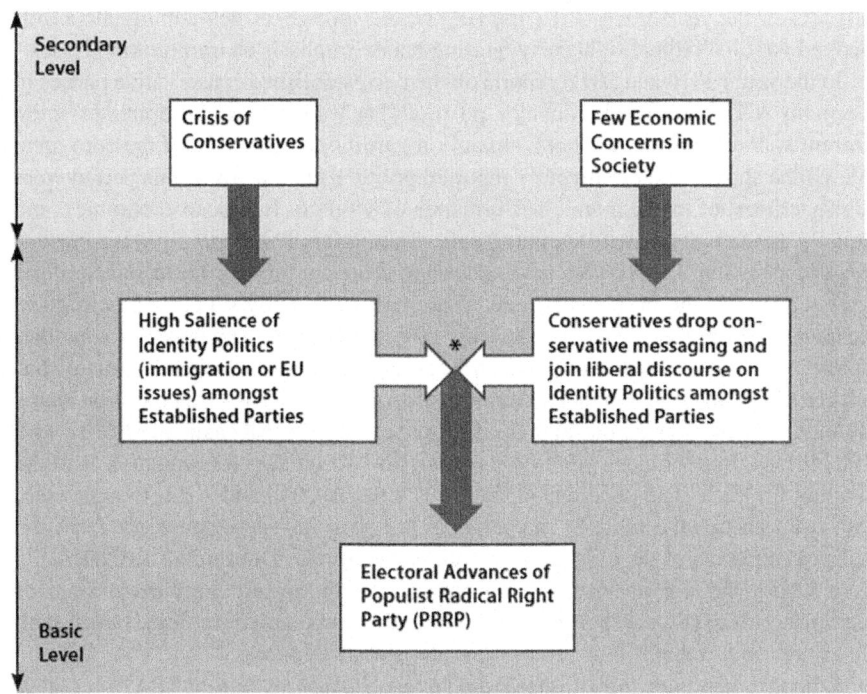

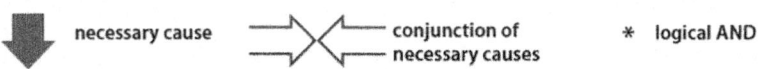

Fig. 9.1 A two-level theory on populist radical right parties in Western Europe—high extension, low intension

extension (more cases covered) and less intension (less precision) looks as follows (Fig. 9.1).

## 9.2 How the Zigzagging Political Messaging of the CDU/CSU Bred the AfD

This adapted two-level theory can reasonably account for the varying polling figures of the AfD in recent years. The low salience of immigration issues prevented the AfD from mobilizing on this issue in its early phase. However, the tacit elite consensus amongst established German parties on EU topics broke in 2010 and 2011. These debates, which were framed as issues concerning the German national identity, eventually opened the electoral niche for the AfD's anti-Euro platform in

2012. Over the years 2014–2016, the AfD would shift gears, developing into a full-fledged populist radical right party, putting major emphasis on immigration issues.[1]

In the years 2010 and 2011, reports on the two established conservative parties in Germany (CDU and CSU) convey a position that leaned toward skepticism of the current state of European affairs—mainly regarding the structure of the euro area. As will be shown, the prominently reported political statements of this period were highly critical of the economic performance of southern European economies, and equally dubious of financial support for these countries. This certainly was a curious development for observers accustomed to the clear-cut pro-European stance of the CDU/CSU over the previous decades. The party eventually supported the highest financial commitment ever offered by post-war German taxpayers to another political entity when it supported all European rescue packages. Germany has backed the European Financial Stability Facility (EFSF) with 211 billion euros (France: 158 billion euros) and the European Stability Mechanism (ESM) with 190 billion euros (France: 143 billion euros), thus accounting for around 27% of the funding for each. The positions of the CDU/CSU in 2010 and 2011, though, stem less from an openly anti-EU campaign of the party as such, and more from the outspoken claims of the CSU party secretary, Alexander Dobrindt. The CDU/CSU as a whole did not necessarily express skepticism toward the current state of European affairs—as other conservative politicians failed to join ranks with Dobrindt—but rather did not contest his statements in public.

When on February 5 2010 the *Frankfurter Allgemeine Zeitung* (FAZ) reported the CSU's insistence on Greek accountability for "cheating with their statistics" in order to enter the euro area, the political solution offered for Greece could only be fierce austerity measures supervised by European—not Greek—institutions. Financial support from northern Europe was clearly rejected: "We must be very thorough in controlling what Greece is doing," said Dobrindt.[2] For reasons that can only be speculated on at this point,[3] neither Chancellor Angela Merkel nor any other prominent CDU/CSU politician has stepped up to refute Dobrindt's claims; despite eventually committing to substantial financial aid for southern Europe, no CDU/CSU politician has publicly made the case for European solidarity or the European project. Instead, the FAZ reports the CSU continuously criticizing financial support for southern European economies. The only clear-cut

---

[1]The elaborations on the AfD largely rely on the writing of the author published elsewhere. Citations to the relevant publications are listed at the end of the respective text parts.

[2]*Frankfurter Allgemeine Zeitung*, February 2, 2010, p. 1.

[3]The *Financial Times* (FT) argues that during certain meetings in 2010 and 2011, German Chancellor Angela Merkel (CDU/CSU) felt blackmailed by US and European partners. The FT reports that Western leaders were trying to push Merkel to significantly increase Germany's financial commitment to safeguarding the euro area with few guarantees from southern European economies in return. These experiences might have led Merkel to refrain from devoting substantial political energy to communicating Germany's commitment to European solidarity. *Financial Times* series "How the Euro was saved": http://www.ft.com/indepth/how-euro-was-saved (last accessed May 7, 2017).

pro-European CDU/CSU positions the FAZ search lists for 2010 stem from Merkel's speech at the German Bundestag in May 2010 in which she defended the financial rescue package for Greece: "If the euro fails, Europe will fail."[4]

Former Chancellor Helmut Kohl—who is not considered a spokesman for the CDU/CSU's position—commented on this situation in October 2010. He expressed his concern that the CDU/CSU could hardly be conceived as a pro-European party in 2010. The FAZ writes, "Kohl used this opportunity to admonish his own party: Following the debate about Greece and the euro crisis, I get the impression some politicians have forgotten how crucial a united Europe is for all of us. Consequently, the CDU/CSU must remain a pro-European political force and must continue heading for European unity."[5]

In saying this, the former chancellor might indeed have been referring to the debate in the media and not to actual policies. The CDU/CSU supported all rescue packages for the euro area with a clear majority, along with the Freie Demokratische Partei FDP, its coalition partner at the time. Still, Kohl's statement reflects the FAZ's reports: the former chancellor does not see the CDU/CSU passionately vindicating European solidarity, even though its policies emphasize it.

In summer 2011, while Dobrindt pondered the end of European integration,[6] the CDU/CSU discussed how to handle these hitherto unknown nationalistic tones within the party. "More Europe eventually translates into less national power," Dobrindt wrote. In doing so, he made the case against purported plans from Brussels to claim more competences from the nation states. Only CDU/CSU politicians from the European parliament rejected his stance. Merkel (CDU), along with Horst Seehofer, chairperson of the CSU, remained quiet. Parts of the CSU interpret this as support for Dobrindt's position. Other politicians from the CDU and CSU are instead concerned about Euroskeptical populism within the party.[7] Again, one can only speculate about the reasons for the rather unassertive conduct of the party leaders of the hitherto pro-European CDU/CSU.[8]

Only in October 2011—a full year and a half after the FAZ reported Dobrindt's first Euroskeptical positions—did reports appear in the FAZ of the CDU/CSU again making a clear case for further European integration. The final draft of a CDU party convention program in November 2011 called for further European integration on various levels, along with the strengthening of EU institutions: "Therefore, the CDU is considering the transfer of national competencies to European institutions within the framework of 'subsidiarity' an appropriate way to safeguard our interests."[9] By the end of 2011, the CDU/CSU had withdrawn all publicly visible Euroskeptic statements.

---

[4]*Frankfurter Allgemeine Zeitung*, May 20, 2010, p. 1.

[5]*Frankfurter Allgemeine Zeitung*, October 10, 2010, FAZ online.

[6]*Frankfurter Allgemeine Zeitung*, June 6, 2011, p. 4.

[7]*Frankfurter Allgemeine Zeitung*, July 21, 2011, p. 10.

[8]See footnote 19.

[9]*Frankfurter Allgemeine Zeitung*, November 5, 2011, p. 2.

CDU/CSU's retreat from their once-prominent skepticism toward the state of European affairs opened an electoral niche for a new political contender running on a Euroskeptical platform. This was the perfect springboard for the Alternative für Deutschland (AfD). The political space for their program opened in the winter of 2011–2012, with the party itself forming in February 2013. In 2013, the AfD ran on a platform of concerns very similar to those voiced by Dobrindt 2 years before. His statements seem—through the lack of other publicly visible CDU/CSU statements at that time—to have framed the public perception of the CDU/CSU's position on European matters in 2010–2011. Like Dobrindt, the AfD was not campaigning against the EU or European integration per se, but against Germany's financial commitments over the past few years and the transfer of national powers to European institutions.

The AfD polled well during the peak of the negotiations over the Eurozone crisis in 2014 and into early 2015. Meanwhile, a right-wing extremist movement calling itself Patriotic Europeans Against the Islamization of the Occident (PEGIDA) held rallies in eastern German cities such as Dresden. Some in the AfD flirted openly with PEGIDA and thereby reached out to further groups of voters. In December 2014, AfD was polling at around 7% (Lochocki 2014).

The party had a hard time consolidating its gains, however. In mid-2015, it became known that the German finance minister Wolfang Schäuble (CDU) was taking a harder line on Eurozone issues, suggesting that Greece should either meet German demands or quit the common currency. Additionally, the AfD was split between the Euroskeptics forming around Bernd Lucke and a nationalist wing around two other leaders, Frauke Petry and Alexander Gauland. Lucke wanted the AfD to be a market-liberal party focused on Eurozone matters; his rivals wanted to expand into criticism of multiculturalism and immigration in order to forge a fully-fledged right-wing populist platform. In July 2015, the split became formal. Petry took over as the AfD's new leader, while Lucke went off to found a new party that has yet to make a mark. Bad press sparked by the disarray, along with the government's ability (thanks to Schäuble) to reclaim Euroskeptical voters, drove AfD down to about 4% in July and August 2015 surveys.

But Petry's widening of the party program paid off later in 2015. In July and August, even as AfD was dipping in the polls, asylum applications were going up. In September, Merkel made her fateful decision to accept the refugees stranded at the Budapest train station, a move that was taken as a signal that Germany would accept not only all who had already arrived, but even those heading to Europe. If migrants reaching southeastern Europe said that they were bound for Germany, authorities there would let them pass. In June 2015, Germany took about 40,000 newcomers. In July, it was 80,000 and in August 105,000. An additional 165,000 arrived in September, and another 550,000 came during the months of October, November, and December. As staggering as these numbers were—more than 900,000 people came to Germany from June through December 2015—they were *not* what led to the AfD's rise in the polls. Three months after this massive surge, the grand coalition's members began arguing among themselves about how to reduce the incoming numbers going forward. In October 2015, the CSU demanded the closure of German borders. The CDU and the SPD said no—giving the AfD an opening to approach conservative voters whom the CSU had mobilized but had then had to disappoint owing to its coalition partners' insistence on keeping the borders open. From its nadir of around 3% in August 2015, the AfD saw its support quadruple to 12% in January 2016. It was this debate amongst the parties of the grand coalition that spurred the AfD's upward trend in the public-opinion surveys.

After widely publicized New Year's Eve attacks in Cologne and other cities, in which criminals with migrant backgrounds sexually assaulted hundreds of women, the AfD added ringing denunciations of multiculturalism to its call for border controls. This did not help the party as much as it might have, however, for in March 2016 the EU and Turkey struck their deal to close off the Balkan migration route, leading to a large drop in the number of new arrivals. The members of the CDU/CSU–SPD grand coalition were back on the same page. Their shift toward restrictionism and conservatism on immigration and integration issues was further confirmed in the wake of a series of July 2016 attacks in southern Germany. These included a Syrian refugee hacking a pregnant woman to death on the street with a machete, a failed asylum seeker blowing himself up outside a music festival, a German-Iranian teenager shooting nine people to death at a Munich shopping mall, and a Pakistani (who had been posing as an Afghan) using a knife and axe to assault a family of tourists from Hong Kong on a train.

While the SPD seems very interested in an open conflict with the CDU on the matter, the constant struggle between the CSU and the CDU keeps the AfD alive. Since the beginning of 2016 the CDU and the CSU have been arguing about how to prevent a major influx of refugees. Such a debate prevents German voters from conceiving of a conservative compromise on immigration matters, which would significantly harm the AfD. This prevents a decrease in the salience of immigration topics and shows the lack of a conservative compromise between the SPD, CDU and the CSU. This explains why the populist radical right party polled at between 10 and 12% over 2016 (Lochocki 2016a, b). However, at the beginning of 2017, Martin Schulz announced that he would be running for the chancellorship for the SPD. This is dire news for the AfD, with the SPD avoiding polarization on immigration issues, but seeking an open confrontation with the CDU/CSU on economic and European matters—running counter to the AfD's winning formula. The established parties have *not* reached a conservative compromise on immigration topics, but have shifted attention to other issues. If this trend persists, the AfD's prime selling point—being the only party with a fierce stance on immigration—loses traction (Lochocki 2017). However, as the latest high salience period of immigration issues did not result in a conservative compromise between the SPD, CDU and the CSU, substantial numbers of German voters still find their demands in immigration matters unmet by the established parties. (It might be worth speculating that the CDU and the CSU did not see the need to reach a compromise as they expected to win the federal election against the SPD without mobilizing conservative voters.) Thus, how the AfD will perform in the upcoming federal elections in autumn 2017 will largely depend on the salience of immigration issues in the election year and whether conservative voters regain trust in the identity politics of the CDU/CSU, along with whether the AfD can

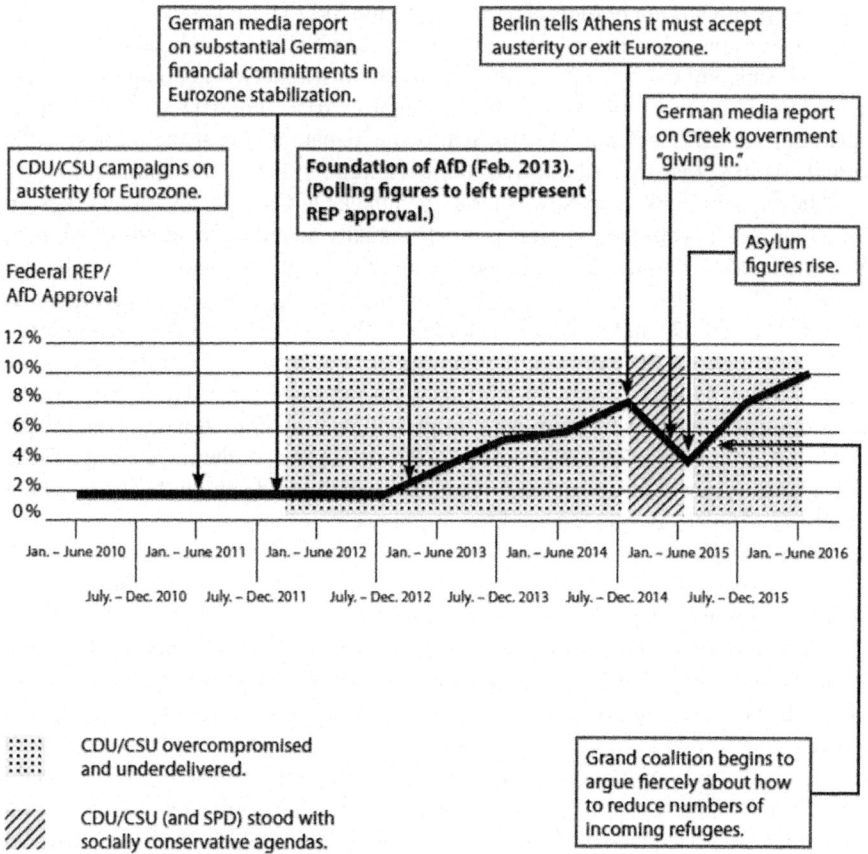

**Fig. 9.2** The rise and fall of the AfD

avoid a new and public internal split, this time between national conservatives around Petry and a more extreme faction. If the latter prevail, the German media might stop reporting on the AfD and it will be very difficult for them to attract bourgeois voters.

The two-level theory explains the ups and downs of the AfD over the past few years extremely well. AfD's advances to the largest extend depend on the CDU/CSU's positioning on issues concerning Germany's national identity. If the CDU/CSU and the SPD reach a conservative compromise (as in the spring and summer of 2015 on Greece), the AfD will drop in the polls. If the established parties overpromise and underdeliver on conservative agendas (as in 2011 on Eurozone issues and in 2015 on refugee matters) the AfD will gain public support (Fig. 9.2).

The 'causes of the causes' as outlined by the two-level theory also match the political mechanisms in Germany. The CDU/CSU increased the salience of cultural matters when facing substantial problems. The CDU's successes at the federal level (up to 20% (!) ahead of the SPD over the last decade) stand in stark contrast to its massive problems at the regional level. Over the last 3 years, the SPD won nearly all Landtagswahlen, depriving the CDU of some its most important power bases. In the winter of 2010/2011 the CDU feared losing its most important regional center—the conservative government of the economic powerhouse Baden-Württemberg. The conservative government was in a very unfortunate situation: the center-left coalition polled well ahead of the bourgeois camp; even worse for the CDU, for the very first time in German history, it was not the SPD lurking to take a state government in West Germany from the CDU, but the Greens. The Greens in southwest Germany are more conservative than other regional chapters and the federal branch. This enabled the Greens in Baden-Württemberg to attract former CDU voters. The CDU thus faced a major challenge in the state home to some of Germany's most important companies and infamous thriftiness. It is of little surprise that the CDU/CSU adjusted its otherwise pro-European political messaging and tried to play hardball on Greece in the months before the regional election in March 2011. However, the strategy failed—Winfried Kretchmann became the first Green Ministerpräsident in German history. He formed a coalition with the SPD as junior partner. While the Greens increased their vote share to 24.2% (+12.5), the SPD gained only 23.1% (−2.1). However, this coalition gathered more votes than the bourgeois camp consisting of the CDU with 39% (−5.2) and the FDP with 5.3% (−5.4).

The second time cultural matters became salient during the period under scrutiny also fits this bill perfectly. In autumn 2015 the CSU entered a fully-fledged confrontation with the CDU and the SPD over refugee policies *not* as the numbers of refugees began to rise, but as the CSU in Bavaria abruptly lost support from September to October 2015. The CSU called for closing the border to refugees *not* when the incomings had been doubling every month in July, August and September. Instead, the CSU put forward and/or supported calls for transit zones, suing the federal government at the constitutional court, and prevented an agreement over asylum legislation in October 2015, exactly after the CSU suffered massive polling loses (Fig. 9.3). Again, another important regional branch of the CDU/CSU was endangered, leading to an increase in the salience of cultural matters in the nationwide debate.

The two-level theory explains the varying salience as being due to the condition of the conservatives, but their position in these matters is dependent on those of their most important competitor—the social democrats. Fitting the theory, the CDU/CSU have been the sole agenda setters in cultural matters since 2010 because of the weakness of German social democracy. As outlined in the two-level theory, conservative parties are inclined to drop their conservative messaging if facing a highly successful center-left camp polling well ahead in a society freed of economic concerns. While the German economy was booming, the German SPD polled up to 20% (!) behind the CDU/CSU in the crucial years 2010–2016. Only after Martin Schulz announced his candidature in January 2017 did the SPD again become a political force whose political messages the CDU/CSU had to seriously take into account. Up 2017, the CDU/CSU heated up matters concerning German national identity whenever it hoped to mobilize conservative voter strata. Which position the

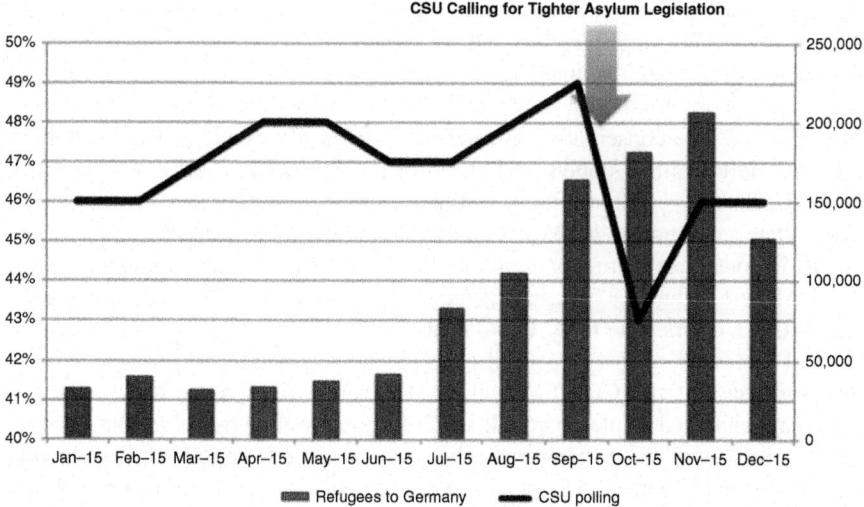

**Fig. 9.3** When the CSU called for tighter asylum legislation

CDU/CSU subsequently took was far more dependent on their internal struggles than the SPD's political messages. Given the bright prospects of the German economy, if a revitalized SPD campaigned successfully on a clear pro-European and pro-migrant platform, this could eventually force the CDU/CSU to alter its political messaging.

## 9.3 How David Cameron Perpetuated UKIP's Rise and Enabled Brexit

The rise of perhaps the most impactful populist radical right party in Europe—UKIP—which eventually led to the UK leaving the EU (Brexit) can also be explained under the auspices of the two-level theory. In the autumn of 2009, the party leader of the British Conservatives (and soon to be prime minister), David Cameron, marked the clear Euroskeptical position of his party by "maintaining the Tory position that they will plan for a referendum if the Lisbon treaty has not been ratified when they come to power, and not let 'matters rest' if it has been."[10] In other words, the British Conservatives promised to renegotiate the very basics of the British relationship with the EU and open this for a referendum if they won the national election in 2010 (which they did). In October 2009, the *Daily Telegraph* reported that the Tories threatened

---

[10]*Daily Telegraph*, October 5, 2009, p. 7.

"Europe's leaders that they face a 'five-year war' with Britain if they installed Tony Blair as new European president."[11]

Cameron maintained the Tories' clear-cut position on the EU after becoming prime minister. In July 2010, he announced that no extra pound out of the pockets of British tax payers would be spent to address the financial challenges in southern Europe.[12] Over the course of that year, he affirmed his highly Euroskeptical position, culminating on October 30 with the declaration: "I'm a Euroskeptic."[13]

Over the course of 2011, the prime minister faced strong internal resistance from the conservative wing of his party when he denounced a popular vote that would enable Britain to leave the EU. "'I don't want Britain to leave the EU," the prime minister said. "I think it's the wrong answer for Britain. People in rooms up and down Britain aren't thinking, gosh, if only we could have a treaty change in Europe."'[14] Despite these rather nuanced statements, Cameron kept the Tories on a clear anti-EU position in the winter of 2011 by publicly accusing "France and Germany of orchestrating 'constant attacks' on the City of London through new EU red tape on the financial sector."[15] The prime minister was in good company here, as a group of 81 Tory MPs formed an anti-EU group in Westminster with the goal of repatriating powers from Brussels, as EU regulations were seen to be hampering the British economy.[16] Cameron insisted that this repatriation of powers must wait, as the prime challenge at the time was the rescue of the euro.[17] In the summer of 2012, the *Daily Telegraph* reported Cameron's change of course: he refused to call for a referendum on Britain's relations with the EU in June 2012.[18] A month later, he once again stressed that he personally thought Britain should stay in the EU.[19] However, he tried to pacify the strong anti-EU wing of his conservative party in emphasizing his rejection of further steps of European integration, even as his Europe minister, David Lidington, was clear in underlining the "new" position of Cameron's cabinet: "Britain must not 'walk away' from the European Union and Conservatives should not be 'emotional' about the issue."[20] At the beginning of December 2012, however, Cameron became the first British prime minister to veto a new EU treaty since the early 1990s (aiming at a far stronger integration of the fiscal sector of European countries to counter the financial crisis).[21]

---

[11]*Daily Telegraph*, October 26, 2009, p. 19.

[12]*Daily Telegraph*, June 22, 2010, p. 4.

[13]*Daily Telegraph*, October 30, 2010, p. 19.

[14]*Daily Telegraph*, October 5, 2011, p. 14.

[15]*Daily Telegraph*, October 29, 2011, p. 1.

[16]*Daily Telegraph*, November 10, 2011, p. 6.

[17]*Daily Telegraph*, December 8, 2011, p. 1.

[18]*Daily Telegraph*, June 13, 2012, p. 1.

[19]*Daily Telegraph*, July 20, 2012, p. 10.

[20]*Daily Telegraph*, December 20, 2012, p. 1.

[21]*Daily Telegraph*, December 10, 2011, p. 1.

The end of 2012 was the first time the United Kingdom Independence Party's (UKIP) share in the polls grew since 2009. The party increased from a 3% national average from 2009 to 2011 to 5% at the end of 2012. UKIP gathered even more voter support in 2013, polling a remarkable 12% national average as Cameron made clear that he wanted Britain to stay in a reformed EU.[22] In January 2013, conservative MPs spread the rumor that the prime minister would campaign on a pro-EU position regardless of how a possible renegotiation between London and Brussels about a repatriation of powers turned out.[23] The British prime minister responded by offering to schedule a referendum on such a renegotiated relationship for 2017 if the Conservatives won the national election in 2015,[24] (a proposal that was admittedly similar to his undelivered promise to hold a popular vote on the Lisbon Treaty after winning the 2010 election).

Two camps defined the Tory position on the EU at the end of 2013: the clear anti-EU faction centered around a few MP backbenchers, and a camp led by Cameron that wanted Britain to stay in a reformed EU. The prime minister tried to cater to the anti-EU faction of his own party by accompanying his admittedly clear pro-EU standpoints with a plan to limit welfare benefits to migrants from Eastern Europe.[25] At this point, UKIP climbed to unprecedented heights in polls for the next national election, and meanwhile remained at around 12–14% from the end of 2013 and was still polling at these levels in September 2014. In the election for the European Parliament in May 2014, UKIP finished as the strongest British party, receiving 27.5% of the votes (an increase of 11% from 2009).

Though this might have passed unnoticed by observers from the continent, the Tories dropped a large part of their Euroskeptical rhetoric in 2012, and changed position significantly in the first half of 2013. This does not imply that the Tories were a pro-European party in 2013; they were merely campaigning on far more pro-European positions than in the years before. For instance, while Cameron said in a widely publicized statement in 2010, "I am a Euroskeptic!", he announced in 2012 that he personally thought Britain should stay in the EU. While up until 2011 conservative politicians had uttered barely any pro-European sentiments, prominent members of the cabinet—such as conservative Europe Minister Lidington—began doing so from 2012 onwards.

This positional shift was strongest in the first half of 2013. Cameron repeatedly made clear that he wanted Britain to stay in a reformed EU, and various Tory politicians supported the prime minister in this stance. This corresponded with the first time that UKIP's voter support rose notably (Fig. 9.4)—by nine percentage points. While the party was polling at around 3% before 2011, it rose to 5% in 2012, and finally reached 12% from 2013 on. This surge in voter support went hand-in-hand with the positional shift of the Tories over the same time period. In line with

[22]*Daily Telegraph*, January 24, 2013, p. 21.

[23]*Daily Telegraph*, January 25, 2013, p. 4.

[24]*Daily Telegraph*, October 9, 2013, p. 20.

[25]*Daily Telegraph*, November 30, 2013, p. 2.

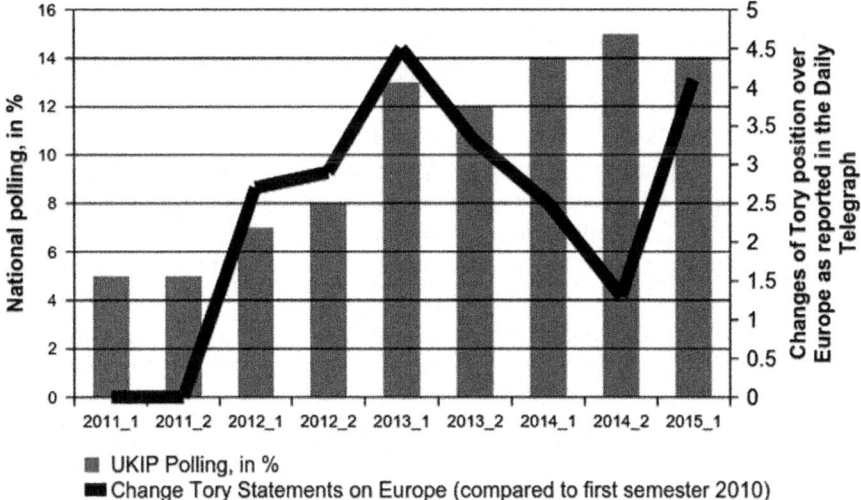

**Fig. 9.4**  The positional shift of the Tories and the rise of UKIP. Source: Lochocki (2015)

these findings, UKIP emerged as the strongest party in the elections for the European Parliament in May 2014 with 27.5% (+11.0 percentage points compared to 2009). As the campaign began for the British federal election in summer 2014, the Prime Minister tried to strike a middle ground between the clear anti-EU faction centered around certain MP backbenchers, and the camp led by Cameron that wanted Britain to stay in a reformed EU. He described EU membership as necessary so "Britain can punch over its weight",[26] while his widely noted speech on Europe in November 2014 stated that major reforms were necessary for Britain to stay in the EU and that the conservative government would cut welfare benefits to migrants from EU countries.[27] After 2012, the statements of leading Tory politicians lingered between the "stay in a reformed EU" stance and clearly pro-Brexit statements. The latter camp faced severe setbacks as the Conservatives' coalition partner until 2015, the pro-European Liberal Democrats, refused to enshrine the call for an in-/out referendum in law in October 2014.[28] As the Tories never reclaimed their anti-EU rhetoric from 2009 entirely and over a longer time, UKIP's support remained steady from 2013 up to the British parliamentary election in May 2015 (Lochocki 2014, 2015) in which UKIP won 12.7% of the votes. After the Tories won the federal election in May 2015, David Cameron lost the Brexit referendum in June 2016 and resigned. This might have been the greatest victory of a populist radical right party in Europe up to the time of writing in May 2017.

---

[26]*Daily Telegraph*, July 24, 2014, p. 4.

[27]*Daily Telegraph*, November 11, 2014, p. 1.

[28]*Daily Telegraph*, October 29, 2014, p. 4.

However, it might have proven a pyrrhic victory for UKIP. Since Theresa May became Prime Minister following Cameron's resignation, the Tories have gained substantially in the polls. While they polled at around 35% under Cameron's tutelage, they have been polling steadily at and above 40% since the summer of 2016. Theresa May's strictly conservative position in pursuing a hard Brexit might deprive UKIP of their prime campaign topic. While the Tories' support increases, UKIP's support is stalling, dropping to about 10% in national polls. One of the most well-read scholars of UKIP, Matthew Goodwin, summarizes the problems of the populist radical right in the UK in almost exactly the same way as the two-level theory of this study:

> But the vote for Brexit and the arrival of Prime Minister Theresa May put a wrench in UKIP's progress. May's high-profile and unwavering support for Brexit, selective education and her clear desire to prioritize immigration reform in the forthcoming negotiations resonated strongly among those who might otherwise have remained in, or joined, the UKIP camp. [...] This development also reflects UKIP's failure to develop a wider message beyond Brexit and immigration. Focusing on these issues in the era of David Cameron made good strategic sense. But in the era of Theresa May, UKIP's voter appeal is being overshadowed by a far more compelling offer—an incumbent government that appears to take their identity concerns, values and aspirations seriously. (Goodwin 2017)

The positioning of the Tories on Europe and immigration thus also explains to the greatest extent the varying electoral advances of the far right in the UK. While both issues dominate the political debate in the UK, the question of varying salience is more difficult to assess. In contrast with the immigration issues in the Netherlands, Sweden and Germany and the Eurozone issue in Germany, the EU issue is affecting the state of the UK in its entirety. In this situation, there are various political players that have an interest in keeping the issue on the political agenda; this suggests that the Tories have far fewer opportunities to decrease and increase the salience on their own. However, the first time the European issue become a highly salient issue for the Cameron-Tories fits the two-level theory perfectly. It was the winter of 2009/2010; these were the crucial months before the parliamentary election in the UK. David Cameron's Tories looked forward to ousting the Labour government led by Gordon Brown. However, the polls did not look promising for the Conservatives. Both Labour and the Liberal Democrats closed in with the Tories on national polls. At times it seemed the electorate was parted evenly between the three parties. This was devastating news for the Tories. In a winner-takes-all system as in the UK it is crucial to come out as the strongest party to win the seat in your voting district and eventually gain the upper hand in the parliament. The Tories had to make sure they mobilized conservative voter strata to ensure wining the crucial percentage points over Labour and the Liberal Democrats. Promising to hold a referendum on the European Union was a key issue to make sure that conservative voters flocked to the polls for the Tories. Similarly to the German CDU/CSU, David Cameron's Tories in 2009/2010 were inclined to mobilize on matters of national identity for strategic gains.

The Tories will remain the sole agenda setter in British identity politics because the UK looks deprived of the two factors that could change the Conservatives' strategy: a society freed of economic concerns and a strong center-left party. While the UK is facing substantial social inequalities, a large part of its electorate will remain concerned about their economic prospects. This in turn will inform the position of British Labour. As long as voters are concerned about economics, center-left parties are hardly interested in running on a clear-cut pro-EU or pro-multiculturalism platform. If economic concerns in the UK were to decrease, the incentives for Labour to campaign on liberal positions would increase. However, their very low polling figures provide little incentive for the Tories to take these liberal messages into account. The decision to pick Jeremy Corbyn as leader seems the personification of this political mechanism: a leader of a center-left party that prevents the party from reaching out to center voters, while campaigning on very ambivalent messages on both the EU and immigration. If this situation is to persist, the Tories will remain the prime agenda setter in identity politics in the UK for years to come.

## 9.4   The Proof of the Pudding: Contemporary European Politics

The party political developments in Germany and the UK over the past few years can be reasonably well accounted for by the two-level theory with high extension and low intension (Fig. 9.1). The CDU/CSU and the Tories use identity politics to mobilize and regain conservative voters. In Germany the Eurozone issues were used for the Landtagswahl in Baden-Württemberg in 2011, as much as the refugee issue to improve the CSU's standing in Bavaria in 2015. In the UK, the EU issue was used to safeguard crucial percentage points for the British parliamentary election in 2010.

The weakness of the German SPD and British Labour explains why neither the CDU/CSU nor the Tories had to take the political messaging of center-left parties in identity politics into account to a substantial degree. The SPD operating in a more benign economic climate than Labour does not affect this mechanism as long as the SPD was polling up to 20% behind the CDU/CSU at the federal level.

Consequently, the campaign platform of both conservative parties was more dependent on internal struggles within their parties. Ultimately, the political messaging of the CDU/CSU and the Tories on Europe and immigration has had a massive impact on the public support of the AfD and UKIP. Whenever the conservative parties kept their conservative promises in identity politics, the populist radical right lost support: Germany's tough stance on Greece in the spring of 2015 and Theresa May's pursuit of a hard Brexit led to the polling figures of the AfD and UKIP decreasing substantially. In contrast, when the center-right parties overpromised and underdelivered on identity politics, the far right received a boost in the polls: the AfD benefitted massively from the CDU/CSU's changing positions on Greece from 2010 to 2013 and the major struggle within the Grand Coalition and between the CDU and the CSU over refugee issues from 2015 onwards; ultimately, UKIP rose due to David Cameron's flip-flopping over the EU throughout his tenure 2010–2016.

# References

Goertz G, Mahoney J (2006) Social science concepts: a user's guide. Princeton University Press, Princeton

Goodwin M (2017) UKIP tanks in 'Brexit Capital'. Politico Europe, 2/24/17. Available at: http://www.politico.eu/article/ukip-tanks-in-brexit-capital-stoke-byelection/. Last accessed 7 May 2017

Lochocki T (2014) The unstoppable far right? How established parties communication strategies and media reporting of European affairs affect the advances of populist radical right parties. GMF Europe Policy Paper 4/2014. Available at: http://www.gmfus.org/publications/unstoppable-far-right. Last accessed 7 May 2017

Lochocki T (2015) How the United Kingdom independence party's one seat has the power to change British and European politics. GMF Europe Policy Paper 4/2015. Available at: http://www.gmfus.org/publications/how-UKIPs-one-seat-has-power. Last accessed 7 May 2017

Lochocki T (2016a) Germany's political center is stronger than it looks. GMF Europe Policy Paper 136/2016. Available at: http://www.gmfus.org/publications/germanys-political-center-stronger-it-looks. Last accessed 7 May 2017

Lochocki T (2016b) The specter haunting Europe: will the German center hold? J Democr 27 (4):37–46

Lochocki T (2017) Martin Schulz, the outsider insider. Politico Europe, 1/26/2017. Available at: http://www.politico.eu/article/martin-schulz-the-outsider-insider-sigmar-gabriel-social-democrat-race/. Last accessed 7 May 2017

Michelot M, Quencez M, Lochocki T (2017) The rise of the front national. Taking stock of ten years of French mainstream politics. GMF Europe Policy Paper 1/2017. Available at: http://www.gmfus.org/publications/rise-front-national-taking-stock-ten-years-french-mainstream-politics. Last accessed 7 May 2017

Sartori G (1984) Social science concepts: a systematic analysis. Sage, Beverly Hills

# Chapter 10
# Conclusion: It's Political Messaging, Stupid!

## 10.1 Research Advances and New Questions: Explaining Party Politics

This book offers two major findings: firstly, it provides reliable and valid empirical evidence for how processes of political messaging benefit or hinder the electoral advances of populist radical right parties; secondly, it explains the reasons for the varying rationales of established parties in debates about identity politics. It elucidates 'the causes behind the causes' (Goertz and Mahoney 2006, 241) in the outlined two-level theory. This study therefore advances existing research in three ways. Firstly, in stressing the pivotal role of supply-side explanations—the interaction and political messaging of established parties—in explaining advances of niche parties: variables related to the demand-side alone (e.g. survey data on voters' preferences or socio-economic factors) hardly account for electoral variation here; this adds to an ongoing debate regarding the fruitfulness of either approach (Mudde 2016). Secondly, an answer as to why established political parties increase the salience of cultural topics and identity politics at seemingly arbitrary points in time is given (Alonso and Claro da Fonseca 2011); it has been shown that party rationale, and not exogenous factors, account for variation here. Thirdly, an answer as to why the positional void, or the electoral niche, for populist radical right parties opens in salient debates over cultural topics and identity politics is given under the auspices of the two-level theory. This enhances published studies, which deal with the positional changes of established parties in a primarily descriptive fashion (Ellinas 2010; Green-Pedersen 2012; Schumacher et al. 2013).

However, this study also faces limitations. As shown with the empirical results, the basic level of the two-level theory is grounded in conditions that are jointly necessary, but not sufficient. This implies that other factors *can* influence the advances and losses of PRRPs that are not accounted for in this book. For instance this study is assessing neither the role of the organizational level of the populist radical right party (Art 2011) nor their media access (Ellinas 2010; Muis 2012).

© Springer International Publishing AG 2018
T. Lochocki, *The Rise of Populism in Western Europe*,
DOI 10.1007/978-3-319-62855-4_10

This implies that the factors revealed in this study are necessary conditions that *must be given* for the advances or setbacks of populist parties, but they do not trigger them automatically. It is worth repeating that they are jointly necessary, but not sufficient. An example helps illustrate this point. If a penalty is granted during a football match, this does not automatically lead to a goal through the penalty kick if the player hits the ball; the player must hit the ball properly, the aim must be good, the goalie must miss, the referee must accept the goal, and so on. However, if the player does not try to take the shot in the first place, it is 100% certain that no goal will be scored. Thus, the player trying to score from the penalty spot is a necessary, but not a jointly necessary and sufficient condition to score. This is exactly how the subject fares with (1) a withdrawal of a conservative position in (2) salient debates about cultural issues among established political players: neither automatically lead to the advances—or (if reversed) losses—in support of populist radical right parties, but are necessary conditions. It is very likely that four factors in combination—(1) a conservative party dropping their conservative messages in a debate about national identity in a (2) salient debate; (3) the proper organizational structure of the populist radial right party and (4) its decent media access—are jointly necessary and sufficient conditions explaining their rise (and if the factors are reversed, their fall). Conversely, if established parties do *not* find a conservative compromise in identity politics and do *not* reduce its salience, it is hardly possible for them to regain votes from populist radical right parties. As shown with the QCA results (Chap. 5) and the case studies on the AfD and UKIP, organizational capacity and media access seems of lesser importance in explaining the losses of far right parties. If established parties can stick with their conservative messaging on identity politics, voters seem to turn their back on PRRPs regardless of their media access or organizational capacity.

The political mechanisms outlined lead to some intriguing questions, namely, when is the threshold reached for conservative parties to prefer certain topics over others? Under which circumstances do they increase the salience of cultural matters and politicize identity politics? And how severe must the crisis of the center-right be in order for the party to shift its campaign from the economic to the cultural axis? And for an agenda shift on the social democrats' part: how severe must the economic threat be, and how weak must the center-left camp be, in order for social democrats to refrain from campaigning on a liberal agenda in cultural matters? It is very likely that the key question concerns intra-party dynamics. Namely, when and why are the conservative wings in the major parties succeeding in setting the agenda (Schumacher et al. 2013)? For a populist radical right party to lose votes, it seems that the conservative wings of the conservatives and the social democrats must succeed, enabling a conservative compromise. This would close the electoral niche for a populist radical right party and reduce the salience of identity politics PRRPs need for their program to resonate with voters.

This research project also provides important lessons regarding methodological questions: Is one quality newspaper *always* sufficient to assess party positions reliably? Given the 25–30 annual claims necessary to assess party position reliably for the given coding scheme, what is the golden path between reliability and validity on the one hand, and limited resources for research on the other? Is it perhaps possible to outline a formula for how many claims are needed in order to assess party positions reliably given a certain coding scheme? If comparable and robust benchmarks of media analysis could be found that would allow party positions to be assessed via quality newspapers without requiring too many resources, should party positions be obtained via media data only in general, rejecting party-manifesto projects (like the CMP) entirely? In comparing the CMP and media data for the German case (Fig. 10.1), the limitations of the validity of CMP data come to the fore: valid party positions in the 1980s are not captured, nor can the manifesto data capture the CDU/CSU's rapid position change that led to the first electoral advances of the REP in the elections for European Parliament in 1989, nor can CMP data display the radical repositioning of the SPD's position in the early 1990s. This begs the question: when should the researcher rely on media data and when on CMP data?

Revisiting the inter-coder reliability tests and the pivotal role the perception of threat plays in understanding the public's reaction to cultural topics, one can speculate as to what might explain various coding outcomes. Could individual character traits primarily account for variation here (as suggested in psychological research), or do these significant variations across countries in evaluating political claims as liberal or conservative suggest that national discourse is more important than personal character traits? A repetition of the inter-coder reliability tests with, for example, 30 Dutch, Swedish and German citizens—with comparable variation in socio-economic variables among all three groups—could offer insights into whether contemporary country discourse or ingrained national narratives take precedence over individual character traits in determining coding variability and individual perceptions on issues concerning the national identity such as immigration and integration.

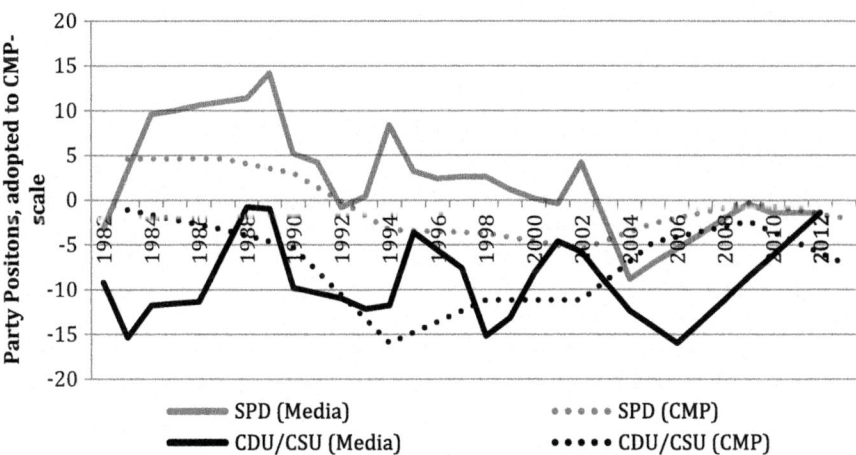

**Fig. 10.1** Comparison of CMP and media data for the German case (adapted to CMP scale)

Finally, if PRRPs are dependent on conservatives legitimating the conservative position on a cultural issue in the first place, are European Green parties or populist radical *left* populists, such as Podemos and Syriza (which are often seen as the counterpart to PRRPs) also dependent on having the door opened to them by the social democrats? If conservative parties move to the right in order to open up new voting strata when they drop in the polls, do social democrats widen their program to far left positions in economics and liberal positions in cultural matters when they do not know how else to mobilize *their* voters? If conservative parties open a space on the far right when facing a successful left camp and favorable economic conditions, do social democrats drop their left and liberal positions, joining the conservative discourse, when they face a successful bourgeois camp and poor economic outlooks? In short, are the breakthroughs of Western European green parties and populist radical left parties the result of the social democrats overpromising and underdelivering in times of strong bourgeois parties and dire economic conditions? Can the two-level theory on the varying electoral advances of populist radical right parties be 'turned around' to explain the advances of the Greens and populist radical left parties?

This argument seems to hold at least for the German case. The SPD increasingly campaigned on liberal demands along the cultural axis in the late 1960s ('Mehr Demokratie wagen') because the party could not take office over the CDU/CSU without mobilizing new strata of voters. The SPD dropped these issues in the 1970s due to the fiercely competitive economic conditions to which Germany was exposed (e.g. the 'oil shock' in 1973) and followed the conservative agenda of the CDU/CSU. Chancellor Helmut Schmidt infamously shrugged off the various claims of the liberal wing of the SPD and the Greens. In so doing, the SPD might have alienated the post-material, left-liberal potential it had mobilized in the first place, boosting the first electoral advances of Die Grünen beginning in the late 1970s. It is worthwhile putting these hypotheses to the empirical test.

## 10.2  The Unintended Consequences of Trying to Reach a Desirable Level of 'Manageable Diversity'

Uniting the empirical findings with their theoretical foundation allows us to formulate a general theory on party politics: the electoral advances of populist radical right parties are the unintended consequences of the political messaging of established parties aimed at altering the level of 'manageable diversity' in their favor.

How and whether established political actors put forward an issue on the cultural axis of political conflict depends on how they think they are evaluated by voters. If conservative parties find their polling figures dropping and are undergoing a crisis, the legitimacy of the conservative party is endangered. As voters seem to disapprove of the conservatives' handling of 'known problems' the conservative party proposes a 'new problem' with an according solution in order to regain its legitimacy (as measured by public support). Conservatives only drop their conservative agenda in identity politics if faced with successful social democrats with a highly liberal agenda. This in turn only occurs if the left camp is leading in the polls while society conceives itself as being spared of economic concerns. At this point, the legitimacy of the social democratic party reaches its peak. It has fulfilled its major raison d'être—it has allegedly solved all economic problems—and is greatly appreciated by the voter. In this moment, the social democrats eagerly counter conservatives' demands for more restrictive policies with a highly liberal agenda. They do so because they conceive of few other social conflicts to manage (because there are very few concerns about economics) and the social democrats' handling of social conflict has proven to be highly legitimate (illustrated by the high polling of the left camp). One could even go one step further: the social democrats might even be 'grateful' for the salience of the new social conflict, because a further enhancement of their legitimacy via (rather absent) economic issues seems difficult. Thus, the social democrats begin to manage this new social conflict according to a social democratic mantra: supporting the interests of minority groups with weak political agency. Consequently, these political mechanisms are dependent on the <u>perceived</u> legitimacy of established political parties (Fig. 10.2).

The subsequent unfolding debate about cultural diversity is constructed as a conflict over the nation's symbolic boundaries (e.g. about immigrants endangering the nation's identity). This debate then decides the fate of the populist radical right parties, because established political parties and their salient debates on cultural issues and identity politics are necessary to *legitimate* radical right populists' agendas: the *symbolic national boundary* must first be *discursively constructed* in salient debates, so that voters demand the supply of this very definition (the conservative position in debates about national identity). After an established actor has introduced this view, but then withdraws from this position in a salient debate, voters' demands for this boundary definition is no longer catered to sufficiently. This opens an electoral niche for a populist radical right party, portraying itself as defending the national identity against the political establishment. Voters then call for a party <u>re</u>introducing this conservative definition of the nation's symbolic boundary. The electoral advances of PRRPs can therefore be understood as the unintended consequences of salient discursive constructions of the socially constructed symbolic boundary of the nation.

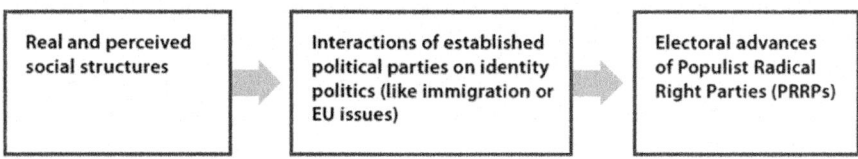

**Fig. 10.2** The link between perceived economic diversity, parties' legitimacy and perceived cultural diversity

Flipping the coin, this explains why salient discourses about national identity alone, or liberal discourses embracing a very low salience, do *not* lead to the advances of PRRPs. If the salient discourse reinforces the conservatives' definition of the nation's symbolic boundary, voter demand is already catered to by the programmatic supply of the established political parties; hence, the electoral niche for a PRRP remains closed (as seen with the positions of the CDU/CSU in salient immigration debates in Germany from the mid 1990s to the mid 2000s for example). In the absence of salient discourse over cultural issues, no conservative voters are mobilized on a conservative position in the first place (e.g. in the Netherlands up to the early 1990s and in Sweden up to the early 2000s). The demand for this position must be created and legitimized by an established actor in the first place. In essence, the rise of PRRPs is the consequence of a debate about the nation's symbolic boundaries, whose form is dependent on the perceived legitimacy of established parties (Fig. 10.3).

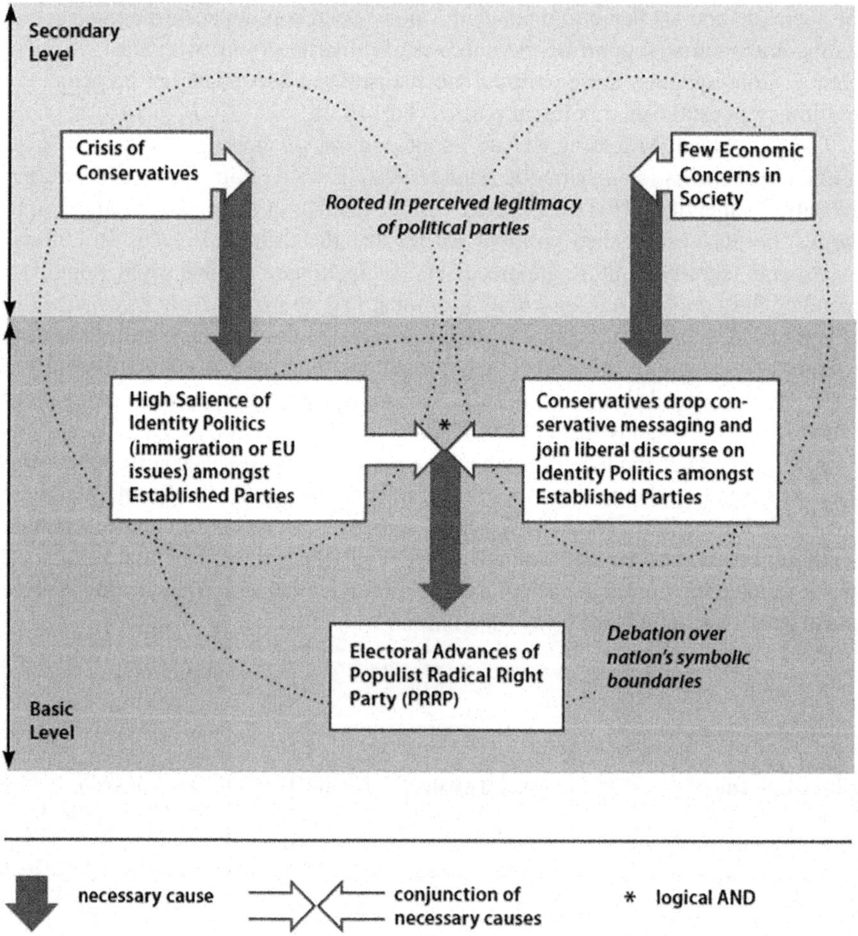

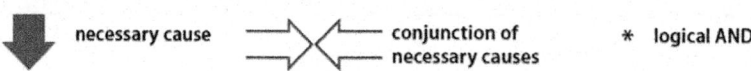

**Fig. 10.3** The two-level theory in the light of theories of social conflict

A new theory of party conduct can be developed based on these concepts. Simply stated, the center-left side of the political spectrum tends to embrace lower socio-economic and higher cultural diversity, while the center-right side allegedly campaigns in favor of higher socio-economic and lower cultural diversity. The data, however, shows that established parties' striving for legitimacy affects this struggle. If the conservatives drop in the polls due to voters' dissatisfaction with their handling of perceived economic diversity, they tend to politicize cultural issues; if the social democrats see that their handling of perceived economic diversity seems to be appreciated by voters (a successful left camp in a society allegedly free of economic concerns), they respond with a liberal agenda on cultural matters—they rhetorically embrace an increase in cultural diversity. Consequently, the reasons behind when and how political parties discuss cultural issues depend on their perception of the level of—in terms of their own interests—desire for diversity in the society in general.

The management of socio-economic diversity is dependent on various exogenous factors beyond the direct reach of national parties (e.g. global trade, foreign banks, international conflicts). However, the management of cultural diversity—as symbolized by debates about the construction of the nation's symbolic boundaries—is mainly dependent on the rationales of national parties. While national parties cannot decide alone which European or migration issues are facing the country, it is mainly up to them how to <u>frame</u> this debate, and to what extent they <u>politicize</u> and <u>polarize</u> these issues (Figs. 10.3 and 10.4).

What characterizes these diversity features is largely decided by political parties themselves. Therefore, established political parties seem keen to ensure a degree of diversity in the public debate they can utilize to enhance the legitimacy ascribed to them by voters. Parties therefore seek to safeguard a desirable degree of 'manageable diversity' in political discourse. Populist radical right parties benefit from this

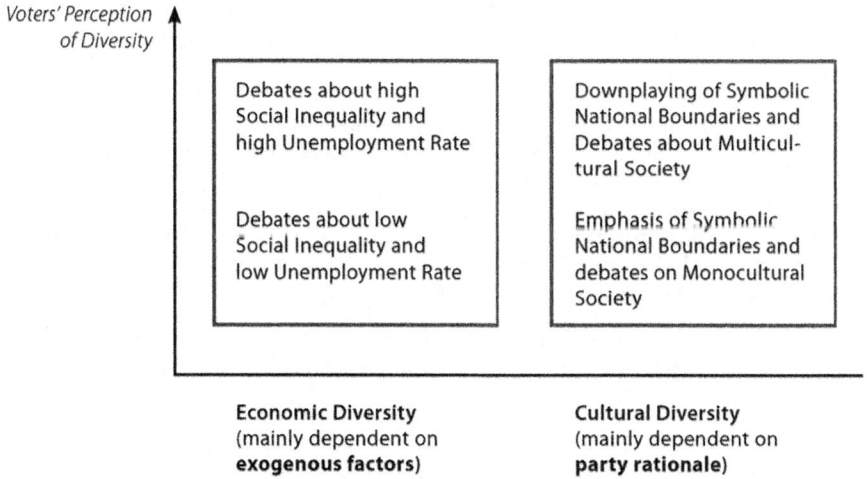

Fig. 10.4  Perceived economic and cultural diversity in comparison

process if the various party rationales outlined lead to a situation in which no
established political party any longer supplies a—previously offered—management
(or rather: reduction) of cultural diversity.

Therefore, the electoral advances of populist radical right parties are the
unintended consequences of the political messaging of established parties aimed
at altering the level of 'manageable diversity' in their favor (Table 10.1). Populist
radical right parties rise in the polls if voters' desire to manage cultural diversity is
substantially exceeding voters' perceptions of the necessity to manage economic
diversity. Conversely, if voters see a far greater need to manage socio-economic
challenges than cultural issues, populist radical right parties drop in the polls
(Figs. 10.4 and 10.5).

The electoral advances of PRRPs are *unintended consequences* because
established political parties themselves are preparing the electoral plane for an
impactful new political competitor. They stem from the *politicized interactions of
established political parties* because the salient debates and the positional void
PRRPs need to advance are driven by established political parties in the first place.
The established parties aim to increase their legitimacy for two reasons: firstly,
because the conservatives are experiencing a crisis and need a new topic (salience)
to enhance their credibility; and secondly, because the social democrats' appreciation of perceived high cultural diversity (eventually leading to liberal discourse
and an electoral void on the right) depends on their desire to further enhance their

**Table 10.1** Explaining the political processes at work in the theory of 'manageable diversity'

| Debate about cultural topics and conduct of established parties | Cultural topics enter the political scene (**high salience**) with a conservative position of the conservatives (**no liberal discourse**) | The conservatives follow the highly liberal agenda of the successful social democrats and drop their conservative profile (**salient liberal discourse**) | The electoral niche on the right is seized by a political contender proposing a conservative position in cultural matters (**electoral advances of populist radical right party**) |
|---|---|---|---|
| Causes (of the causes) | **Crisis of conservatives** | **Successful left camp** in a **society allegedly free of economic concerns** | **Salient debates about cultural issues and liberal party discourse** |
| 'Manageable diversity' | **Conservatives** fail to legitimate their agency due to—in the eye of the voter—insufficient management of economic diversity; they **put forward the need of—until now not expounded as a problem—management/ reduction of cultural diversity** | Social democrats propose a highly liberal agenda due to—in the eyes of the voter—**their successful management of economic diversity; conservatives follow, eventually and thereby failing to manage/reduce cultural diversity in the voter's eyes** | In the eyes of the voter, no established political actor any longer offers a substantial reduction of the saliently debated cultural diversity— **demand and support for a party offering a previously offered 'management/reduction of cultural diversity'** |

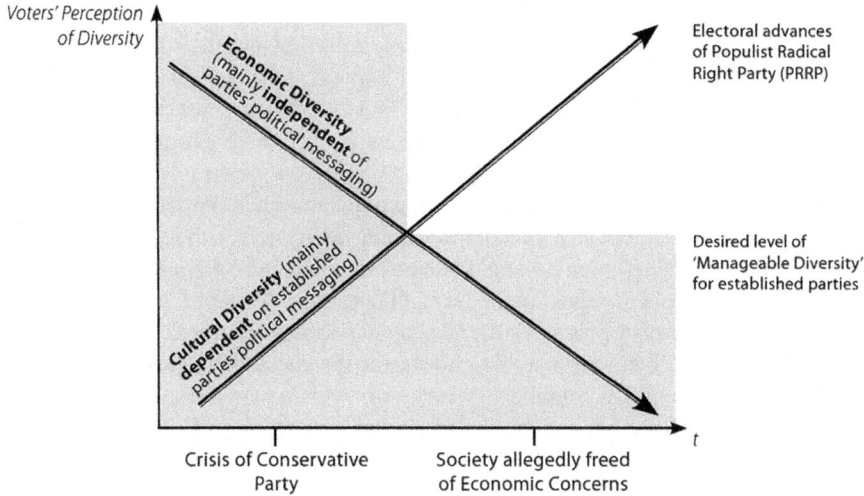

**Fig. 10.5** How established parties' attempts to renegotiate the level of 'manageable diversity' affect the voter and the electoral fortunes of populist radical right parties

legitimacy in times of promising polling figures in a society allegedly free of economic concerns. And finally, they aim to renegotiate the level of 'manageable diversity in political discourse' because the party discourse amongst established political parties on issues of cultural diversity are dependent on their perceived legitimacy, which, in turn, is largely based on handling other textures of diversity to which the society is exposed.

## 10.3 It's Political Messaging, Stupid!

Especially since Donald Trump's victory and the UKIP-induced Brexit, the seemingly unstoppable rise of populist radical right parties has given them almost mythic status. This study shows that there is hardly anything mysterious about their rise (or their fall). The successes of populist radical right parties are neither unavoidable, nor unexplainable. Instead, they follow generalizable political mechanisms that are very similar across Western Europe. It is important to stress that national particularities—e.g. national history or the electoral system—barely accounts for variation here. To entirely demystify their rise, their advances are to a large extent dependent on factors entirely beyond the control of the populist radical right parties themselves. The most decisive factor is the intonation and political messaging of established moderate parties. Populist radical right parties are thus dependent on the parties they despise.

The interaction and political messaging of established moderate parties is not the only factor accounting for variation in the advances of the far right. However, the dropping of conservative messaging by bourgeois parties in a salient debate over identity politics is a jointly necessary condition. This implies that if these two factors are given, populists face the perfect context in which to rise. In turn, if identity politics are not salient or the debate is defined by a conservative compromise led by a bourgeois party sticking to its conservative promises, populists cannot rise, and subsequently lose support.

Economics do play a role, but contradicting popular opinon. Populist radical right parties do not rise if the country's economy is doing badly. In fact, the exact opposite is true. Populist radical *left* parties—e.g. Podemos in Spain and Syriza in Greece—rise due to economic problems, but not the far right parties in Western Europe; they need the salience of cultural topics and suffer during passionate debates about economics. They also require a benign economic climate for the social democrats to staunchly oppose the conservatives' political messaging, which can eventually open the electoral niche for the populist radical right parties to fill (Fig. 10.6).

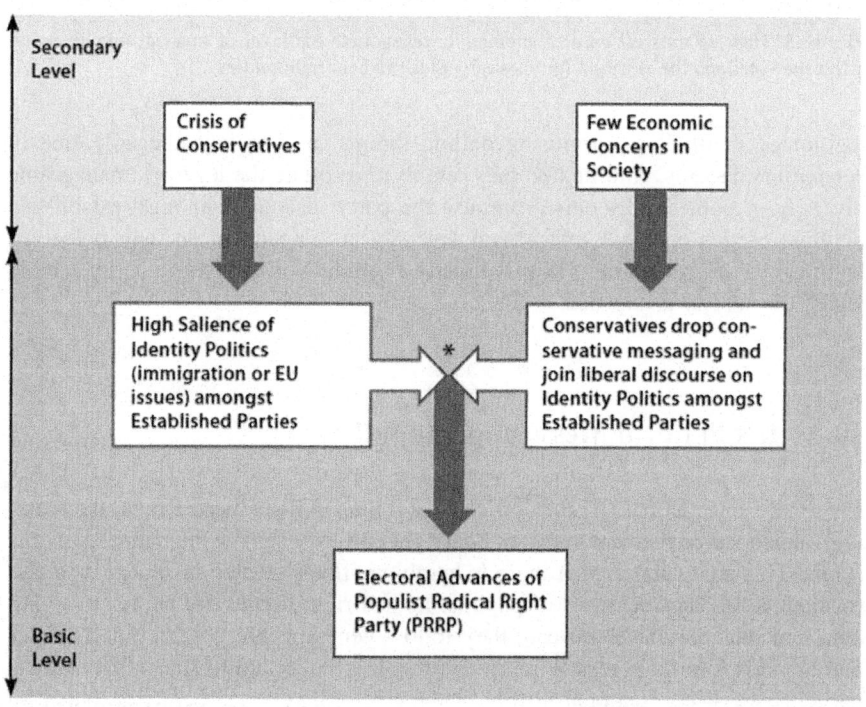

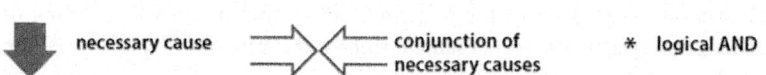

**Fig. 10.6** A two-level theory on populist radical right parties in Western Europe—high extension, low intension

Only in recent years have identity politics extended from migration matters to European and foreign policies. The politicization of immigration politics almost had immediate consequences 'only' for migrants and the national debate. However, instrumentalizing foreign policy matters to mobilize conservative voter strata can have far more implications. Brexit is the best example. Bourgeois parties considering mobilizing on EU issues in particular, or foreign policies in general should carefully ponder how much of a price they are willing to pay for short-term political gain. If they mobilize on European issues, they can either significantly damage the EU, constrain the country's international leverage, hurt their long-term national interest in polemicizing and gambling over international cooperation (best example: Brexit) or breed a populist radical right party on their doorstep.

This illustrates that the rise and fall of PRRPs has very little to do with actual policy changes; rather how they are framed via political messaging. This does not imply that voters would not care about immigration policies, the state of the EU or international cooperation. But if and to what extent this affects the chances of far right parties mainly comes down to how these issues are discussed amongst established parties.

If and how identity politics are debated largely depends on the interaction of the two most influential European parties—the center-right conservatives and the center-left social democrats. Both are catchall parties, trying to reach for the center voter as much as to the electoral fringes. Consequently, they both rely on a more centrist and a more right-leaning or respectively left-leaning wing. It is worth hypothesizing that the more influential the centrist wings, the lower the probability of a politicization of identity politics. However, if identity politics turn salient, it seems that populist parties rise if the left-leaning wing of the social democrats is stronger than the right-leaning wing of the conservatives. Then, the social democrats take a liberal position, while the conservatives are keen to follow a centrist position, opening the electoral niche for a far right party. In turn, populist radical right parties seem to lose if the right-leaning wing of the conservatives is more influential than the left-leaning wing of the social democrats. Then, the conservatives can close the electoral niche on the right, while the social democrats accommodate their messages in a conservative compromise, leading to the decreasing salience of identity politics.

To emphasize one last time, the advances of PRRPs are not dependent on actual policies, but on how the debate is framed. Consequently, there is a massive difference between what parties campaign on and what they implement in government. Very conservative political messaging can come along with policy aspects that are very liberal, and vice versa. However, if populist radical right parties have secured seats in the national parliament, both the debate and the policies affecting the national identity become significantly more conservative; eventually, populist radical right parties aim for an 'illiberal democracy' (see Chap. 2). This leads to an intricate paradox: once identity politics have become salient, liberal interests seem best safeguarded in the long haul if the capacity for thought-through conservative messaging with the social democrats and the conservatives are strengthened. Then populist radical right parties can be blocked from rising and from triggering processes that eventually lead to not very conservative, but illiberal policies. In times of salient identity politics, working against an illiberal democracy seems to call for backing the conservative messengers within European social democratic and bourgeois parties.

# References

Alonso S, Claro da Fonseca S (2011) Immigration, left and right. Party Polit 18:1–20
Art D (2011) Inside the radical right. Cambridge Publishing, Cambridge
Ellinas A (2010) The media and the far right in Western Europe: playing the nationalist card. Cambridge University Press, Cambridge
Green-Pedersen C (2012) A giant fast asleep? Party incentives and the politicisation of European integration. Polit Stud 60:115–130
Goertz G, Mahoney J (2006) Social science concepts. A user's guide. Princeton University Press, Princeton
Muis J (2012) Pim Fortuyn. The evolution of a media phenomenon. Ridderkerk
Mudde C (2016) The study of populist radical right parties: towards a fourth wave. C-Rex Working Paper Series 1/2016. Available via https://www.sv.uio.no/c-rex/english/publications/c-rex-working-paperseries/Cas%20Mudde:%20The%20Study%20of%20Populist%20Radical%20Right%20Parties.pdf. Last accessed 7 May 2017
Schumacher G, De Vries C, Vis B (2013) Why do parties change position? Party organization and environmental incentives. J Polit 75(2):464–477

Printed by Printforce, the Netherlands